Varieties of Transition

Varieties of Transition

The East European and East German Experience

CLAUS OFFE

The MIT Press
Cambridge, Massachusetts

First MIT Press edition, 1997
© 1996 Claus Offe
English translation of chapters 1, 7, and 9 © 1996 Polity Press
English translation of chapter 2 © 1996 Claus Offe

This book was printed and bound in the United States of America.

Library of Congress Cataloging-in-Publication Data

Offe, Claus.
  Varieties of Transition: East European and East German experience / Claus Offe.
      p.   cm.—(Studies in contemporary German social thought)
  Includes bibliographical references (p.   ) and index.
  ISBN 0-262-15048-2 (hardcover: alk. paper).—ISBN 0-262-65048-7 (pbk.: alk. paper)
  1. Post-communism—Europe, Eastern. 2. Europe, Eastern—Social policy.
3. Europe, Eastern—Social conditions—1989–   . 4. Europe, Eastern—
Politics and government—1989–   . 5. Democracy—Europe, Eastern.
I. Title. II. Series.
HN380.7.A8038   1996
306'.0947—dc20   96-9046
                                                              CIP

Contents

Contents

Preface and Acknowledgements

I have found the upheaval in East Europe and the consequences this has had for the post-Communist societies in transformation exceptionally interesting and the individual chapters of this volume are the result of this fascination. This upheaval prompted me, like many others, to attempt to overcome a certain limitation in my own way of viewing the social problems of Western democracies, a narrowing of perspective that had been encouraged by the Cold War and the difference between the East and the West. And, although I do not have the requisite linguistic tools or knowledge of the region to do full justice to it, I have endeavoured to explore some of the aspects of the process of transformation in Central and East European countries using the politico-sociological categories of transformation research in West and South Europe that have proved their worth in Latin America. I undertook this work in the context not just of the intellectual attraction of current events, but also of both the preparations for a research project sponsored by the Volkswagen Foundation and a year spent as a Fellow of the Institute for Advanced Studies in Berlin (1991–2).

I would like to thank the following friends and colleagues for reading individual chapters and commenting on them: David Abraham, Bruce Ackerman, Frank Bönker, Michael Brie, László Bruszt, Wolfgang Eichwede, Jon Elster, Ulrike Götting, Adalbert Hepp, Karl Hinrichs, Stephen Holmes, Herbert Kitschelt, Peter A. Kraus, György Markus, Milan Otahal, Ulrich K. Preuss, Claudia Rose, Friedbert Rüb, Quentin Skinner, Jirí Vecernik and Helmut Wiesenthal. I would like to thank them all for their criticism and encouragement.

Most of the essays in this volume were written in English and appeared in German translation in my book *Der Tunnel am Ende des Lichts* (Frankfurt: Campus, 1994) and have in part been revised and updated for this edition. Earlier versions of some of the chapters also appeared in English. Parts of chapter 2 were originally published in English in *German Politics and Society*, 22 (1991), pp. 18–32; the English translation is reprinted by permission. Chapter 3 was presented at the First Plenary Session of the International Political Science Association (IPSA) Congress, Buenos Aires, Argentina, in July 1991 and was subsequently revised and published in *Social Research*, 58, 4 (1991), pp. 865–92. A much shorter version of chapter 4 appeared in the *East European Constitutional Review* 1, 1 (1992), pp. 21–3, as well as in the *Budapest Review of Books*, 3, 1 (1993), pp. 6–13. Passages from chapter 5 were published in *Archives Européennes de Sociologie*, 33 (1992), pp. 195–201, and an extended version (of which major sections are reprinted here) came out in the *Journal of Political Philosophy*, 1, 1 (1993), pp. 17–44. Chapters 7 and 9 are published here in English for the first time, while chapters 6 and 8 have not previously been published in any language. Chapters 1, 7 and 9 have been translated for this volume by Jeremy Gaines.

Varieties of Transition

1

The Structure of Industrial Societies: the Joint Characteristics and Shortcomings of State Socialist Societies and Democratic Capitalism

Viewed from the East, the Federal Republic of Germany also has a wall. It does not serve, like the Berlin Wall, to prevent citizens from leaving, be it for political or any other reasons for that matter, but instead it functions for economic reasons to prevent specific foreigners from entering. I wish in this introductory chapter to consider some of the complex logical symmetries of this sort and the reciprocal negations which characterize the relations between the forms of state socialist society which came to an end in 1989 and the democratic capitalism of the OECD countries, in other words the two known structural models for industrial societies.

'Scientific socialism', the dominant theory of state socialist societies, refers with 'hyper-rational' pathos to society's ability to plan its structure and changes as well as to render social life as a whole an object that society can control. Typically, state socialist societies do not have the simplest preconditions for reliably and accurately monitoring themselves. With regard to self-observation, they remain far more opaque than is manifestly the case for liberal democratic societies, which have perfected techniques even for shedding light on their remotest nooks and crannies without, however, using the insights thus generated as a lever for deliberate global self-change. Is it perhaps the case that on the one hand the more you know, the less you can do, and on the other the greater your ambition to act, the more you try to avoid reliable information?

Other than Karl Deutsch's ingenious definition of power,[1] there is hardly a better illustration of this paradoxical relation between action based on planning and knowledge than the provisions by means of which the regimes in state socialist societies blinkered themselves. They do not have a rational calculation of capital resources and therefore have no basis at the level of either individual plant or the state economy for calculating or assessing the efficiency of the apparatus of production, be it in detail or as a whole. They do not have the artistic, scientific and political liberties which alone enable an articulation and reflection of the perception members of society have of that society. Equally, there is neither an independent judiciary that is in a position to sort social states of affairs in terms of a code of 'legal/illegal' nor a formal, rational bureaucracy that is able to discern whether something in the inflow of communication inundating the administration falls within its scope or not. It is this self-induced inability of the state socialist system to monitor itself[2] which Wolfgang Engler has in mind when he speaks of 'de-objectification', of 'a privatization of the political'. And it is also what he means when he talks of the fact that the operative rules of interaction between the administration and its clients remain so opaque for both that 'any individual life of any sort of importance can become a doubtful case' (1992: 6).

As a rule, the practical side to the social sciences is that they foster society's knowledge of itself and disseminate such knowledge. But this has a negative impact: the destruction of myths, ideologies, impossible assertions, assumed trends and incorrectly construed causal chains – just as the cost analysis conducted by businesses uncovers faulty allocation of resources or the civil judiciary rejects illegitimate claims. The social sciences require free scope precisely in order to fulfil such a negative, corrective function, however, a freedom they did not enjoy in most state socialist societies.[3]

What interests social scientists about comparing the Western capitalist democracies with the collapsed state socialist systems are the specific forms of institutionalizing a rationality of knowledge and action in the two types of society and their system-specific weaknesses, with the weaknesses of the one often mirroring those of the other. Thus state socialist societies spawned achievements in the field of the natural sciences and technology, above all in areas of military relevance (the 'Sputnik shock'), which, when compared with their general economic state of development, must be given their due and regarded as proof of the existence of a quite exceptional ability to mobilize resources and plan their coordination. On the other hand, for all the efforts to integrate the 'scientific and technological revolution' and its achievements into the production process and into the material living conditions of the population, there were quite staggering failures, because the state socialist systems did not have any mechanisms of technological innovation and its consequent diffusion at their disposal. In the West this function was fulfilled by competition and the constant devaluation of obsolete technologies, products and plant that this brings with it. State socialist society 'creates' material assets and modern technologies, but it is not able to allow existing plant and technologies to be 'abolished' when they are technologically or economically out of date. In fact it functions to prevent precisely this from happening.

The market, by contrast, is an agency which engenders judgements on who or what should not be continued, judgements that in the most favourable case do not jeopardize the social consensus and are constantly innovative. Where the market does not exist in such a capacity, there is no mechanism of selection and devaluation that functions anonymously, intervenes 'from outside' and does not operate according to some intentional logic. In such instances there is simply no spontaneous control of the macro-economic process of modernization. The assertion that capitalism 'fetters' the productive forces and state socialist society 'unleashes' them is thus one of the most unfortunate of the errors of historical materialism. In such cases where, by dint of both the party's monopoly on power and the apparatus of the state, decisions can be taken on everything, there can no longer be any decisions on the overall results which come from all the decision-making.

In democratic capitalist societies there is no overall social objective that is placed on a pedestal as the measure of all things. Societies of this type are 'pluralist'. They do not relate to the age in which they exist as if it were the implementation phase of a global and dominant 'project'. Instead they exhibit a constant dynamic of multi-dimensional change that is predominantly perceived after the event. The opposite is the case with state socialist societies. There is definitely an official developmental goal, namely 'Communism', which, however, coexists with factual economic stagnation and the conservation of 'pre-modern' cultural and political structures – at any rate, there is no steady change in the direction of this goal. State socialist society, and this is no doubt the across-the-board consensus in the mid-1990s, is not a suitable vehicle for approaching Communist goals. The idea of wishing to achieve the emancipatory goals of Communism with the institutional means of state socialist society simply does not hold, or rather no longer holds, any prospect of success.

On the one hand we have control without self-observation, on the other self-observation without control; on the one hand technological creativity without the economic destruction of obsolete structures, and on the other (frequently) destruction without creativity; on the one hand a macro-social project goal without change, on the other change without a goal. The search for the typical faults in the structures of the two social orders that were 'competing systems' until 1989 uncovers a series of additional reciprocities. In the capitalist countries and their market economies micro-planning at the individual company level is coupled with macro-anarchy at the level of the national economy. This is the object of well-founded Marxist criticism. Conversely, the macro-planning of state socialist societies is not really able to control the micro-anarchy at the level of the individual companies, that is, the actions of the persons involved in the production process, which are inadequately coordinated because they are motivated by opposing interests that are simply not acknowledged as such. It therefore again appears to be a misleading euphemism if we speak of 'planned economies' when we have the state socialist systems in mind. These were admittedly economies in which there was planning; but precisely for that reason they were economies which did not function according to plan, but were instead susceptible (and vulnerable) to unpleasant surprises 'from below' – to the friction that resulted from the fact that it was not possible to coordinate actions 'on site' effectively or discipline them sufficiently. In order to regulate such friction and unsolved problems of the collective good, state socialist society, which does not have the disciplinary means of market-based sanctions to fall back on, would have to tap an enormous (and to an enormous extent parasitic) quantum of power – like a power station that requires more than 100 per cent of the power it generates to illuminate its own plant and offices. The consequences of these symmetrical deficits of the two systems are insoluble problems of macro-economic control on the one hand and severe shortfalls in productivity on the other.

In the capitalist countries in the West, queues form in front of the unemployment offices and the same happens in the state socialist societies in front of the butchers' shops. In the former there is a 'reserve army' of labour, waiting for employment, and a 'reserve army', or rather 'mountain', of commodities waiting for buyers. In the latter there are managers waiting for workers and workers waiting for key supplies. This arrangement of queues in the two systems has the following effect: the very few countries in which poverty is known as a mass phenomenon are all capitalist countries and yet at the same time capitalism is unable to get any nearer to finding an economic or political solution to poverty even though, given capitalism's superior technology, this is a practical possibility (see Przeworski 1991).

The two systems show a similar symmetry in the system-specific pathologies of their respective political public arenas. In capitalist democracies you can say what you want, but nobody really listens and the political public domain is fragmented into innumerable different groupings round particular issues or forms of communication. The main problem is attracting 'attention' for communications. In the former Comecon countries you were by no means able to say what you wanted, but this very fact meant that people certainly pricked up their ears (and not just the police informers) in a particular way. The art of carefully 'reading between the lines' of the official communiqués was pronounced in the state socialist societies.

The organizational principle underlying capitalism involves economic activity to a great extent being independent of collectively reached decisions and the citizens' public approval. Nevertheless, such approval is in fact widely given. Conversely, the state socialist societies, where they are even halfway able to function, rely on a type of person who selflessly, responsibly and devotedly acts for the common good and regards this as being good for him or her. Yet such a person and his or her active concurrence with the conditions of production and distribution were not only not spawned by the state socialist societies, but in fact systematically discouraged by them. The great and perhaps historically decisive advantage of capitalism is that it desists from making moral claims. Capitalism is a play that is successful even if most of the roles are those of rogues. Capitalism is not choosy when it comes to structures and as a consequence what could be termed 'congruent socialization' proceeds infinitely more simply within it. In other words the system generates with (comparatively) little effort those types of persons it requires to enact its rules and mechanisms. Capitalist societies, because of their absence of moral claims, are much more capable of such congruent socialization than is the case in state socialist societies. For the latter were structurally much more demanding in this respect and yet to a quite destructive degree then engendered cynical and 'privatistic' attitudes and mentalities that were widely described as apathy, as the 'you scratch my back, I'll scratch yours' approach and as petty corruption.[4] The mental retardedness of the 'economic ethics' of state socialist societies, the economic culture of the 'uncivil economy', to use Richard Rose's term, will place a grave strain on the transformation process and hinder its progress. The state socialist economies on the one hand tyrannized their citizens with deficits and repression; yet on the other, or precisely because of this, they afforded their citizens opportunities for obstruction and for private aggrandizement that, on aggregate, had a fatal impact. With respect to production decisions to be made in the framework of a mechanism of property rights and market forces that is not linked to political power, capitalism does not need the agreement of citizens. Yet it nevertheless generates more agreement than state socialism, which, unlike capitalism, can function only given the robust agreement of the 'working citizens'.

The state socialist system did not succeed in winning the enduring loyalty of its working citizens. In the final analysis its downfall was probably caused by this 'moral deficit' and the attendant economic consequences. This cannot be taken to mean, however, that socialist theories and projected socialist societies definitively have no future prospects. The preferences human beings develop for particular economic and political institutions are subject to so many contextual influences, ambivalences and changes in perspective that any hypothesis of the 'finality' or even the 'end of history' are from the outset categorical errors.

Whether capitalism *per se* is preferred to socialism *per se* depends completely on whether the respective factual system is being discussed or whether debate focuses on some exemplary idealized version of the two alternatives. If one takes this difference into account, then the following order of preferences seems to have a great deal of moral plausibility, or could at least come to have such in future political conflicts: exemplary socialism, exemplary capitalism, factual capitalism, factual socialism. The calculation becomes somewhat more complex if one examines, on both sides of the borderline between the systems, which particular socio-structural positions apply to the choice of the one or the other. In this context the difference again holds good that only a small portion of the underclass in capitalism opts for Communist parties, while in socialism a large section of the middle class also opts for the 'capitalist road' (or the road to capitalism). This preference in turn depends on the factual experiences that people have during the transformation process. Thus the distress and uncertainties of the political and economic transformation of the former Comecon systems have led everywhere to the authoritarian and protectionist care that state socialist regimes paid to the welfare of their citizens being posthumously granted a moral credit which it never enjoyed during their actual lifetime. It is not only the clear losers of the transformation process who in the mid-1990s have quite unexpectedly helped the former Communist monopoly parties to attain strong positions of power in many East European countries.

Conversely, the political protagonists of democratic capitalism now also clearly have very plausible grounds for harking back to the days before the decline of their 'systemic' rivals, for it was easy to demonstrate economic and moral superiority in the face of such rivals. The societies of the OECD world are no longer simply able to legitimate themselves by referring to themselves antithetically as the 'better' of the two. Today they have to prove that they are 'good', that is, convince citizens that they are worthy of recognition and preservation on the basis of their own characteristics and achievements. Or they simply have to jettison the attempt to justify themselves normatively by citing the 'good reasons' of peace, liberty and justice. In the latter case they would obviously become intricately caught up in the crisis of state socialism itself, with all its attendant unforeseeable consequences.

The state socialist and democratic capitalist systems are symmetrical in another important respect if one considers the prevailing forecasts of the one as to the long-term potential for survival and adaptation of the other. From the very beginning one fixed dogma in historical materialism was that capitalism, owing to its intrinsic coordination problems, was characterized by the dynamics of crisis and class conflict which would inevitably lead to the historical collapse of this social formation. To date there is no instance of this theory having been confirmed – partly, no doubt, because this forecast sparked reactions that made it 'self-destroying'. Conversely, the negative predictions made in the West in respect of the ability of the social orders established in Eastern Europe were always and increasingly held only by intellectual minorities and outsiders. And it was they who turned out to be right – even if in the mid-1990s there is no clear account of the political, economic, social and historical reasons which would explain in concrete terms the collapse of the regime in 1989 (see Szelenyi and Szelenyi 1994).

This leads directly to the final aspect of a comparison of the systems, namely the question as to the relative ability of Western as opposed to Eastern societies to learn to innovate and shape themselves. In this context Western societies were privileged to enjoy continuity, whereas the Eastern social systems were marked by incisive discontinuity. It would seem obvious again to propose a mirror-image scenario here, with a clear discrepancy in the pressure to learn and the capacity to learn in the two systems. Certainly democratic capitalist societies are with some justification proud of their stable, institutionalized ability to learn and their capacity for adjusting in an ongoing and flexible manner to new problematic conditions. Proof of this would be the basic institutional framework of Western democracies, such as the system of competing parties, federalism and the division of power, corporatist negotiation systems and production steered by market forces. At the same time, however, there is a danger that this institutionalized ability to learn is not sufficiently challenged and that its potential thus remains untapped, because the externally induced pressure to learn and cooperate no longer exists and the new challenges that have emerged since 1989 can be answered by saying, with a shrug of the shoulders, that the problems of the (erstwhile) 'Second' World are its own and no one else's. In addition, the post-Communist systems exhibit the joint weakness of clearly being exposed to an extremely high pressure to learn while even the tried and effective capacities to learn in the shape of an open, perceptive and stable guaranteed state and social 'governing capacity' have themselves been caught up in the systemic crisis and have accordingly been weakened. The West has changed the East, be it merely through the simple fact of its being there, its visible existence as a successful model. The structural upheaval in the East is at the same time in the process of casting the factual and normative premises of the West into question and subjecting them to an unprecedented test. It is, at any rate, unclear whether we have adequately perceived this retroactive impact of the changed East on the West, that is, grasped the completely new reality of the 'post-Communist West'.

The problems of transformation to which the post-Communist systems are exposed will be discussed in this volume in the context of an analytical framework which can be construed as a 'magic' triangle. It is a threefold task that has to be solved in these societies, and for the first time in history all three aspects have to be solved simultaneously. The validity of a new economic order, a new legal order and a new constitutional order and also new rules of social integration (that is, rules of social recognition and membership) has to be asserted on the large scale of complete societies. Resources have to be generated and distributed, rights defined and implemented, and respect for (national, ethnic, civil) identities has to become a practised reliable part of life, even in the context of the territorial organization of the post-Communist societies. The multifarious forms in which the three levels interact and contradict one another will be elaborated in chapter 2 with reference to Germany and in chapter 3 with regard to post-Communist societies as a whole. The typology devised in chapter 7 for the various 'families' of post-Communist societies rests on the same fundamental conceptual structure. Chapter 6, which was written with Franz Bönker, focuses on problems of economic integration, and chapter 4 concentrates on the renewed topicality of the ethnic, nationalist and territorial definitions of social identity. Chapter 8 explains why a post-war transition to democracy, as it occurred in West Germany in

1949, is counter-intuitively more easily accomplished than the 'civilian' case of East Germany in 1989.

Two 'transitional' problems differ from these three 'constructive' problems. The one is that of the friction in social and distribution policy that has to be handled in the course of the new foundation of a political and economic system and a new national and/or territorial definition of the 'unity' of society. I have addressed this complex elsewhere (see Offe 1993). The other transitional problem is that of the change in elites and in the political and legal treatment of functionaries in the old regimes by the administrators of the new regimes. I will discuss this in chapter 5. Finally, some of the remote or long-term effects of the collapse of the state socialist regimes on the political world in the Western democracies will be outlined in chapter 9.

2

Prosperity, Nation, Republic: Modes of Societal Integration and the Unique German Journey from Socialism to Capitalism

It seems obvious in the mid-1990s that future historians will recognize the break-up of political, economic and military order in Central East Europe as having initiated a new historical epoch. At this point it is too early, in one respect, to try to provide a definitive analysis of the driving forces behind the changes and their long-term consequences. But in another respect it is already too late to stick to the view, so popular in the years 1989–90, that describes these changes as uniform and as having taken the same course in all the countries that have emerged from state socialism. In spite of their common past each country and its path of change must be considered a special case. One of these cases is that of the former German Democratic Republic, some of whose special features I wish to analyse in this chapter. A comprehensive discussion of parallel 'particularities' of the other post-Communist countries is presented in chapter 7.

Major historical changes are 'revolutionary' to the extent that they alter the basis of unity and integration of a society, or the building blocks of its identity. The outcome of such changes is a new 'social contract' that involves some widely shared understanding at the basis of the new order as to who belongs to it, who will have which rights and responsibilities and how individuals and functions of a society shall be coordinated and held together. In the present discussion I distinguish three possible ways (cultural, political, economic) in which the coherence and integrity of the new social order can be built.

First, unity can be proclaimed and corroborated (on the part of elites), as well as experienced and supported (on the part of non-elites), in terms of an appeal to the shared territory, history, culture and language of a nation. In the German case this notion of the hitherto divided parts of the nation 'belonging together' was invoked by, among others, Willy Brandt in his remark that the unity of the nation will eventually come about due to its shared history and culture. Secondly, unity can be 'political'. Here the ultimate reason why members of a political community recognize each other as belonging to that community is due to collective agreement on the principles of the political order which provides and protects peace, freedom and justice to all of them. Finally, unity can be constituted by the adoption and successful implementation of principles of economic organization, pertaining as a specific 'mode of production' to both production and distribution of economic resources. Needless to say, the analytical distinction of these three types of macro-social integration (cultural identity, political regime, mode of production) is probably fuzzy at the edges; it is also not meant to suggest that one of these modes of integration will anywhere be the sole support of social unity, but that societies can be distinguished according to which of the three mechanisms of integration is dominant. One way of answering that question is, of course, to establish which of the three media a particular society relies upon when its unity and coherence are seen to come under stress and strain.

I also wish to pursue the hypothesis that, depending on the predominant unity-enhancing mode chosen, the post-revolutionary social order will be more or less robust and sustainable. My background intuition is that political principles are better than economic performance, and economic performance better than cultural identity, as a source of macro-integration. The way in which the new social order was created will determine its degree of vulnerability, and hence the extent to which a relapse into a 'state of nature', or post-revolutionary decay, can be prevented. Which of these models of social integration became valid and dominant during the revolutionary change starting in October 1989 in the GDR?

Ever since the creation of the GDR in 1949, as a result of the Second World War and the beginning of the Cold War, it has been clear how the question of inner unity of the state and society can be accounted for in the GDR. It was never a distinct nation, but always remained, in the view of non-elites if not always the elites, part of a more encompassing nation. Nor was it constituted by an autonomous revolutionary act proclaiming certain political principles as binding (with the exception of a negative, that is 'anti-fascist', principle that supposedly sufficed as the founding idea of the state). Instead it was created from the outside, by the occupying forces of the Soviet Union and by the constitutional order devised and imposed by them.

As a consequence the GDR had nothing but a distinctive, as well as increasingly more consistently implemented, economic system on which to build its identity and coherence, namely the state socialist mode of economic organization, comprising centralized allocation of investment and production, state-organized international trade, international division of labour within the Council for Mutual Economic Aid (CMEA), collectivized agriculture and administered prices. The GDR had no identity other than in terms of its economic organization and thus represented a pure and consistent (and, perhaps for that reason, relatively successful) instance of a 'socialist' society.

Turning now to the breakdown of that regime and the subsequent emergence of a new social order in a comparative perspective, we can distinguish three very different patterns of events which led to the transformation of the state socialist systems. First, in the majority of 'continuity' countries the national unit and base of integration were maintained, while the economic and political order underwent major alterations. Secondly, a 'new' or (as in the case of the Baltic states and Slovakia) re-created national state emerged alongside the political and economic reorganization. Thirdly, the new social order involved the simultaneous abolition of the economic order, political order and, following unification with some other state, the (always rather nominal) national 'stateness' of the old system. The GDR is the only case so far that falls into this last category of transition patterns.

Thus, as much of the identity of the GDR built up since 1949 was predominantly based on its type of economic organization, the ruins that remained after its breakdown were predominantly to be considered an economic problem – that of transforming and modernizing a defunct apparatus of production – and not one of coming to terms with surviving political institutions or national identities, of which there were virtually none. The transformation of the GDR is essentially a project of economic reorganization that was to be implemented by the West German economic and political system into which the GDR merged on unification day, 3 October 1990. Nor was the breakdown itself brought about by other than mainly economic reasons: the GDR's elite had lost all confidence that the state socialist economy could ever be revived to a sustainable level of efficiency and sustainability, and the oppositional segments of non-elites were inspired less by ambitions for political liberty (which were dominant at best only during a few weeks around the turn of the year 1990, those few weeks when the democratic civil movement determined events with the cry 'We are the people') than by dissatisfaction with standards of living and their further lagging behind the West German reference population.

The striking absence of ambitions for a genuine reorganization of the political system of the GDR might be explained by the lack in the collective memory of GDR citizens of any experience of liberal democracy and of pluralistic political conditions that could serve as a model of reform and source of inspiration. In the case of the GDR any experience of a better past that could guide aspirations to liberation dates back to the time before 1933, that is, further into the past than in any other state socialist country except for the Soviet Union itself. For that reason, and in contrast to the condition of the West German transformation after the Second World War (see chapter 8), there was no 'older generation' in the GDR that could conceivably have been reactivated in the service of building a new political order. Also, in contrast to Poland and Czechoslovakia, due to the regime's practice of granting selective exit permits to West Germany to potential leaders of political opposition (or expatriating them outright) there were no active counter-elites (such as Dubček, Havel, Wałesa) or organizations (such as Charter 77, Solidarność) which would have become visible to the public in the past by struggle, defeat and acts of repression, and which would then have been instrumental in the breakdown of the old regime and the establishment of the new.

Although the GDR called itself a 'democratic and republican' form of regime, no official explanation of those concepts agreed with the model of a liberal, legal and constitutional state, once the pathos of an 'anti-fascist' creation had quickly been exhausted and compromised. Instead the official line was directed at the 'leading role of the party of the working class' and therefore at the mechanism of a bureaucratic economic organization.

The process that was concluded by the event of German unification was thus not propelled by the struggle for a new political order, nor was it inspired by longings for national unity. It was premised upon an economic fact, the precarious viability of the GDR's economic order and performance, and it left behind another economic fact, the need to reorganize and modernize a vast landscape populated by submarginal economic units. Given the GDR's dismal economic situation (as well as its minority position in the new united polity in which its population comprised just 20 per cent of the total), issues of autonomous political reorganization (which were taken over and resolved by West Germans anyway) lapsed into insignificance, leaving issues of economic recovery and of a rapid equalization of prosperity levels in East and West dominating the scene of unification strategies. This emphasis on economic order, however, raises two questions. First, how can unity be preserved and fostered as long as vast disparities remain in terms of economic performance? After all, the decline in economic output after the breakdown of the old regime, euphemistically referred to as the 'transformation crisis', is of such an order of magnitude that ex-GDR output levels are expected to reach those of 1989 in 1995 at the earliest, that is, six years and many hundreds of thousands of millions of transferred Deutschmarks after the end of the old economic regime. Secondly, how realistic is it to assume that, even after full economic integration and equalization are accomplished (which may well be a matter of a full generation), such unified economic order will serve as a sufficiently robust support for the unity of German society? Concerning the latter question, and *a fortiori* the former, a number of concerned and alarmed voices are to be heard pointing to the deficiencies of prosperity, even after it has been achieved within a unified and reasonably homogeneous national economy; they suggest that it is no reliable glue for societal coherence and that therefore additional unifying mechanisms must be relied upon if the results of the formal merger of the GDR with the FRG are to make compelling sense to the citizens of both of these formerly antagonistic states. The standard phrase by which these additional unifying mechanisms are known is 'inner unity' – a rather mysterious quality of national existence that hardly anyone is able to define. Nor can anyone specify ways in which it might be brought about. What this need for 'inner unity' boils down to is, in my view, a set of compelling arguments providing good reasons as to why citizens of the enlarged state should recognize each other as belonging to the same political community, share burdens and recognize responsibilities stemming from common historical legacies and liabilities. The need for a set of arguments serving those demanding purposes is aggravated by two circumstances. First, the accession of the GDR was not a matter in which the West German majority was asked for its assent; it was rather a unilateral decision of the first democratic GDR government (elected in March 1990) on the basis of the opportunities that section 23 of the West German constitution offered to it. Secondly, given the vast disparities between the performance of the West German economy and that of the East German economy after it was removed from the CMEA, massive transfers of funds to East Germans from West German tax payers, consumers, investors, local and state governments and wage earners will be required for the unforeseeable future; in 1995 these amounted to 170,000 million Deutschmarks per year, or about 18 dollars per capita per day for 16 million inhabitants of the new *Länder*. Such figures suggest that 'good arguments' are indeed called for to induce West Germans to accept this kind of burden, as well as to induce East Germans to accept the new institutional environment and severe economic uncertainties to which they have been exposed as a consequence of unification. The apparent solution to these many-sided problems of meaning and obligation is an appeal to national modes of macro-integration.

Being born within this functional dilemma of providing compelling reasons for redistribution, the special feature of the new German nationalism is its instrumental and somewhat artificial character, the way in which its proponents respond to the needs emerging from the economic process of unification. Strategic considerations in the use of nationalist symbols and modes of obligation are visible in four respects.

First, the strategic use of nationalism dominates the relationship between the (former) GDR population and the wealthy (old) FRG. The slogan 'We are *one* people', which soon replaced the democratic revolutionary maxim 'We are *the* people', was inspired by the obvious intent to provide a meaningful commitment to desperately needed economic support from the Federal Republic. Secondly, the same pattern of calculated nationalism proved to be useful for the relationship of the Federal Republic to the GDR. Only if West German tax payers could be persuaded to feel a sense of national 'happiness' (such as Chancellor Kohl has tried to encourage) based on the newly won German unity would it be possible, without political risk, to impose the considerable sacrifices necessary for the quick recovery of the economy in the GDR. The willingness of the West German population to make such sacrifices and, beyond this, to agree to uncertain commitments for the future would have been drastically reduced if control of the resources flowing to the East had not ended up in the hands of a unified national leadership, that is, a leadership dominated by the Federal Republic. Transformation via national unity was a way to make sure that control over transfers of funds would remain in the hands of the West German political elite. Thirdly, the expression of longing for national unity proved itself to be an instrument in the negotiations of the two German states with the Allies of the Second World War. Its purpose was to make sure that the absolute right of Germans to national unity and sovereignty was presented as a goal so desirable that the Allies were unable to refuse its recognition without political risk to themselves. Finally, a relaxation of relations between

West and East Germany, as well as *vis-à-vis* their common history, in the name of national reunification might also have been a motive for emphasizing the value of national unity. If the moral catastrophe of the war initiated by Germany, along with the destruction of the Jews, stood until recently at the centre of (a therefore weak) West German historical and national consciousness, reunification offers an opportunity to former West Germans to have this burden relativized and, at least partially, to exchange it for the lesser burden of overcoming the past of the GDR with its systematic and massive violation of human and civil rights.

The new nationalism in Germany in the 1990s is not therefore the nationalism of an emotionalized *Volk*; in fact a large number of West German citizens expressed reservations about reunification that were of a cost-conscious nature. Instead a calculated and moderate 'elite-nationalism' exists which was designed to set the stage for, as well as to provide compelling meaning for, the hurried-up process of economic integration.

Economic integration at this fast tempo was not a foregone conclusion. As far as the government of the Federal Republic was concerned, haste resulted from the uncertainty of domestic politics in the Soviet Union and the fate of Mikhail Gorbachev, together with anticipation of the danger of a structural 'implosion' of the GDR brought about by the migration of much of its economically active population and the total lack of a will, on the part of that population (in 1990), to preserve any of the political, economic or moral heritage or ambition of the GDR. Even after the GDR, as a result of its first and last free elections on 18 March 1990, had become a state worthy of its name by Western standards, no widely supported project of building a 'better' GDR was advocated. The overwhelming majority of its voters, organized along Western party divisions, wanted not a 'better', more democratic GDR, but none at all. Yet the economic elite of the Federal Republic, including the Bundesbank, explicitly pleaded for a slower process of gradual integration of the two German states via a confederation in the first half of the 1990s, and they did so with definite rational arguments from a purely economic perspective. Only the functionalized sentiment of 'national unity' determined that in this conflict between political and economic rationalities the proponents of the 'quick' variant maintained the upper hand.

To be sure, neither GDR society nor its government opposed this process. It is indicative of the conditions in GDR society – anaesthetized and 'depoliticized' for forty years by state socialism and in stark contrast to the Hungarian, Czechoslovak and Polish cases – that the political, moral and organizational resources for an independent political reform and self-extrication within the boundaries of the old state were simply not present. Initiatives therefore came almost completely from the government in Bonn.

The strategy of the West German government was based on creating irreversible conditions quickly by executive decision and international contracts, while pushing the costs of the rapid transition into the future or leaving them to the market to absorb. This involves a strategy that is based – literally as well as figuratively – on extremely high and very poorly secured credit. Be it out of naïvety or cynicism, the originators believed, or pretended to believe, that a second economic miracle would automatically unfold in the GDR. This faith has not been borne out by any facts to date.

West German investors first adopted a 'wait and see' strategy: the longer the economic decline of large sectors of the industrial basis of the GDR – which was largely incapable of surviving after the dissolution of CMEA trade links – the more painful the economic and social consequences and the cheaper the takeover of remaining enterprises. The decline of the GDR's industry was accelerated by the rapid expansion of marketing and retail trade into the new *Länder*, which resulted in the availability of West German goods in every corner of the former GDR – goods of mostly superior quality, but also consistently perceived as being of preferable symbolic value. Immediately after the currency reform in July 1990 Western-made goods started to displace not only local industrial products, but even local agricultural goods from the market. For a while East Germans boycotted not only their own state, but also their own economy. And the chance to protect the East German economy temporarily through the erection of tariff barriers was no longer there as the barriers themselves had been removed.

The result of sometimes near-catastrophic conditions in areas such as communication, transportation, energy supply, real estate, health care and education facilities was that chances for the recovery of the economy, in the new market of open and unrestricted competition, declined instead of improving during the second half of 1990, and with them went the chance for autonomous economic recovery.

Considering insurmountable adjustment problems, structural collapses, massive and lasting levels of unemployment and future uncertainties, the economic crisis triggered by the rapid transformation strategy is probably the most difficult (to be precise, the only major) economic crisis experienced by the population of the GDR in its entire forty-year history. The destructive drive for adjustment can, of course, be interpreted as a quick, drastic and above all inescapable shock along the road to prosperity and security. It still remains to be seen

how many citizens of the former GDR will share this optimistic interpretation and for how long, and what those people who oppose it
intend to do. Results of federal elections in October 1994, in which the
former Communist Party, now called the Party of Democratic
Socialism (PDS), made gains of between 15 and 20 per cent, point
towards a demonstration of the disintegrative political consequences
of a failed crash course in economic modernization.

The disappointment, frustration and anger of the East German population are exacerbated by the fact that the economic realities of the
defunct GDR can be remembered, and are remembered from a distance in quite rosy colours. Bleak as the long-term prognosis of the
state socialist economy was, this gloomy outlook was not common
knowledge in the last years of the regime. At any rate, the collapse did
not result from an acute economic crisis. The economy of the GDR created largely tolerable economic conditions – even superior ones, when
compared with standards of economic efficiency of other Comecon
countries – at least with respect to the production and distribution of
consumer and investment goods, albeit less so with respect to infrastructure and housing. To be sure, the efficiency of the system lagged
far, irretrievably, behind that of the Federal Republic. The GDR economy attained only 50 per cent of the labour productivity of the FRG,
yet consumed 124 per cent of the West German consumption of
energy per capita (resulting in the extreme environmental damage
caused by, among other things, the use of brown coal).

Most important on the positive side of the economy of the GDR, as
seen by its former worker-citizens in retrospect, is that the system was
able to provide a high degree of social security and employment stability, which is sorely missed today. The supply of consumer goods
has been adequate and even relatively good since the 1960s, partly
due to a gigantic subsidy of basic goods, transportation and housing.
During the 1970s and 1980s social scientists in the FRG investigating
the satisfaction of GDR citizens with their living conditions agreed
overwhelmingly that a political destabilization of the GDR resulting
from economic discontent could be excluded as a likely possibility.
Rather, social scientists, and gradually also Western political elites,
became convinced that the economy and politics of the GDR were
characterized by a slow, unbalanced, yet irrevocable process of consolidation. Only this circumstance explains why conservative politicians,
in particular, advocated the granting of large amounts of credit to the
GDR. The leadership and the population of the GDR, in their turn,
had every reason to expect the continuity of such external subsidization, especially as it was based not only on Western interest in the
relaxation of tensions that might result from the GDR's economic diffi-

culties, but also on the GDR's ability to 'pay' in terms of a gradual relaxation of repression and the granting of exit permits for categories of its own population. An additional stabilizing factor was the prospect, given the position of the GDR as a *de facto* member of the European Community, of selling cheap mass products (such as furniture, car tyres, some textiles) into West European markets. These (deceptive, as it turned out) indicators of stability and continuity blinded most Western observers to the enormous deficiencies of the GDR economy and the resulting delay in modernization. Hence the actual collapse was entirely unexpected and surprising. What are the factors that contributed to it?

The collapse of the GDR was not caused by acute and dramatic disturbances emerging from within the system of economic organization and its mode of operation – despite some of its obvious deficiencies *vis-à-vis* West European welfare states and their economies. The critical defect of the system was not an economic but a moral flaw: it was a system dependent for its remarkable stability not only on physically restricting its own working population (that is, refusing to allow people to leave), but also on denying it basic political rights, such as freedom of opinion and of publication, freedom to organize, to strike and to vote in meaningful elections. The GDR had in effect precluded all normal and formal 'exit' and 'voice' options. The functional correlation between a socialist economy and political repression is obvious: only if social interests alien to the plan are prevented from manifesting themselves, and the temptations to abuse or exploit which the system itself generates are rigorously repressed, is it possible to maintain a tolerable level of production and productivity.

Furthermore, the functional need for repression inherent in any economic system of state socialism was considerably intensified in the GDR because of its proximity to the FRG. Through its substantial, if gradually declining, hostile political acts and positions and also, probably more importantly, through its mere presence and visibility the Federal Republic and its society presented a dangerous environment for the political-economic system of the GDR. This threat essentially implied that at any time any GDR citizen could acquire full legal status as a citizen (as well as, given the common language, cultural status) upon request in the FRG, if only he or she managed to find a way over the Wall and barbed wire. The presence of FRG media throughout the GDR also meant that Western lifestyles and consumer models penetrated, without censorship, the consciousness of every GDR citizen via radio and television. To a certain (even if astonishingly small) extent this situation helped to stimulate a desire for stronger participation and voting rights among the GDR population; in turn, the state apparatus of the GDR felt compelled to invest in a gigantic system of 'excess repression', by forcing an expansion of its capacities for supervision, control and manipulation.

The greater the capacity of means for repression necessary (or thought necessary) in this environment, the greater the risk of the system's continuance once the repressive apparatus collapses. Two things can happen: repression-induced explosion or, its opposite, decompression. For example, the repressive apparatus can fail when its actions generate such levels of protest and rebellion on the part of the population that additional methods of repression are no longer available or are rendered impractical. In this case the repressive apparatus collapses under the weight of being excessively challenged. This is hardly appropriate to events in the GDR. Another scenario is much more applicable: due to external, accidental and unforeseen causes the capability of the repressive apparatus is suddenly so reduced that even a limited and relatively harmless manifestation of opposition and resistance in the population has devastating consequences on the stability of the system. This was without question the course of change in the GDR.

What, precisely, immobilized the repressive apparatus of the GDR during the fall of 1989? The causes lay exclusively in the area of foreign policy, that is, they were due neither to newly arising liberal trends in GDR politics nor to the interior collapse of repressive mechanisms. The immediate cause was the unwillingness of the Hungarian government to prevent GDR citizens who had originally come to Hungary as tourists from travelling to the Federal Republic. Another reason was the clear signal from the Soviet Union, caught up in the politics of *perestroika*, that it would refuse to support political repression by giving the GDR 'fraternal help' in the form of either military or political assistance, in contrast to what happened in Czechoslovakia at the height of the Brezhnev doctrine in 1968. Thirdly, a mass escalation of repression on a major scale had become unthinkable (except in Romania) because of world-wide denunciation of a massacre such as was carried out by the Chinese leadership against the democratic movement in Peking in July 1989. All of these external circumstances, together perhaps with a proliferating loss of faith and determination on the part of segments of the political elite, contributed to the massive devaluation and in the end outright capitulation of the state's repressive capacities.

The demise of the regime was thus caused, in the last analysis, by the loss of repressive pressure, not the rise of counter-pressure. A democratic movement as such did not surface in the GDR until the government's control of repression was in the process of collapsing, and as a consequence the citizens' movement was able to develop in relative safety. It was not the movement that brought about victory. It was just the opposite: the obvious weakness of the state apparatus encouraged and triggered the growth of a democratic movement. Unlike in Poland and Hungary, in the GDR there were only weak attempts at creating opposition movements during the 1980s. These consisted of religious groups, intellectuals, artists and members of the professional world; also natural scientists, physicians and lawyers, from whose circles came the political elite during the transitional period of 1990. Their most important themes were civil and human rights, peace and disarmament, as well as environmental concerns. The connection with the politics of the new social movements as they became established in Western Europe in the 1970s and 1980s was clear from the content of the demands, forms of (non-violent) action, organization and social base of these oppositional forces in the GDR. Unlike the Polish Solidarność movement, these urban protest movements in the GDR were limited to relatively primitive forms of organization and certainly did not result in the formation of oppositional parties or unions. Civil rights and protest groups which developed before the fall of 1989 were unable, with their issues and strategies, to gain support or sympathy from within the industrial working class or the rural population, to say nothing about parties loyal to the regime or the state apparatus. Members of the social science, humanities or literary intelligentsia were conspicuously rare in their ranks: simply no room existed structurally in the GDR for a leadership role such as that assumed by Vaclav Havel in the CSR, precisely because of the lack of a distinctive 'national language' in the former country, a circumstance that enabled dissident writers to leave for West Germany with ease, and sometimes even to leave at the instigation of the regime, which preferred to see them abroad than to let them become involved in 'hostile' political activities.

The weakness of democratic opposition forces was evident not only in their late appearance, but also in their early decline. In short, they represented a short-lived and politically hopeless minority position, which, to be sure, was strong enough – given the unexpected weakening of the weak repressive apparatus – to promote the regime's breakdown and to provide direction to the process of its accelerating disorganization for several weeks. At the same time they were much too weak and inarticulate to be able to define the ends and the means of the subsequent post-Communist transition. As long as the old regime survived, the dissident movement was somewhat immune from repression in that it exhibited some loyalty to the GDR as a state and society, if most definitely not to its existent regime. But a positive image of what should and could be accomplished within a reformed society and polity after the demise of the monopolistic party in terms of a 'third road' of democratic socialism never became clear, let alone hegemonic.

The decisive factor that brought about the definitive end of the GDR was not democratic protest, but the perfectly legitimate, as well as urgent, desire for economic prosperity and, following in its path, a massive emigration of people made possible by the crumbling of the Wall on 9 November 1989. The GDR revolution was an 'exit revolution', not a 'voice revolution'. It was not that a victorious collective struggle for a new political order marked the end of the GDR, but that the emigration of individuals and their shared desire to let the West Germans take over rendered its economic existence as a state socialist mode of production unsustainable.

How should things continue politically? Which traditions and institutions of the GDR might conceivably be saved? Which constitution and parties, what territorial organization and degree of sovereignty for the area of the GDR should be preserved? All these questions were in effect left to the West German government to decide. A new draft constitution proposed by representatives of the civic movement as the result of round-table negotiations was not even admitted for consideration by the newly elected parliament of the GDR in April 1990. The people of the GDR were not consulted and did not demand to be heard – so long as prospects of their participation in West German prosperity remained a sign of hope for a better future. At the bottom of it lay a lack of moral and political involvement on the part of the GDR population, a total lack of loyalty towards its own political existence. The people of the GDR emerged not as the winner of a revolution, but as a bankrupt estate in search of a new management. What happened next was left to the discretion of the West German government (which was committed to unification by its constitution), fully aware that the bargaining power of the East German government was virtually nil. Accordingly, without resistance, even passively and fatalistically, the West German party system was allowed to take over first, and then in rapid succession the currency, the economic and social security systems and finally the private and constitutional laws of the FRG were imposed on its newly gained eastern territories. The Unity Treaty that was negotiated between the two governments during the summer of 1990 stipulated that, at midnight of 2 October 1990, one of the two sovereign parties to the treaty would cease to exist. The ease with which this contractual self-annihilation of the GDR was agreed upon confirmed in retrospect that the statehood of the GDR, its political integration as an entity of the international system, had always been rather fictitious – in spite of the formal international recognition it had earned in the sixties and seventies. It turned out that the GDR had not been solidly recognized internally, that is, by its own people.

How far the GDR had been from becoming a 'nation' through its own collective self-confidence and identity became apparent in the lack of a voice of its own during the process of unification. A distinctive and respectable tradition worth preserving and insisting upon was not present in the GDR, according to the vast majority of the political forces that emerged after the regime's breakdown. Initial efforts to appeal to particular political and cultural attributes and achievements on which a sense of 'national' pride and identity could be built soon proved to be futile. At best one came up with optical illusions: what might have been taken for components of a specific GDR identity (for example, a culture of helpfulness, leisurely and solidary conduct of life and modesty in a society of 'niches' and bottlenecks) soon turned out to be just artefacts engendered by the authoritarian rule of the party monopoly and command economy. These artefacts were soon seen to evaporate together with the conditions that had given rise to them.

Instead of proclaiming or trying to preserve traces of some GDR identity, the newly established East German political elite was anxious to assimilate itself and to become fluent in the language and style of Bonn politics. In the meantime former dissidents and members of the civic movements concentrated on looking back in an attempt to 'come to terms with' the history of the GDR, and to uncover and denounce the enormous network of security operations and systematic abuse of human and civil rights that had occurred under the old regime – rather than trying to play a role under the new political conditions. In contrast to the situation after 1945, when the 'anti-fascist' rejection of the past regime and its crimes implied very clear proposals for the shaping of the future, no such programmatic forward-looking 'anti-state-socialist' message was taken up by the victims and opponents of the old regime (see chapter 8). Thus virtually the only way in which the former opposition contributed to the unification process was in expressing its suffering under the old regime. The single exception to this pattern of either eagerly looking to the West or self-commiseratingly remaining fixed to the past is to be found in the former Socialist Unity Party (SED), restructured by new personnel and programmes and now renamed the Party of Democratic Socialism (PDS), which in the federal elections of 1994 established itself as an East German regional protest party with rather uncertain 'socialist' ambitions.

The 'identity' and international role of the GDR was built upon the increasingly stable and relatively prosperous economy that it was able to build in the course of its forty years of existence, and it literally disappeared from the map due to its sudden and unanticipated economic collapse. The loyalty of its citizens was contingent upon the state's ability to supply them with rising standards of living and high levels of social security, which in turn was premised upon repression and the prohibition of escape. Thus the collapse was triggered by the sudden breakdown of the exit barrier that now turned out to have been the decisive 'force of production' of the regime. After the Wall came down, the regime was unable to rely on any obligations of national identity or political legitimacy as potential alternative sources of its citizens' loyalty.

The collapse was not induced by a widely shared intrinsic desire for national unity with West Germany, nor by an intrinsic desire for liberal-democratic forms of political life. To be sure, the latter desire was voiced by the short-lived democratic-revolutionary civil movement, which, however, was the product rather than the moving force of the collapse. I suggest, for these two negative reasons, that the dramatic and unexpected breakdown of the GDR cannot be explained in terms of any category of 'collective will' or in terms of the historical logic of a coming to a head of long-inherent crisis tendencies, but must be accounted for in terms of a contingent and rather 'accidental' chain of events to which the economic mode of integration, the only one the GDR was based upon, eventually fell victim.

Was it a 'fortunate' accident, we might ask. That is certainly the case if we look at the immediate results, which now enable a larger population to participate in liberal-democratic forms of government and legal guarantees denied them until very recently. The definitive end of the Cold War and the dangers of military conflict stemming from it should most certainly also be welcomed. Less certain, however, is the balance sheet concerning the internal and international dynamics of a newly unified German state with its large post-socialist component. At least, it is still uncertain what mode (and what degree) of integration, cohesion and self-recognition is likely to be achieved underneath the formal and tenuous cover of formal unified statehood. The question remains whether this formation will be able to avail itself of the forces of internal integration and cohesion – the forces whose absence within the GDR suddenly revealed itself in 1989 and caused its sudden disintegration.

I have already mentioned the syndrome of 'elite nationalism' as the proposed glue of unity. Throughout the first half of the 1990s German political elites, not only those governing in Bonn, continued to rely upon the notion of national unity as a 'blessing' to be cherished as a value in itself. The extent, however, to which the sentiments of pride and duty invoked by this formula carry weight within the people of the united nation is highly uncertain. Surveys indicate that, if asked whether they see themselves more as 'Germans' or as 'East Germans', almost half of the Easterners opt for the latter. And nor does the term 'blessing' seem to be an accurate reflection of the sentiments of West Germans, who have become increasingly weary of the economic burdens imposed upon them by transfers of funds to the East. In short, the idea of 'blessing' does not mirror the feelings of the population; it was created, rather, by political elites in an effort to motivate people and to win support for the heavy burdens and sacrifices that the process of economic integration imposes upon both parts of the country.

It is hardly surprising that recognition of the suggested 'duty to sacrifice out of national solidarity' is qualified by economic interests. Solidarity and a national sense of belonging, which have been appealed to by political elites, are obviously constrained by distributional considerations, as well as structural differences, such as these: the population of the FRG is almost four times as large as that of the GDR; the FRG is much more prosperous and will remain so for a long time; public life in the FRG is shaped to a much greater extent by the two major Christian denominations than is the case in the 'atheist' (and otherwise mostly Protestant) GDR, which, for instance, provided a very different status and role for women. Dialects and other linguistic differences make it easy to classify most speakers according to their origin in East or West.

Such differences in terms of the respective experience of political and economic developments and style or habits, along with many mostly unflattering mutual stereotypes reflecting the awareness of these differences, have become more visible as a consequence of unification, and new distribution conflicts between the two territories continue to dominate the scene of unification politics. Quite obviously, there will be winners and losers on both sides. If these conflicts and potential conflicts are to be mitigated by the medicine of the sentiments of national unity and appeals to national duty, it is not unlikely that dangerously high doses of it will be required.

But even in the absence of such dangerous escalation a 'national sentiment' is unpromising as a legitimating resource for the management of unification conflicts. The legitimating reference to the 'unity of all Germans' inevitably generates as many conflicts as it possibly solves. First, because not all people of German cultural identity live within the borders of united Germany. Thus appeals to German-ness will be perceived by Poles, in spite of contractual agreements concluded between the two states, as a continuing threat that the national

Right of the FRG will encourage German residents of Poland, and eventually the German government, to proclaim rights to the 'German East'. Secondly, conflicts can also develop from the reverse situation: not all people who live in Germany have a German cultural identity, but many come originally from Mediterranean countries – in large cities as many as 10 per cent of the resident population. In addition to 'guest workers', there is an increasing number of undocumented immigrants and of people applying for political asylum. As domestic policies are strengthened by the concept of 'national unity', material living conditions are clearly put into jeopardy, along with the civil rights and the cultural opportunity for recognition of the non-German population.

Thirdly, the preoccupation of the federal government with the enormous problems associated with unification and 'national unity' is likely to result in a corresponding decline in the attention paid to all 'non-German' issues and all responsibilities that are not exclusively 'national' in scope. Responsibilities such as Third World aid, global environmental problems, support for other East European countries and, further, all 'non-productivist' issues might suffer under the newly found priorities of an inward-looking focus on integration and reconstruction of the eastern parts of the country.

Since its very inception the West German state, together with its society, has derived its identity and its remarkably robust inner cohesion from what could be described as an institutionalized superiority complex. With respect to the political and constitutional order, modelled after the example of the Western liberal democracies, this sense of superiority related to the 'totalitarian' order of its own Nazi past, as well as to the East German and East European state socialist present. Concerning its post-war 'economic miracle', its highly competitive and export-oriented industrial economy and its development of a 'social market economy', the West Germans and their political elites prided themselves on having accomplished an unparalleled success story. But in the 1990s these two underpinnings of social cohesion and undisturbed order have come under stress and strain from the dual challenges of German and European integration. In such a situation a relapse into a predominantly 'national' mode of integration (routinely described by conservative and some liberal politicians as a 'healthy' national awareness) presents itself, particularly after the demise of the totalitarian external opponent to whose existence the old Federal Republic owed much of its contrastive sense of identity.

The new Federal Republic has forgone the opportunity to reconstitute itself through the formal act of adopting a new constitution (as in fact called for by section 146 of the Basic Law) and thereby specifying the basis of a binding post-anti-totalitarian political consensus. Had such a constitution been adopted, it would have created and stipulated the obligations to each other that citizens of the German state must fulfil. No appeal to national sentiment would be necessary to legitimate such obligations, and no resentment against this appeal would be nurtured. The constitution of the FRG founded in 1949 was, of course, described by itself as a provisional one. The constitutional democratic order it established was not founded through democratic procedures (such as a constitutional referendum or an elected constitutional assembly), as the transitory nature of the project was thought to make such formalities unnecessary. All the more reason to have a formal constitution-making act after 1990.

Such an act was required because of, among other things, a condition in section 23 which allows any part of Germany presently not covered by the Basic Law to 'accede' to the Federal Republic by the unilateral declaration of its wish to do so. It was via this stipulation that the fusion of the GDR with the Federal Republic took place on 3 October 1990. The implication of the choice of this accession procedure is that neither the population of the FRG nor the population of the GDR was ever given the chance to agree expressly (through methods other than a mere international contract) to the conditions governing the new combined state. They were not given the chance, that is to say, to express a formal commitment and binding willingness to accept the responsibilities and share the burdens involved in the fusion of the two states. In other words each citizen, each interest group, each regional government and each political party can in future conflicts and with some justification take the line that unification just resulted from some inter-governmental emergency operation, dictated by at the time uncontrollable circumstances, which therefore does not have the force and the quality of a lasting and binding contractual commitment engaged in by the people themselves. The conditions in which this agreement came into being are too weak to exclude the opportunistic questioning of its validity and bindingness. But the point of a constitution is precisely to function as a barrier to opportunism: a constitution operates in the temporal pattern of a *futurum exactum* in that it provides the future with a past which it cannot ignore and from which it cannot escape.

At the same time the need for such forces of self-binding and widely supported validity will surely increase. Everything indicates that the self-righteous triumph of conservatives and liberals – whose views of the superiority of the order of the capitalist market and of property seem to be irrevocably justified by history – will be short-lived. Feelings of triumph undermine people's learning capacity; even in

capitalist countries the problems of work and employment, of relations between the sexes, generations and ethnic groups, of social justice and the responsible treatment of natural resources have not
moved an inch closer to their solution through the demise of Eastern
European socialism. The now unreal and unproductive contrast
between the capitalist and the socialist blocs has come to an end, while
marking the beginning of an intra-capitalist dynamic of conflicts and
contradictions that can no longer be resolved by means of economic
growth and welfare state provision. As a comparatively harmless
example I cite the predicted five-fold increase of cars in East Europe
within the nineties – an ecological nightmare exceeded only by that of
an explosion of ethnic particularism in a greater, barrier-free geographical area. The more unpredictable these turbulences and their
explosive potential, the more important it seems to be able to rely on
rules, rights and procedures that are not easily and opportunistically
bent in response to the vagaries of business cycles or nationalist sentiments. As a result a great deal of optimism is required to believe in
the ability of the newly created German state to establish unity based
not on precarious growth and predictably short-lived national enthu-
siasm, but on the adequate and binding constitutional principles of a
German democratic republic worthy of its name.

3

Capitalism by Democratic Design? Democratic Theory Facing the Triple Transition in East Central Europe

Convergence theories of the sixties and seventies predicted that the two rival political economic systems would more or less rapidly assimilate each other and inevitably move towards each other. The East was to be enriched with market elements, while the 'mixed' economic order of Western capitalism had already adopted elements of state intervention in production and distribution processes. The problem with this theory, as is now becoming apparent, was that only the West was capable of 'mixing', whereas the socialist societies were constantly on the verge of 'capsizing' through concessions made to political liberalization (party competition, freedom of opinion), national independence, decentralized forms of ownership and competitive price formation, to say nothing of 'economic democracy'. Western 'admixtures' in terms of economic or political organization were not allowed or were taken back, with Hungary adopting the boldest reform moves. Everywhere the self-transformation of socialist societies foundered on the political elites' fear (justified, as it turned out) of downward paths. The 'oil-spill thesis', which predicts that the entire system will be spoiled when just a single 'alien' element or move is introduced, proved not to apply to precisely those systems for which it was considered to hold true in the twenties by von Mieses, that is, Western capitalist democracies. It was corroborated all the more clearly, however, by the state socialist regimes. As is shown by the results of the debates of the sixties and seventies over economic reform in the Eastern bloc, these regimes did not manage to incorporate their opposite principle in both sufficient and harmless dosage.

Resolute 'reforms from above' were ruled out in the eyes of the Soviet leadership, for it was suspected they would lead to incalculable complications and destabilizations – even to dangerous encouragement of 'reforms from below' or, still worse, a 'revolution from below'. What was left in this blocked situation was a way out which seemed as unlikely before as it looks inevitable after the fact: the way of a 'revolution from the top', for which the name Mikhail Gorbachev stands. This Soviet revolution from the top created the conditions necessary for the success of the reforms and revolutions from the bottom which followed on its heels in the other countries belonging to the crumbling Warsaw Pact and the CMEA.

This upheaval is a revolution without a historical model and a revolution without a revolutionary theory. Indeed its most conspicuous distinguishing characteristic is the lack of any elaborated theoretical assumptions and normative arguments addressing the questions of who is to carry out which actions in which circumstances and with what aims, which dilemmas are to be expected along the road, how ought the new synthesis of a post-revolutionary order be constituted and what meaning should be assigned to the notion of 'progress'. In all of the revolutions of the last two centuries some kind of answer to these questions had been available before revolutionary action was undertaken, though most of them proved wrong. The answers of revolutionary theorists were formulated independently of the immediate contexts of action and were known to those participating; in that sense they were theoretical answers. In the case of the Eastern and Central European upheavals of 1989–91, however, these questions remain for the time being unanswered or are given only tactically coloured answers in the form of self-explications and situation-bound *ad hoc* assessments by participants. The rapid flow of events not only broke out unexpectedly, it was also not guided by any premeditated sequence, or by proven principles, interests and organizational forms about which the participants were clear. Instead of concepts, strategies, mediating bodies and normative principles there are individuals and their discoveries of the moment, with their deliberately opaque semantic content. Among them are the catchwords *glasnost* and *perestroika* and the metaphor of a 'common European home'.

The distinctly 'a-theoretical' character of the upheaval is reflected in the literary forms which accompany it. Entirely absent are all analytical expressions and grandiose directives by revolutionary intellectuals, of which Lenin's *State and Revolution* of 1917 remains a model.

Where the social theorists express themselves at all, they do so not in the form of global interpretations of the events and their driving dynamics, but rather in more modest descriptions of single aspects, if not in the role of mere citizen and concerned person and without claiming any professionally privileged insight. This upheaval, so it seems, for the time being has forced the ideologues and theoreticians to a welcome silence, while being simultaneously the great hour of such literary forms as the diary, reportage, the letter, the interview and the autobiography. In the absence of any valid or, for that matter, any kind of prescriptive 'ex-ante' revolutionary theory in the East (or a positive and predictive theory of the demise of the Soviet empire in the West), the task of the social scientist is to understand in retrospect what actually happened.

Since the early eighties, under the label 'transition to democracy', an important and successful research branch in the social sciences has concerned itself with comparative studies of political modernizing processes since the Second World War (O'Donnell et al. 1986). Three groups of countries stand at the centre of these investigations: the 'post-war democracies' (Italy, Austria, Japan and West Germany); the Mediterranean democratic processes of the seventies (Portugal, Spain, Greece); and the collapse of the authoritarian regimes in South America during the eighties (Argentina, Brazil, Uruguay, Chile, Paraguay).

The suggestive temptation to add a fourth group to these – that is, that of the Central and East European states – and to analyse them with the proven instrument supplied by this research tradition turns out, however, to be at least partly unsuitable and misleading. The 'revolution' (if that is still the right term, given the above particularities) taking place in the former socialist countries is basically different in two respects from the transitions in the countries mentioned above. First, in the case of the post-war democracies (with the exception of divided Germany) and the South European and South American countries the territorial integrity and organization of each country were largely preserved and the process of democratization did not occasion any large-scale population migrations. These states retained their population, and the populations remained in their states. In Central and East Europe the situation is different: there the scene is dominated by territorial disputes, migrations, ethnic and other minority conflicts and corresponding secessionist longings (again this does not include the German exception of the so far only national merger of the two previously separate states). Following the breakdown of the Communist regimes in Central East Europe all four of the ethno-territorial moves that were largely unknown in the other transitions dominate the scene: (1) erecting new borders through secession or demanding local and regional autonomy for minorities; (2) negating the legitimacy of existing borders; (3) moving people across borders, ranging from 'voluntary' mass exodus to 'ethnic cleansing'; and (4) negating previously recognized ethnic differences through forced assimilation.

Even more important is a second difference. In the above-mentioned cases of 'transition to democracy' the modernizing processes are of a strictly political and constitutional sort, that is, they concern the form of government and the legal relationships between the state and society, whereas at the end of socialism the additional task of reforming the economy is the order of the day. In the countries that underwent a transition to democracy in the other three groups capital remained largely in the hands of its owners and as a rule the owners remained in charge of their capital. The Soviet Union and its former satellites are faced with an acute and altogether different, as well as more demanding, problem: the transfer of the hitherto state-owned productive assets to other forms of proprietor and, to this end, the creation of an entirely new class of entrepreneurs and owners in a way that has to be decided and justified politically and through politically visible agencies. The political installation of an entrepreneurial class (that is, of a previously non-existent category of people whose existence was explicitly abolished at the point at which the old regime was established) whose members are now to participate in market competition on the basis of ownership rights means reversing the economic order, a task which none of the previous transitions had to accomplish (and which is rather belittled by the revolution's being described as just 'catching up', as in Habermas 1990: 179–204).

Three levels of the political universe

The unique and unprecedented nature of the East Central European process of transformation – and the challenges to democratic theory emerging from it – is fully highlighted only if we remind ourselves that any operative political system is the combined outcome of three hierarchical levels of decision-making (Easton 1965: chs 10–13). At the most fundamental level a 'decision' must be made as to who 'we' are, that is, a decision on identity, citizenship and the territorial, as well as social and cultural, boundaries of the nation state. At the second level, rules, procedures and rights must be established which together make up the constitution, or the institutional framework of the 'regime'. It is only at the highest level, that is, within the parameters of those two previous premises, that those processes and decisions occur which are sometimes mistaken for the essence of politics, namely the decisions on 'who gets what, when and how' – both in terms of political power and economic resources.

Arguably, each of the three levels stands in close affinity to and invokes one of the three human capabilities that early modern political philosophers distinguished. The first relates to passions, virtue, honour and patriotism, the second to reason and the third to interest.[1] This three-tiered model clearly suggests links of upward determination: 'normal politics' that is going on at the third level is embedded in identities and constitutions. In most political systems this determination is unilateral and causal rather than intentional. By 'unilateral' I mean the asymmetrical relationship whereby the lowest of the three levels determines the higher ones, and the causal arrow only rarely, if ever, points in the opposite direction. For instance, the constitution will govern normal politics much more often than it becomes the object of normal (or rather exceptional) politics of constitution-making, resulting in constitutional change. There is simply not much retroactivity. By 'causal' (as opposed to intentional) determination I mean that the effect the lower level(s) will have upon the higher one(s) is not due to some purposive action or design on the part of interested parties. It is precisely because procedures are made certain by constitutions that outcomes are contingent, as Przeworski (1991) has argued.

Inserted between the three levels there are veils of ignorance which limit the range of intentionality prompted by particular interests. These veils of ignorance result from, among other things, the markedly different temporal structure of our three levels: we tend to believe – and experience tends to confirm – that nations last for centuries, constitutions for many decades and governments or positive law passed by the legislature for just a few years. If this is so, how could any conceivable individual design the boundaries of a nation state with the purpose of thereby determining the much more contingent downstream phenomena of constitutions and regimes, governments and the allocation of rights and resources? As long as decisions at the two lower levels must be taken as fixed, the system is highly path-dependent, and its parameters are strategy-proof.

As far as the third of these three levels is concerned, democratic theory provides good answers, both positive and normative. Troubles and paradoxes begin if we move down one level: should the players be allowed to decide on the rules of the game they are in the process of playing, as well as the scope of what the game is 'about'? And, if so, under what precautionary conditions may they do so? Can democracy itself be democratized, including the option of abolishing democracy by democratic means (cf. Holmes 1988)? And, if the answer is no, in what sense can we still speak of a 'democracy' and its presumption of 'popular sovereignty'? Even more thorny questions relate to the first level, that of nationhood, collective identity and territorial boundaries. Whatever the constitutional rules are, only those who already enjoy citizenship rights are admitted to an active role in the game. But does that mean that those basic admission rules can be based only on the unilateral decisions of those who are, due to their place of birth or inherited citizenship rights, already admitted to the game or, alternatively, can they be based on the brute facts of international or civil wars, at best constrained by the fragile web of international law and transnational regimes? Or can democratic theory transcend its home territory of 'normal politics' and provide criteria according to which both constitutional change and the definition of boundaries can be ascribed the quality of being more or less 'democratic'?

In the first half of the 1990s these questions have moved from their secluded place on the agenda of philosophical seminars into widely perceived practical problems covered in daily front-page news. What used to be the Second World of the Soviet empire is now undergoing a triple transformation affecting all three levels: nationhood, constitutional order and the 'normal politics' of the allocation and distribution of positive rights and resources through legislatures and executives. The very simultaneity of the three transformations generates an unprecedented load of decision-making. Unlike in the Western democracies, there is no time for slow maturation, experience and learning along the evolutionary road of nation-building, constitution-making and the politics of allocation and distribution. And there are neither model cases that might be imitated nor, for that matter, a victorious power imposing its will from the outside, as was the case with the new East and West European postwar regimes. As a consequence the decisions made on all three of these levels may easily turn out to be incompatible and thus to obstruct each other, rather than forming a coherent whole.

The risk resulting from simultaneity is exacerbated by a second one. The situation of extreme contingency invites opportunism, and the veil of ignorance is lifted. Now people are in a position to see which constitutional design and which ethnic boundaries of a state will best serve their interest in policy outcomes. The situation is replete with opportunities, rightly perceived to be unique in their scope, to improve one's 'original endowment' or, for that matter, to take one's revenge. Correspondingly, there is an increase in the amount of 'moral effort' required to overcome the temptations generated by a situation that is no longer strategy-proof. In the absence of the requisite amount of such effort everything – boundaries, rights, procedures and the allocation of power, legal rights and material resources – will be argued for and advocated in consequentialist, acquisitive and hence potentially divisive terms, rather than on the basis of historical antecedents and principles of justice, freedom and peace.

The dilemma of simultaneity

In view of these two added dimensions the revolutionary transformation in Eastern Europe can be analysed only with conceptual means whose use has not been called for in almost all of Western and Southern Europe since the First World War. Simultaneously at stake in the Soviet Union and most of its former satellites are:

the territorial[2] issue, that is, the determination of the borders for a state and a population, and the consolidation of these borders within the framework of a European order of states ('common European home');

the issue of democracy, that is, the dissolution of the monopoly claims of a party and its replacement by a constitutionally tamed exercise of authority and party competition in the context of guarantees of basic human and civil rights (*glasnost*);

the issue of the economic and property order and the orderly political management of pressing production and distribution problems (*perestroika*).

The stages of a process, which in the case of the 'normal' West European examples were mastered over a centuries-long sequence (from the nation state to capitalism, and then to democracy), must thus be gone through nearly simultaneously in Eastern Europe (just as both components of a 'modern' political economy, namely democracy and private property, had also been simultaneously abolished by the October Revolution). This occasions not only gigantic decision-making burdens, but also the effect of mutual obstruction. It may well be that each one of those problems can be solved only when the situation makes it possible to assume that one or even both of the other two problems have already been solved or are presently not in need of a solution. In the following discussion I wish to examine the phenomenon of the mutual obstruction of solutions to problems and thereby to show that although the proverbial advice to do 'one thing at a time' rather than 'everything at the same time' may have good grounds in its favour, the protagonists may well find themselves in the tragic situation of having to reject this piece of advice and to decline recognizing these good grounds on the basis of equally good grounds.

All of this would amount to idle contemplation if it were shown that the opening of a hitherto planned economy to a market economy and the democratization of the political decision process do not exclude and impede each other, but rather facilitate and enhance one another. In point of fact there are analyses of the existent socialist systems which attempt to establish that such an interaction takes place between the two goals – already desirable in themselves – of economic and political modernization. Considering the political and economic development in Czechoslovakia prior to 1968, Jirí Kosta has tried to show 'that the process of reforming the economy [which was forced on the regime at the beginning of the sixties by the manifest inefficiency of the planning procedures] . . . would over the course of only a few years change to a democratic movement, which would sweep away the old leadership' (1991: 302ff). To be sure, there remained the problem that the virtuous circle allegedly obtaining between economic liberalization and political democratization was broken by the third issue, that of the integrity of national borders and the sovereignty of state power, by the events of August 1968 and the proclamation of the Brezhnev doctrine.

A Pandora's box of paradoxes

In the mid-1990s, on the other hand, the field in all the concerned disciplines and political camps is dominated by rather pessimistic vicious-circle assumptions. The only circumstance in which a market economy and democracy can be simultaneously implanted and prosper is the one in which both are forced upon a society from the outside and guaranteed by international relations of dependency and supervision for a long period of time. This, at least, is arguably the lesson offered by the war-ruined post-war democracies of Japan and, with qualification, of the Federal Republic of Germany – and perhaps also of the political and economic space of the former German Democratic Republic. Otherwise there reigns everywhere an asymmetrical antagonism: 'The market requires the development of a democracy, but democracy does not demand the emergence of a market . . . If *perestroika* founders, then it will also soon be over for *glasnost*.' The members of the former Polish, Bulgarian, Romanian and Soviet bureaucracies who are newly oriented towards economic reform may be in complete agreement with this resolutely free-market message when they plead that what is now required is the iron hand of a strong presidential regime and not a 'premature' democratic opening, which they fear would invite all kinds of counter-productive conflicts. The Stalinists who rescued themselves to the shores of post-Communism diverge from the free-market thesis only to the extent that they proclaim that if *perestroika* is not to founder, then *glasnost* must be forgotten.

A further dilemma may be outlined as follows: a constitutional and democratic political system finds its appropriate content of issues and divisions, the smooth processing of which in turn continuously reinforces its legitimacy only if a certain measure of autonomous economic development has already taken place and if interest coalitions and mediating bodies, together with their divisions and themes of conflict, have – in contrast to what is the case in the forcibly homogenized societies of state socialism – emerged from the system of the social division of labour. Only a somewhat developed free-market society with a relatively high level of wealth enables competitive democracy to work as a procedure for the arbitration and reconciliation of interests (cf. Lipset 1981: 469–76). In a society in which a labour market is unknown and the overwhelming majority of the adult population consists of so-called *Werktätige* (working people, *trudjascijsja*) with similar incomes and uniformly regulated educational, housing and living standards, competitive democracy lacks, due to this 'atomized' (Schöpflin 1991c) social structure of 'repressed difference', sufficiently formed protagonists, associations and issues considered worth processing through the machinery of democratic politics. Or, alternatively, the lack of a developed complexity in civil society leads to the dominance of themes which, albeit suited to conflict, are not also equally suited to compromise. In both of these seemingly polar cases, perfect homogeneity and deep antagonism, the social structure lacks the requisite degree of differentiation, namely the division of labour, status, interest and cultural identity that only a developed market society will generate. But homogeneity may just be the surface appearance of repressed antagonism. The Polish sociologist Jadwiga Staniskis has that case in mind when she writes: 'As long as the economic foundations for a genuine civil society do not exist, the massive political mobilization of the population is only possible along nationalist or fundamentalist lines' (1991: 326). She implies that such themes of mobilization would lead to the rapid perversion of democratic openness into a populist authoritarian regime hostile to internal or external minorities. As a consequence not only the free-market economy but also democracy itself would be ruined if the latter were too hastily introduced. What this seems to suggest, again, is that the market must precede democracy.

On the other hand even before introducing private property and the market economy it is necessary to have procedures which hold the political elites accountable and enable participation on the part of the majority of the population – in other words at least rudimentary democratic procedures are necessary at the initial stage of the transformation. This is so not only because democratic concessions, apart from being a minimum condition for much needed economic aid from abroad, are alone able to appease the indignation at the arbitrariness and paternalist authoritarianism that were practised by the old regime, but also because from a certain point of view democratization appears – despite the three points to the contrary made before – to be the precondition of economic transformation. In contrast to that of its Western companion, the market economy that is emerging in Eastern Europe will be, if it in fact emerges, 'political capitalism'. It is a capitalism designed, organized and set into motion by reform elites. Its driving force is not the pre-political datum of owners' (Lockian) natural right to their property and its free enjoyment. Rather, the driving force is what in the case of the Western countries was discovered only subsequently as a welcome functional side-effect of an economic order based on the freedom to own property, namely that an efficient economic mechanism serves, at least arguably and in the long run, the overall interest of society. Thus the reform elites, by taking responsibility for and helping to start a capitalist economic mechanism, represent the interests of society without, however, being able in the process to rely upon and comply with the demands of an already existing class of capitalist owners and their interests, power and ideological propositions.

Again the contrast to Western patterns of the growth of capitalism is obvious. In the West a class of proprietors claims rights which it bases upon moral and ideological arguments that are critical of the forces and institutions of the absolutist, mercantile and feudal old regimes; efficiency, economic growth and eventually prosperity are mere by-products of the victorious ideological initiatives taken by early entrepreneurial and commercial protagonists. In the East, in contrast, privatization and marketization are not rights-driven, but outcome-oriented; not class-based, but elite-initiated; not creeping and halting, but sudden and highly visible; not supported by moral and ideological arguments on rights and freedoms, but defended in the name of vehemently and universally desired economic prosperity.

That the introduction of property rights and market mechanisms is in the interest of society as a whole is, however, typically not reliably recognized and appreciated by the empirical will of the majority of the population. Such reluctance to believe in the desired beneficial outcomes proclaimed and promised by reform elites is due to two quite sound reasons: first, the population has grounds to suspect that the privatizing initiatives of the new reforming elites might not necessarily serve the universal improvement of economic conditions, but rather contribute in the first place to the enrichment of the members of the state apparatus and its clientele. Secondly, no one can guarantee that the envisaged improvement of the economic situation will in fact occur, and that it will come about without massive and at least passing absolute economic deprivation of a sizeable portion of the population. These two misgivings – that the powerful will enrich themselves and that the powerless will fall victims to the market – can be overcome, and their destructive potential restrained, only if the elites in charge of reform secure a solid democratic mandate for their privatizing initiatives and recognize a fair accountability to the majority of the people. Such a mandate can in turn be obtained only via democratic means – which leads to the paradoxical result that in the case of the economies of the Soviet type and when a state-managed withdrawal of the state from the economy is to be undertaken, democracy is a necessary precondition of economic transformation. This is obviously the exact, albeit no less compelling, antithesis of the inferences set forth above.

Even though in many instances and according to the reformers' doctrinaire aspirations the reformed economic order may represent a 'purer' variety of capitalism than is to be encountered anywhere in the West, it remains a political project according to the post-socialist mode and its statist form of realization. This 'capitalism by design' (or capitalism without capitalists as active promoters of their class interests) depends in every detail on highly visible decisions which therefore require justification, and its development cannot rely on blind evolutionary emergences, which has largely been the pattern in the history of pioneering Western capitalisms. The new class of entrepreneurs (and, correspondingly, the new class of employees, into which the previous 'worker-citizens' see themselves falling) is created according to a blueprint designed by political elites.

In any event this blueprint contains multiple parameters, each of which is contingent and might be set in numerous different ways (cf. Stark 1990; Stark n.d.). Should all productive assets be privatized, or should state enterprises be maintained? In which sectors and over what stretches of time should the structural transformation take place? How should the new owners acquire their property – for example, via the gratuitous distribution of the capital stock (or a portion thereof) to the population, or to the employees or managers of enterprises? Or should it happen by auctioning off the capital stock to any possessor of financial capital? Or by being returned to the possibly still living former owners? Or even to their heirs? Should it be returned only to native or also to foreign interested parties? With or without liberalization of the capital market? With or without qualifications concerning such vital issues as categories of persons authorized to purchase, upper limits of capital acquisition per capita, maximum prices and minimum wages, licences to engage in foreign trade and dozens of further variables. It is barely conceivable that one could take a single step into this vast arena without arming oneself with strong legitimating reasons, which cannot be gained otherwise than through democratic politics.

Even if an extensive societal consensus favouring a 'capitalist' constitution of the economy (that is, the introduction of private property and marketization of goods, services, capital and labour) were to be assumed, this factual consensus could not suffice as a substitute for a formal and explicit democratic mandate for such reform initiatives. The point is precisely what is meant in operational terms by the only seemingly unequivocal concept of 'capitalism' or 'market economy' – to say nothing of 'social' market economy. But not even such a global and diffuse consensus in favour of capitalism – as a structure and process, as opposed to prosperity as the supposed outcome of both – can seriously be assumed to exist. For the situation which took place in the Soviet Union after the 'revolution from the top' and which set the ball rolling in the other countries of Central and Eastern Europe cannot be compared to the overwhelming imperative force of the 'zero hour' as it hit the Germans in 1945 after their total military, moral and material defeat and implied an inescapable commitment to a new political beginning whose parameters were fixed and enforced by the occupying powers. The Romanians and the Bulgarians are not alone today in seeming far removed from the consciousness of such a commitment, and no one can block the conceivable path back to some form of a state-managed economy from which these two countries never moved effectively away. Instead the political majority culture of an 'authoritarian egalitarianism' that seems to prevail in at least these two countries stands in the way both of a market economy and of democracy as uncontested goals for the process of reform. This pattern, as cultivated by and inherited from the old regime (and, beyond that, much of the East European historical experience; cf. Schöpflin 1991c), does not allow a market economy to unfold. For the latter functions under the premise that a general increase of output can be achieved only at the price of a minority's being in a position to increase its income far more substantially and more rapidly than the rest, who, at least for an interval of unknown duration, may even lose out. The market economy produces, along with the growing output of goods, a growing inequality – a tendency which is resisted by the egalitarian resentment. As for democracy, it is reproached with burdening the decision process with frictions, uncertainties and discontinuities, which threaten to interfere with the already precariously poor level of economic performance. This constellation of expectations and fears (which can of course also be activated by the memory of frustration with so many failed attempts at reform and broken promises in the past) would obviously have the consequence that, precisely because the economic situation is so dire, promising attempts at economic reform – and at its democratic legitimation – are blocked by a majority of the population.

To summarize the propositions that I have discussed so far: a market economy is set in motion only under pre-democratic conditions. In order to promote it democratic rights must be held back to allow for a healthy dose of original accumulation. Only a developed market economy produces the social structural conditions necessary for stable democracy and makes it possible to form compromises within the framework of what is perceived as a positive-sum game. But the introduction of a market economy in the post-socialist societies is a 'political' project, which has prospects of success only if it rests on a strong and explicit democratic legitimation. And it is possible that the majority of the population will find neither democracy nor a market economy a desirable prospect. If all of those propositions hold true at the same time, then we are presented with a Pandora's box of paradoxes, in the face of which every 'theory' – or, for that matter, rational strategy – of the transition must fail.

The core problem of the political and economic modernization of the former socialist societies resides in their lack of any non-contingent 'givens' which would be suitable fixed parameters of the politics of reform. Precisely because the system is at such a deadlock, everything becomes contingent and nothing can self-evidently remain as it is. The absence of a fixed set of trustworthy or at least uncontested social facts and binding institutions forces the reform politicians to some gigantic 'bootstrapping act' (Elster). For this reason also the quest for reliable foundations of societal and political accord clings to national identities and desires for ethnic self-assertion. Or, as Staniskis reports from Poland, it clings to 'exemplary communities' and doctrines such as the Roman Catholic social doctrine, which is now called on as a binding force in the strategy to maintain political order. Others raise the doctrines of neoclassical political economy to the status of a revealed doctrine of salvation. Still others think that they have found the 'Archimedean point' at which reform policies can be levered into place if in their countries they simply reproduce minutely one of the tested Western constitutional systems (such as the German Basic Law). These attempts at inventing traditions, exemplary models and dogmas can hardly be promising given the clear element of arbitrariness with which the political movements and elites choose these allegedly 'pre-political' fundamental truths or 'correct lines' and proclaim them as their programme.

This unavoidable circularity is particularly patent when, as in Poland, Bulgaria, Romania and Czechoslovakia (up to 1992), the newly elected parliaments also function as constituent assemblies. This indeed means nothing other than that the players determine the rules by which the future game will be played and by which it will be decided who will be a fellow player. Individuals are judges in their own case. Even though in the struggle over constitutional principles they appear as persons arguing in accordance with norms, they will be defenceless against the suspicion that in reality they are conducting their deliberations solely with their own interests in mind.

This suspicion is radicalized by the citizens' movements in the Eastern and Central European countries. The 'logical' difference between their way of proceeding and the activities of 'new social movements' in the West lies in the fact that the Western movements operate within the context of already created and solidly established democratic institutions and focus on overcoming some of the built-in biases, deficiencies and blind spots of these institutions. In so doing they can base themselves on a core of institutionally stable principles.[3] At times they have criticized political elites and constitutional practices by referring to the 'spirit' of the constitution itself and established principles of political culture. No such 'spirit', or set of generally approved principles and traditions, is yet in place in any of the post-Communist states.

In Eastern Europe the movements of former dissidents, as well as those of ethnic or religious fundamentalists, often have an unconditionally anti-institutional, if not outright 'anti-political', bent to them, which is all too understandable in view of their past experiences. Because they cannot refer to already established routines and call for the redemption of the principles embodied in them, they are exposed to the danger of wearing themselves out in idle contemplation, of overrating romantically direct democracy and extra-parliamentary forms of action, and of thereby overlooking the capacity for negotiation and compromise which would alone be capable of converting social mobilization into political power. As is to be expected, if this transformation fails, the mobilization will collapse and, in an abrupt reversal, give way to symptoms of apathy, cynicism and withdrawal into privacy among the majority of the people. At the end of such a cycle the initial atomized state of the post-totalitarian society would not be somehow overcome, but rather reproduced and reinforced. Because the negative coalitions of dissidents and citizens' movements had no coherent political and economic project of their own, they fell victim to the risk of failing to come to terms with the inexorable 'routinization' of their initial charisma. The former dissidents become politically sterile at the very moment when the bureaucracy of the old regime is deprived of its power and is thus eliminated as the only factor on which the opposition is united, and they disappear from the scene if they fail to take the turn away from lofty principles to the functional and pragmatic requirements of 'normal politics'.

In a series of recent works Jon Elster (1990) has attempted to explore and conceptualize the interdependencies and antinomies which arise in the process of carrying out political and economic reforms. In the case of economic reform the two components at issue are those of price reform (deregulation and the dismantling of the system of permanent subsidies provided for by soft budget constraints) and property reform (privatization). A price reform without a property reform would induce the temptation in the managers of state-owned firms to ignore price signals and to keep on squandering public capital by using it inefficiently. A price reform with a property reform would of course establish a complete capitalist system of control, that is, one with labour and capital markets, which is to say one with extensive lay-offs and business collapses. In the mid-1990s it is entirely unclear – though on the whole it seems rather improbable – whether in this respect promising and feasible intermediate solutions are available. They could be democratic with regard to the enterprise level (that is, of a cooperative sort): in that case one would have a capital market without a labour market. Or they could be democratic as regards the economy as a whole: there would then be a labour market without a capital market, and in place of the latter the investment funds would continue being allocated through some state agency. But, interestingly enough, no such mixed or halfway solutions to the problem of economic reform seem to have had much support among Central East European intellectual and political elites since 1989.

The political reform also consists of two measures: constitutional guarantee of civil rights and the accountability of state power through checks and balances. The first without the second would amount to a classical liberal constitutional state, in whose framework, as was shown above, the vast decision-making burdens of the project of 'political capitalism' could not be handled. Additionally, liberal constitutional guarantees would easily be exposed to the opportunistic grip of political elites, if the risk of their being democratically voted out of office did not stand in their way: 'Power must be divided to ensure that the constitution will be respected.' The second measure without the first (for example, mass democracy without freedom of the press) would be equally absurd and in Eastern Europe would have to boil down to forms of authoritarian populism, for it lacks sufficiently powerful intermediary bodies (political parties, associations, trade unions, churches, local governments) which could exercise a function of control *vis-à-vis* the demagogic presidential regimes.

From these assumptions in the model Elster draws the conclusion that property and price reforms, as well as the guarantees of freedom and democracy, condition each other mutually, that the guarantee of liberty and the reform of property stand in a harmonious relationship, but that there must be an irreconcilable antagonism between democracy and property and price reforms if the consequences of both of these economic reforms (namely unemployment and inflation) prove as disastrous for the former countries of the CMEA as was to be anticipated. The core of this antinomy is obvious: people do not want to wait until the blessings of the market economy reach them too and the shock waves of the transition have subsided. And nor are they willing to see the new economic elites (which may often be composed of elements of the old ones) becoming rich at their expense. In this mixture of fear, resentment and envy they are encouraged by their own dispositions acquired under the old regime, as well as by the interested parties in the 'conservative' circles of the old political elites. Add to that the fact that there are few intermediary institutions and people who would be capable of making the individual costs and risks of the transition a subjectively acceptable load and of guaranteeing that the pains and burdens of the economic transition are shared fairly in the present and compensated for by equitable returns in the long run.

One way to elaborate and refine Elster's model further might be as follows. Each of the two reforms, constitutional and economic, involves three steps: institutional framework, unfolding process and desired outcome. Democratic reforms thus consist in setting up a constitutional framework of civil rights and parliamentary government. These will supposedly lead to 'normal' competitive democratic politics and the allocation of power and material resources through it. The overall result is the peaceful resolution of social and political conflict. Similarly, economic reform consists in property rights and privatization, an unfolding process of competitive price setting and the desired result of productivity gains, growth and prosperity. Moreover, both chains of structure–process–result are intertwined and are supposed mutually to reinforce each other. If this is the theory, practice may have a number of unpleasant surprises in store. The seven most likely and plausible of them are these:

democratic politics may block or distort the road to privatization and hence marketization;

privatization may succeed, but fail to lead to marketization and hence to growth and prosperity; this could be due to the conservation of cartels and monopolistic structures which make the transition one that occurs not from 'plan to market', but 'from plan to clan' (D. Stark);

privatization may succeed, but lead to the obstruction of democratic politics through powerful interferences originating from domestic or international owners of capital;

democratic politics may evolve, but fail to lead to the peaceful resolution of social conflict as it is dominated by ethnic, territorial and minority conflicts that do not lend themselves to democratic forms of compromise;

marketization may succeed, but fail to generate the reality of (or even the widely perceived prospect of) an equitable distribution of its benefits;

accumulated disappointments and frustrations with these failures may give rise to demands for a type of 'democracy' that is based on an institutional structure other than civil liberties and representative government, such as populist presidential dictatorship;

conversely, frustrations with economic performance and distribution may also lead to demands for marketization without private property, for example, a return to state ownership of productive assets.

The tunnel effect and the political economy of patience

The temporal structure of processes is decisive. This applies not only to the macroscopic level, where, as the Western model teaches us, a sufficient time interval between the discrete modernizing thrusts (nation state, market economy, democracy and finally the welfare state), as well as different degrees of rigidity among our three levels, fosters their cumulative success, but also to the microscopic level of individuals. They must, if the simultaneous mastery of all the tasks of modernization is to succeed, be ready to muster a large measure of patience, confidence and trust. As macro-events have assumed an incredible speed, the painful task of patient waiting falls upon the individuals. They must quickly adapt themselves to the new circumstances and then be ready to wait for a long time for the fruits of this adaptation. They need this patience in order not to interfere with the 'creative destruction' which will follow the price and property reform in a perfectly intended manner, though by making use of their newly won civil rights they would be quite capable of doing so. Not only must they be sufficiently disciplined to willingly undergo shock therapy, but in the process they must also hold fast, in spite of commonly available evidence to the contrary, to the (perhaps self-fulfilling) belief that the shock will be a therapeutic one. What is required is therefore the very virtues and moral resources – flexibility, patient waiting, deliberating, probing, weighing one's short-term against long-term and individual against collective preferences, tolerance of highly unequal distribution patterns – which over the course of two (three in the case of the Soviet Union) generations of the 'construction of socialist society' were either discouraged and entirely under-utilized or excessively put to the test and frustrated as a result. Who would predict with any confidence that these virtues would flourish now?

Albert O. Hirschman (1981) has discussed this problem of the ability to wait, or of the political economy of patience, using the metaphor of the tunnel effect. The analogy is that of a tunnel for cars in which there are two lanes going in the same direction. There occurs a nasty traffic jam. In both lanes the cars come to a standstill, and no one sees what is going on. Suddenly the cars in the right lane begin moving and pass by the vehicles still blocked in the left lane. The occupants of the latter are now enduring a cognitive and emotional dynamic ranging from hopeful relief ('Well, after all, it'll soon be our turn to go!'), through envy of the lucky ones and indignation at an obviously unfair traffic regulation, to the open aggression that is displayed by those who try to force themselves illicitly into the moving traffic of the right lane and through the ensuing collisions bring the traffic to a renewed complete standstill. The question is, why is it that this nightmare scenario sometimes unfolds quite swiftly, sometimes quite slowly, while at other times it does not unfold at all? – the last on the happy occasion when the civilized behaviour and patience of the less fortunate ones prevail until the jam clears itself or when, for that matter, some of the more fortunate drivers in the right lane voluntarily cede their right of way. And there is the additional question: is it possible to generate this kind of patience and civilized behaviour where they are lacking by the judicious use of political resources and institutional reforms?

Transferring this question to the political economy of the postsocialist transformation processes yields at least four conceivable categories of answers. The first and simplest one is that, thanks to advantageous circumstances, not much patience is necessary in the first place. This corresponds to the case of the 'economic miracle', or a vigorous take-off into self-sustained growth. The gains in prosperity are so rapid and steady that all the participants find it an obvious dictate of good sense to keep to the rules; and, in the process, getting used to the value of the rules comes easily and compliance with rules thus becomes more robust.

The second response is a mixture of positive and negative encouragements and incentives, arising from the international system. The external supports of the new order (Marshall Plan, occupation regime) were – along with, and as a necessary condition of, the 'economic miracle' – the key to the success story of the Federal Republic of Germany and other post-war democracies. Since in the case of the Eastern European transformation it is a matter neither of a post-war nor of a Cold War situation, military threats have no role to play here – or only negatively, in the strategy of the discontinuation of military threat, that is, of a consistently continued politics of disarmament and *détente*. Besides, this policy of refraining from the threat of military intervention would have the desired effect of cancelling some of the conceivable pretexts for intervention on the part of the former Warsaw Pact countries' military. Some form of military intervention would, however, have to be kept in reserve in case 'reactionary' regimes in the south-east of Europe should try to resist transformation by military aggression and civil war. But, in contrast to the situation after the Second World War, there is no obvious 'patron power' that would be a natural candidate for the task of supervising and enforcing the peaceful nature of the transition process.

Nor is there an obvious candidate who would be able to dispense the carrot along with the stick. It all depends on the robustness and the capacity to act of supranational regimes such as the European Community and the Conference on Security and Cooperation in Europe. The reward would consist in a policy of granting international credits and transfers of funds, whose function, so to speak, would be to subsidize the population's patience. Built into such loans for the external subsidization of the transition would be the soft, disciplining threat that those granting credit could suspend their aid or favourable trade agreements if the intended integration of profitable economic and political developments in the countries benefiting from the credits failed to materialize. This strategy of providing 'support from the outside' poses difficulties for a number of reasons. The necessary volume of loans may exceed the capacity of the lending countries, who may have more narrowly defined priorities. Or the lenders may expose themselves to the beneficiaries' suspicion (justified or not) that the real intention behind the loans is not the subsidization of patience, but rather the long-term exploitation of the recipients, which would consequently be more likely to cause impatience. Or the transferred funds may have the unintended effect not of subsidizing patience with the uncertainties attached to the process of economic and democratic renewal, but on the contrary of making bearable the costs which arise from the conservation of structures, thereby encouraging the slowing down or outright absence of renewal.

A third method of buying time and engendering the moral credit and trust required for the simultaneous transition to a market economy and democracy consists in an effective socio-political mitigation of the pains of transition by continued and fine-tuned mechanisms of internal redistribution. Granted, such mitigation has thus far not occurred even under the extraordinarily favoured special conditions of the former German Democratic Republic. Presumably tolerance of a transformation towards a market economy, in the course of which inequality inevitably increases (for some must do much better quickly in order for all to do somewhat better in the long run), will be more likely to be generated if the danger that a substantial part of the population will be absolutely worse off, and for some extended period of time, is ruled out. Here the design question boils down to whether you want to provide status security to the economic core groups or the unconditional guarantee of an adequate subsistence minimum for everyone. At any rate, the beneficiaries of the transformation to a market economy would have to be made to compensate the victims of the transformation with some kind of welfare state security and unemployment benefits. This would certainly constitute an inversion of the sequence of Western constitutional development as it was postulated by T. H. Marshall (that is, liberal constitutional state, democratic state and then welfare state), and the welfare state would be recognized as the precondition for both the market and democracy (just as democracy, in another inversion of the Western 'model', would be the precondition for the market, as argued above). So far this has succeeded nowhere; at best it foundered in such a way that (as in the case of Argentinian Perónism) a kind of welfare state was designed to serve as a permanent substitute for liberal democracy. The difficulties are plain to see: the resources which are earmarked for the social insurance against 'creative destruction' make the latter less destructive, but they may also make it less creative. Correspondingly, the prospects for a politically successful privatizing of the system of production and for concomitantly governing the distribution of incomes and services by means of state guarantees are viewed pessimistically nearly without exception (cf. the essays in Deacon and Szalai 1990) – and all the more so since social security and protection can also easily be denounced as ideas that were inherited from the old regime and thus interfere with the unfolding of the new economic order and its hoped-for fruits.

Even more difficult to realize would be a fourth solution to the problem of patience, which would consist in forming intermediary bodies such as associations, federations, trade unions, parties and local authorities within an emerging East European 'civil society'. If each person could be assured of enjoying the protection of a robust representation and negotiation capacity represented by such mediating bodies, whose constitution would have to make it impossible for them to form 'exploitative coalitions' or 'clans' which would work against excluded third parties, then at least some of these fears would diminish – fears which otherwise might turn into a 'democratic' blockage of the transformation towards a market economy and eventually make democracy itself, due to its allegedly adverse economic consequences, pointless. These mediating bodies could not be allowed to be state artefacts and would have to enjoy constitutional guarantees that would make them relatively unavailable to opportunistic strategies of co-optation by governing elites. At least they would be able to 'deliberate' and find 'synthetic solutions' to the conflicting preferences that prevail within their respective constituencies. Also, they would have to be able, due to the representational monopoly granted to them and the strength they derive from it, to explore their opponents' availability for cooperative strategies without running the risk of ending up as the 'sucker' (cf. Bates 1988). Thirdly, they would have to have a moral basis in the feelings of solidarity and mutual obligation within 'civil society'. If such a combination of the institutional and moral patterns of 'civic republicanism' cum 'democratic corporatism' is a rarity even in the affluent societies of the West, how could it flourish on the soil of the atomized social structures of post-socialist societies? Instead of that, and corresponding to the atomized state of the society, we see ahead of us, at least in some of the countries undergoing the triple transformation, a type of 'charismatic' politics and presidentialist constitution-making unmediated by intermediary structures, in the shadow of which the forces of a civil self-organization beyond market, state and ethnic 'community' are finding it exceedingly hard to assert themselves.

4

Ethnic Politics in East European Transitions

Large parts of the Western public in general and liberal intellectuals in particular are dismayed by the outbursts of national and ethnic politics and ethnic strife that have emerged in post-Communist societies. The mood is nicely captured by the *Financial Times* (8 May 1993: 9), which refers to one of those societies as 'a distant part of the world ruled by medieval passions, which are the antithesis of everything modern man stands for'. This moralizing dismissal of nationalist values, attitudes and practices as pre-modern and unenlightened is, however, just one of .two responses that are to be found among the Western public. The other, diametrically opposed response takes the revival of nationalism and ethnic movements, while reprehending some forms of its violent manifestation, as proof that modernity has by no means effectively done away with, but rather presupposes and relies upon, national identities,[1] which are seen, as they were seen by Max Weber in his famous inaugural lecture of 1895, as the core essence of political life. This essence may have been hidden or temporarily rendered obsolete in the West, but it has now reasserted itself in the East.

Both of these positions are based more on normative approval or disapproval than on explanation. Marxists and liberals, the holders of the first of these two views, 'never seem to ask themselves why nationalism survives ... Most of [their explanations] boil down to a dismissal of nationalism as "irrational", "tribal" or something that other, "less civilized" countries suffer from. For the most part, the question "why" is effectively ignored' (Schöpflin 1991b: 51). It is particularly in the age of West European integration that those who hold fast to nationalist and ethnic categories of political life are routinely considered backward in their thinking as well as dangerous, ill-intentioned or blind concerning the practical consequences of their thinking.

I wish to argue in this chapter first that the 'ethnification' of the politics of transition[2] is the outcome of powerful (if in no way 'natural') causal forces that manifest themselves through rational strategic individuals operative in post-Communist societies and cannot easily be wished away, and secondly that it is exceedingly difficult to design universalist institutional or constitutional arrangements that would pave the way for the peaceful coexistence of ethnic groups within East European states. The ills of ethnic politics have strong causes and weak cures. What follows is a sociological balance sheet intended to substantiate both of these points.

What I mean by the 'ethnification' of polities and politics is a number of interrelated strategies of individuals and bodies, social as well as political. They are all embedded in a cognitive and evaluative frame according to which ethnic identity is a primordial and trans-individual set of highly valued qualities that have been formed in a long collective history, are acquired through birth and primary socialization and are inaccessible, even incomprehensible, to others not born with these qualities. From this frame follow a number of practices or strategies. First, territorial boundaries are drawn in a way that maximizes ethnic homogeneity. Secondly, policies are pursued which differentiate the rights and privileges of citizens according to their ethnic affiliation. Thirdly, policies are proposed, advocated and resisted, and associations and political parties are formed, in the name of fostering the well-being of an ethnic community at the expense of excluding those internal or external groups who are not considered to belong to it. Fourthly, ethnic (and, often concomitantly, religious, cultural and linguistic) issues take precedence over class issues and class politics. Implicit in all these practices is the 'reductionist' notion that self-ascribed ethnic identities are more durable, more consequential and somehow more dignified than any other differences that exist between individuals. In a quasi-religious fashion these identities are seen as the ultimate source of meaning, rights and obligations. In all of these strategies ethnicity plays the role of the dominant division, and it is the source of symbolic representations used in the service of political mobilization and collective action.

This syndrome of views and practices, while certainly not limited to East and Central Europe, still seems to have a particular affinity with the region and its history. Thus historians rely on the typological distinction between a 'Western' and 'Eastern' type of nationalism, the latter being much more determined by ethnic factors than the former (for example, Schieder 1991). While the former is said to be associated with bourgeois revolutions and the effective formation of a strong national state, the latter thrives in societies which often have not experienced these steps of political modernization and whose identity is seen to reside in their culture. In the Western case nationalism emerges from the successful overcoming of internal obstacles to sovereignty, mostly the nobility. In the Eastern case nationalism is the ideological underpinning of the struggle against externally imposed rule, such as the Turkish, Habsburg or Soviet-Russian 'yoke' (cf. Stölting 1992).

At the same time ethnicity is an elusive concept. This becomes apparent as soon as we try to measure it. Measurement can proceed on two kinds of indicators, objective and subjective. Objective indicators, such as the language being spoken at home or the ethnic identification of ancestors, will usually yield a large portion of mixed cases. For instance, half of the married couples living in the territories that were contested by Serbia and Croatia in the first half of the 1990s are said to be of ethnically mixed origin. Alternatively, we can use subjective indicators by asking people which ethnic identity they consider they belong to. Here the typical result is that neither the number of individuals within each ethnic category nor the number of ethnic categories itself tends to be stable. Taken together, these two somewhat perplexing facts make for a considerable volatility of ethnic identifications.

The first of these two ambiguities is easily explained. People experience strong incentives, both positive and negative, to simulate or dissimulate, adopt or reject identification with an ethnic group. Thus ethnic surveys based on self-identification can be highly misleading; the Gypsies in Romania, for instance, prefer to a large but unknown extent to misidentify themselves as 'Hungarian' (Ionescu 1992). Conversely, the miraculous multiplication of people claiming German ancestry in Russia is clearly connected to the fact that under a treaty negotiated between the Soviet Union and West Germany ethnic Germans have become eligible for the status of *Aussiedler*, which grants them not only the right to free emigration from the Soviet Union, but also access to full pension entitlements once they have arrived in Germany. Ethnic identification is susceptible to positive and negative incentives.

The second ambiguity is a bit more puzzling. If asked for their ethnic identification in open questions, people either refuse to answer at all (as many 'Yugoslav' intellectuals or fewer 'Czechoslovaks' did in the 1990 census), thus simply rejecting the ethnic code, or answer by naming ethnic identities that are not commonly recognized as such (in

Czechoslovakia, a country which most people think of as being ethnically divided into just Czechs, Slovaks and perhaps Hungarians, large segments of the population claimed, among others, 'Silesian', 'Ruthenian' or even 'Moravian' identity). Obviously there is no objective universe of ethnic groups people can belong to, and hitherto unknown ethnic groups and solidarities can be strategically invented and manufactured out of territorial, historical and linguistic markers. Given this ample room for strategic behaviour both in the choice of groups with which to identify and in the choice of individual identification among these groups, it is not easy to draw a line between 'authentic' and 'strategically' adopted, revived or invented ethnic identities.

Nor is it easy to define ethnic politics in operational terms. The presence of explicitly ethnic parties (as in Bulgaria, Slovakia, Hungary, the Czech Lands or Romania) would provide a clear indication of the presence of ethnic politics. But the explicit (constitutional) prohibition of ethnic political organization[3] in an ethnically divided country, and hence the absence of ethnic parties, can also be an indication of ethnic politics, as it privileges the majority ethnic group and denies the minority the right to organize along ethnic lines by not even acknowledging its existence. Both the recognition of difference and the refusal to recognize (or allow the political representation of) difference can be manifestations of ethnic politics.

Types of ethnic conflict

I propose to chart the field of ethnic conflict by introducing three distinctions. The first is quantitative. While a conflict is always a relationship between (at least) two parties, we may distinguish cases where the active part which initiates the conflict and feels most strongly about it is an ethnically defined minority or a majority. The whole of which a majority is a majority and a minority a minority can be a national, regional or local territorial unit. Rarely do national majorities also form a majority on all the lower territorial levels. This creates the particularly precarious situation of national majorities being minorities within national minority territories, such as the Serbs are in Kosovo, or ethnic Bulgarians in the predominantly Turkish districts of Bulgaria. Secession may make the former majority and minority swap round, as happened to the Russians in Estonia.

Majority ethnic conflict occurs when citizens of a nation develop hostile feelings and engage in hostile activities against minorities which do not even need to share an ethnic identity, but are made up of a multi-ethnic residual category of 'foreigners', 'strangers' or 'immigrants'. This phenomenon of the majority ethnic politics of xenophobia, together with its dramatic repercussions on the level of party politics and voter mobilization, could be observed in the early nineties in national as well as regional elections in Germany, Austria,[4] France and Sweden. On the other hand ethnic conflict can originate with an ethnically defined minority which feels oppressed and deprived of its rights, while the majority, at least at the beginning of the conflict, may hardly be aware of the nature of the minority and its concerns (Turks in Bulgaria, Slovaks in Czechoslovakia). There are also cases where the conflict is initiated by an ethnic group of approximately equal size to its opponent group(s), as in Bosnia-Herzegovina, where the population is about equally divided into Croat, Serb and Muslim segments. Most cases, however, seem to follow a clear-cut majority against minority pattern, with either of the two playing the role of the oppressor or the oppressed. Table 4.1 combines these two distinctions, with examples in each box.

Table 4.1

	Minority	*Majority*
Victims	Hungarians in Slovakia 1	Albanians in Kosovo 2
Oppressors	3 Serbs in Kosovo	4 Bulgarization of Turkish names in 1985

Secondly, distinctions may be drawn according to qualitative features of the groups involved. Qualitative criteria can be of an absolute sort (one group is richer than the other) or of a relational sort (one group feels superior to or exploited by the other, which may cause indignation or resentment on the part of those who feel unfairly treated). Even major absolute differences among ethnic groups do not need to translate into the perception of relational differences, though they often do in fact. But a strong ethnic division of labour, whereby each group has its 'typical' trade, occupation or institutional sector and its concomitant economic status, does not always lead to conflictual ethnic relations, particularly if there are many ethnic groups involved, as we see in the North American multi-ethnic societies.

Conversely, strongly perceived relational differences, the feeling of superiority or inferiority, need not be based on any sizeable absolute differences, at least not differences in economic or legal status, between the groups involved in the conflict. In such cases, of which the conflict between the Croats and Serbs may be an example, it is not easy for the outside observer to determine what the conflict is 'about' and which valuable items are to be allocated or redistributed as its outcome. What the conflict is 'about' may be some tangible privilege or inferiority inherent in inter-ethnic relations; it can also be the fear of such imbalance, its mere anticipation based upon historical precedent, mutually imputed characteristics and intentions or outright paranoic fantasies.

Often the potential gains to be obtained by one of the parties involved appear minuscule (if obtained at all) when compared with the likely and foreseeable losses affecting all parties in the conflict, which is likely to turn õut as a negative-sum game. The agony of Yugoslavia illustrates such a game of dramatic proportions. In the case of a minority claiming rights, resources or symbolic recognition from a majority two questions are often hard to answer: why does the minority insist upon its demands with such intensity and passion,[5] and why does the majority refuse to grant what the minority demands?

To come closer to an answer to these questions I wish to distinguish between two qualitative types of ethnic conflict, which can be rooted in issues of recognition or in issues of distribution. Conflict about recognition between the ethnically defined groups A and B (both of which can be either minorities or majorities) originates according to the following logic. First, A feels that B considers A inferior in some relevant way (for example, lazy, filthy, dishonest, aggressive). A's belief about B's belief can draw upon stated opinions of members of B which are held, rightly or not, to be representative of the entire group. It can also be based upon acts of members of B which are thought by members of A to provide conclusive evidence of B's contempt for or view of the inferiority of A. Still more indirectly, A's belief about B's belief can be based on some action of members of B that occurred in the past, with the assumption being that such active expression of non-recognition has been motivated by the deep-seated and lasting attitudes of B towards A that are still operative in disguise at the present time. Whatever the source and evidence of B's perceived attitude and belief about A, the perception itself gives rise to reciprocal negative valuations of B on the part of A. Those people (B) who treat us or have treated us as or hold us to be inferior are inferior themselves, as they violate the norm of treating us, their neighbours and fellow citizens, as equals. That is to say, the intensity of conflict grows with both the negative attitudes that B is perceived to hold against A and the nominal validity of norms of equal and mutual recognition among citizens. In the presence of the former but absence of the latter members of group A will have little choice but to endure the situation, or to try to escape it by whatever means are available to them. It is only the invoked normative backdrop of formal equality and mutual recognition within the framework of some shared citizenship status that allows A to reciprocate with a moral verdict against B – a condition that makes the conflict virtually self-igniting: by treating 'us' as inferior (according to some substantive value or norm), you betray 'your' own inferiority (according to some formal standard of reciprocity and fairness).[6] It is probably the psychology of humiliation that provides a clue to the question of why the denial of recognition and fair treatment can evidently trigger such enormous anxieties and aggressive energies.

The other type of issues which are at stake in ethnic conflict has to do with the distribution of valued resources. Here the conflict is not focused on A's beliefs about B's beliefs about A's inferiority, but on B's quite tangible and measurable superiority in terms of control over or access to resources such as income, wealth, power, status and rights, and the control over military means of violence and the institutions and media of cultural reproduction. Any demonstrable advantage of the members of one ethnic group can be suspected by the members of the other ethnic group of being acquired in unfair, discriminatory or exploitative ways, thus turning 'difference' into 'unfair advantage'. In order to prevent the raising of issues of inter-ethnic distributional inequities it has been a common practice of Communist regimes to keep statistical data that would provide proof ·of such inequities almost a state secret.[7]

Issues of inter-ethnic distribution can be resolved in three different ways. First, one can adopt the conciliatory view that the past cannot, and therefore should not, be undone. After all, all multi-ethnic societies show a more or less marked pattern of ethnic division of labour, which may even be thought of as a mechanism that fosters their social coherence. As a consequence of this division of labour a limited amount of inter-ethnic difference in the control of material resources is likely to occur. But it must not become the source of strife, conflict and the feeling of deprivation, particularly as institutionalized discrimination and exploitation can reliably be considered a matter of the past. Let us therefore basically leave things as they are, especially since the dominant imperative is efficient allocation, not redistribution. Given the strength of ethnically based resentment, hatred and feelings of discrimination, this complacent attitude is unlikely to muster much support. The second conceivable solution is to install fair distributional rules which are carefully designed to minimize the importance of ethnicity. Universal positive rights applying to all citizens, inter-ethnic quota, lotteries and coupon-based privatization schemes are conceivable instruments by which this philosophy could be implemented. Thirdly, one could adopt an aggressive and rigorous philosophy of reversal, following the rule: what belonged to you in the past will belong to us in the future, and justice must be implemented through compensation. Given the interpenetration of recognition and distribution issues, it is this last and most radical solution that is likely to prevail.

The two types of ethnically contested issues – issues of symbolic recognition and of material distribution – are in fact likely to interact. If there is a strong sense that the dignity of an ethnic group is being violated (or has been violated in the past), there is an almost irresistible temptation to compensate for the resulting indignation not in terms of newly introduced legal safeguards of equal recognition and citizenship rights, but rather in terms of a redistributive reversal of former advantages and privileges. Inversely, as the formerly state-owned property must be privatized and as the determination of who should be entitled to acquire property is inescapably a political decision (as I argued in chapter 3), nothing is more likely than that property rights will be allocated – or in discriminatory ways restored – according to ethnic codes.[8]

A third analytical distinction applying to ethnic conflict phenomena is motivational. The distinction I have in mind here (cf. Walzer 1992) is between genuine, sincere and authentic feelings of ethnic identity and its valuation on the one hand and strategic uses of ethnic symbols on the other.[9]

There are four distinct types of relationships between the citizen and the modern state. First, the state, being the effective monopolist of the means of violence, constitutes a potential threat to the citizen, who is essentially a potential victim of state power; the principles of rule of law and the guarantee of basic liberties form the appropriate antidote to this threat. Secondly, the citizen is the ultimate author and legitimating agent of the democratic state. Thirdly, the citizen as client depends upon state-organized provision of material security and welfare. And, finally, the citizen is a member of a cultural community, as defined by a shared language, history, artistic tradition and way of life, which is also protected and cultivated by *Kulturstaat* institutions and programmes. My point here is that all four of these accomplishments of the modern state – rule of law, democracy, welfare state and national *Kulturstaat* – are unavoidably vulnerable to being put to unintended, that is, selfish, exclusionary, exploitative or hostile, uses. None of the rights and institutions that shape the four dimensions of citizenship is strategy-proof, perhaps most obviously so the institutionalized claim to cultural identity and community.[10] Thus both leaders and followers of ethnic groups and movements may just pretend to be motivated by values of ethnic identity in order to promote interests which are less likely to be satisfied if openly declared as such. An example would be unauthentic use of national and ethnic symbols for the sake of acquisitive ends. On the other hand groups might suffer serious setbacks in terms of their material position as a consequence of their claim to ethnic identity and still stick to their community. This would indicate that ethnicity is cherished for its own sake and in authentic ways. This distinction helps to analyse mixed cases and routes: followers may be authentically motivated, while leaders are not, or vice versa (should that case exist at all). Or an ethnic conflict may start as the sincere defence of the worthiness and recognition of the community and its cultural identity, but later 'degenerate' into a strategy in a distributive game, or go through the reverse sequence.

A further distinction that is helpful in understanding the dynamics of ethnic conflict – and the differences in ethnic politics in general – concerns the territorial structure of ethnicity. Ethnic groups differ according to their location in space and time. At the one extreme of this conceptual axis we find groups in compact and sharply demarcated settlement patterns whose 'homeland' is known to have been inhabited by members of the group since time immemorial. We might describe such an ethnic group as one with high and vested territoriality. At the other end of our scale we might think of scattered settlement patterns or situations where ethnic groups live, such as on a group of islands. The territoriality value is even lower for those groups who do not have an inherited and recognized 'homeland' of their own, but, due to recent (im)migration, at best ethnic neighbourhoods and ghettos within cities. The other variable that determines the dynamics of ethnic conflict is the presence or absence of a patronage state. At one extreme is the presence of a strong and immediately adjacent state that considers 'our people abroad' as part of its responsibility and shows willingness to devote legal, political, economic and, if need be, perhaps also military resources towards the protection of the ethnic group and the advancement of the group's interests. At the other extreme is the situation where no patronage power exists (other than perhaps transnational organizations and human rights groups), or where the 'reference state' is too weak or too distant or politically ill-disposed to assist its presumed diaspora population. Dichotomizing these two variables produces table 4.2, which gives illustrative cases.

Table 4.2

		Territoriality	
		Yes	No
Patronage state	Yes	Hungarians in Romania	Turks in Western Europe
		1	2
		3	4
	No	Basques in Spain	Jews (prior to State of Israel); Gypsies

The prevailing situation in Eastern Europe is represented by box 1. Here the decisive question is the effectiveness of bilateral international diplomacy and the supervisory and disciplinary powers of various transnational agencies. The guest-worker syndrome (box 2) of dispersed ethnic groups with some support from a home state is best represented in East Europe by the example of Russians in the Baltic, as well as other non-Russian fo. mer Soviet republics. Here the critical variable is the willingness of the governments of newly formed nation states to grant their (former elite) 'guest workers' political and economic rights, in spite of the historical record of Russian 'occupation' and 'foreign rule'. The third case, ethnic groups with nation-state aspirations but without external support, is probably the most explosive. The Czechoslovak 'velvet divorce' is a glaring exception to the rule that the governments of titular states and majority nationalities are not easily persuaded to 'let our people go', as the Chechen, Ukrainian and Turkish cases suggest, particularly if there is no history of independent statehood on the part of the secessionist minority. Finally, box 4 is a speciality of Eastern Europe (comparable in some respects to the aborigine population of the United States and Australia, but not New Zealand and South Africa) in that the ethnic minority (the Gypsies, or Sinti and Roma) is so poorly integrated into the legal and political culture of the majority society that it does not even manage to lay effective claim to the rights of citizenship and self-defence through the use of organization and mobilization. This explains why the (arguably) most blatant case of massive ethnic discrimination in the region is at the same time the most inconspicuous case in terms of political conflict and collective action (cf. Offe 1994a).

The 'rationality' of ethnic politics

Given the situation in which individual and collective protagonists find themselves in post-Communist Eastern Europe, ethnification must appear to them as a rational strategy. This is the main thesis that I am going to explore here. If this is true, it is no longer enough to persuade political leaders of these societies that ethnification is dangerous in its consequences and/or inconsistent with Western principles of universalism and political modernization, that is, constitutionalism and human rights. What is called for, instead of moral exhortations, is a change in the parameters and rules of action[11] of these leaders and strategists that would make it both preferable and affordable for them to refrain from pursuing or supporting otherwise perfectly rational strategies of ethnification and 'ethnocracy' (Wolkow 1991).

In what sense can it be said to be 'rational' for individuals and groups to engage in ethnic politics? Rationality has to do with intended and preferred consequences of action (however short-sighted, local or unrealistic they may be) and the selection of courses of action with these consequences in mind. Starting with this 'thin' notion of rationality, ethnic politics can be selected for economic, political, 'constitutive' (to use a term suggested by Bruce Ackerman) and military rational reasons (cf. Senghaas 1992: 117–25). Economic rationality prevails when the insistence upon ethnic divisions and identities is expected to help people to acquire or protect economic resources. Political rationality is served if elites maintain (or counter-elites win) political power positions by mobilizing along ethnic dividing lines, or by justifying their rule in terms of national aspirations. Constitutive rationality is a variant of ethnic politics that is expected to help the foundation of a political unit through establishing borders, that is, uncontested criteria of inclusion and exclusion. Finally, military rationality may call for reliance on ethnic politics in order to strengthen the sense of duty, obligation and the willingness to sacrifice both in an anticipation of future conflicts and in order to strengthen military power in an actual conflict.

The theoretical alternative to the 'rationalist' interpretation pursued here is the communitarian view that the longing for ethnic purity and community is as basic, as universal and hence as legitimate a political force as is the pursuit of interest or that of individual liberty. According to this view, 'nationalism is the politicization of a community's culture', and this culture is in turn the community's mark of collective identity and its 'storehouse of moral precepts', thought to be embodied in language, history, territory, religion, rituals and symbols (Schöpflin 1991b: 52–3). The celebration and, if need be, the assertion and defence of this identity also provide for, according to this theoretical approach, the affective, expressive and emotional dimension of the life of the community and are clearly to be given preference over mere 'characterless citizenship' (Walzer). At any rate, communities and tribes *'ought to be allowed to govern themselves'* as 'tribalism names the commitment of individuals and groups to their own history, culture, and identity, and this commitment ... is a permanent feature of human social life' (Walzer 1992: 165, 171).[12]

While the ubiquity of some measure of valuation of ethnic and national community can hardly be denied, the problem with this approach is its virtually tautological structure. The appearance of ethnic politics at a particular point in time and space is assumed to emanate from a universal force of political life, which in turn is supposed to explain the phenomenon in question. Appearance is the manifestation of some essence which is itself postulated on the basis of appearance. This type of circular reasoning precludes any fruitful consideration of the question as to why some people, masses and elites alike, should imagine, invent, construct, adopt, resort to or be mobilized by ethnic and national codes under certain conditions, while others under different conditions attribute at best marginal significance to ethnic codes and aspirations and find no reason to resort to ethnic symbols and divisions in the pursuit of their military, political or economic interests.

It is evident from the conflicts in the post-Communist world in the 1990s that ethnic politics, apart from the emotional gratifications it may have to offer, involves a number of serious dangers (Koch 1991: 29). Most importantly, ethnification will greatly increase the danger of civil war and international war.[13] Furthermore, ethnification involves diseconomies of scale and vast inefficiencies,[14] as it tends to stand in the way of trans-ethnic cooperation, commerce and division of labour. Finally, ethnic politics, together with its unpleasant symptoms, such as discrimination, civilian violence, deportation and forced assimilation, interferes with the orderly working of democratic politics, violates the idea of citizenship and emphasizes a division that is particularly resistant to bargaining and compromise.[15] While the first and the third of these dangers are quite commonly observed, the interaction between ethnic politics and economic development is less well understood. On the one hand nationalism is often seen as a defensive response to the disruptive forces of economic modernization,[16] or to provide comfort in conditions of manifest failures of economic modernization, or to present scapegoats for economic frustrations. On the other hand it may itself contribute to slowing down the economic modernization process by holding fast to an economic regime of protection and static efficiency, thereby inhibiting the evolution of dynamic efficiency. These hypotheses must be weighed, however, against the more optimistic view that a strong reliance on ethnic and patriotic symbols might be instrumental in mobilizing efforts conducive to economic growth.

Given the uses to which ethnic sentiments, identifications and antagonisms can be put, the ongoing politics of ethnification appears as necessary a response of rational strategic individuals in post-Communist societies as it appears dangerous in its long-term and collective consequences. With these tragic implications in mind, we may ask why people still find it rational to pursue the politics of ethnification. The following explanations, partly interrelated and overlapping, may apply.

Overcoming the old regime In post-Communist societies there is a strong need for members of the political elite to dissociate themselves from the old regime, particularly if they are under the suspicion of having been its former supporters.

The Communist experience in many Central East European countries is framed, not only in retrospect, in terms of both a forced separation and a forced transnational alliance, namely forced separation from the West and forced integration into the East and its economic, political and military structures. East Germany, Poland, Czechoslovakia and Hungary have suffered from the dual predicament of having their historical and cultural ties with the West severed and of being forced to live under military, economic and ideological Soviet rule. While the dominant political divide in the immediate post-Communist period was clearly that between the 'old regime' and the 'new freedom', a bifurcation within the nascent 'new regime' soon set in. This secondary divide is about which of the twin features of the old regime is considered more important and is therefore invoked as the focal point of post-Communist politics. Schematically speaking, the divide falls between those modernizers who have embarked upon the 'return to Europe' and those conservative, Christian, populist and rural forces who have preferred the 'return to ourselves'. Virtually everywhere in Central Europe the first of these two post-Communist political forces has turned out to be much weaker than the second. The reasons that explain this predominance are fairly straightforward. Communism was 'constructing and enforcing artificial supranational bonds. It is only natural that the collapse of communism has brought about the articulation of ambitions to restore and to re-acquire the national past, to rediscover national identity' (Markus 1992: 12). But why has the rival paradigm of mobilization, namely 'the endeavor to "join Europe" not only in the narrow sense of economic and political integration, but in a broad social and cultural sense', remained so weak? The 'modernizers' work with a scenario that sets some 'bright (liberal capitalist) future' against the dark past of Communism, while the nationalists set a 'dark past' of Communism against the 'bright past' of a pre-Communist 'golden age'. Given the opposition of the two frames of reference in which the respective political initiatives are embedded, the modernizers (with their appeal to urban life, civil society, the market, human rights, secularism and moral tolerance) are clearly bound to lose as they confront voters and citizens with a volume of uncertainties and ambiguities that are extremely hard to sustain in a society in which none of these values is widely shared as an established principle and in which, in addition, the pursuit of these values does not involve a credible prospect of desired consequences such as prosperity and security. It seems to be a game of (backward-looking cultural) 'pride' versus (forward-looking economic) 'hope'. In the absence of some overarching constitution of a political space mediating between the two and of compelling reasons for economic hope, the longing for 'pride' is bound to hold sway.

Under these conditions, and with the economic costs of the transition becoming ever more evident, the longing for 'joining Europe' may easily fall victim to 'sour grapes' responses (Jedlicki 1991: 16). The striking asymmetry of the two scenarios is due to the fact that the 'golden past' provides certainty (even if it is the certainty of a carefully crafted myth), while the future does not. It is the strategic and programmatic weakness of the 'modernizing' section of post-Communist political forces that nurtures the overwhelming support for their conservative, nationalist, populist and religious opponents. And the old regime's scandal of forcing people to live with, even being ruled by, 'strangers' maintains the upper hand, as a point of negative reference, over its other scandal of separating people from their Western 'neighbours'. As the dust of the immediate transition settles, ethnic divisions, cultural particularisms and nationalist appeals prevail over class and other socio-economic divisions – in spite of the fact that the carrying out of the latter has so significantly contributed to the political and economic modernization of Western Europe. This prevalence does not preclude hybrid approaches such as that of the Hungarian Democratic Forum (HDF): economic modernization and economic as well as military integration into the West, alongside what is given the highest priority, the protection of 'Hungarianhood from the cosmopolitan cultural and social influences'.

Engaging in ethnic and nationalist political initiatives also helps to symbolize one's distance from the old regime. At least in the

Romanian and Bulgarian cases, but arguably also in the Soviet Union itself, the ethnic movements of Hungarians, Turks, Lithuanians and Armenians greatly contributed to the disorganization, international discrediting and eventual breakdown of the Communist regime. As the old regime was notorious for consistently repressing ethnic divisions and the resultant conflicts, and as it designed the borders of most administrative districts so as to be incongruent with ethnic divides (Wolkow 1991: 37), the easiest way to dissociate oneself is to switch to using ethnic codes. Ethnicity provides for a 'clean' identity, one that is untainted by the status a person has acquired or the associational affiliation he or she was involved in under the old regime.[17] The stronger and the more justified the suspicion of complicity, the stronger the pressure and temptation to resort to this way out, which may explain the strength of nationalist sentiments expressed by former Communist (now turned nationalist-populist) leaders in Serbia, Ukraine, Bulgaria, Slovakia, Croatia, Moldavia and Romania. As can be demonstrated by the cases of Yeltsin, Kravchuk or Landsbergis, the only conceivable strategy for new political leaders trying to win political support is to 'seek popular acceptance as nonpartisan patriotic forces eager to represent the overriding interests of their citizens' (Zaslavsky 1992: 113). A related move, particularly relevant in the former Soviet Union, is to get rid of the (overwhelmingly Russian) power holders and other elites of the old regime by replacing them with 'our' people, that is, people with the local ethnic background.

In many countries historians[18] – where they are not already strongly over-represented in the ranks of the new conservative political elites, as in Hungary until the 1994 elections – are put to work to discover and describe the greatness of their nation's past,[19] or the vicious deeds of former (and hence potential future) enemies belonging to a different nationality or ethnic group. In some other cases (Russia, Slovakia, Bulgaria)[20] former Communist elites have openly joined forces with extreme nationalists in order to resist or obstruct the process of political and economic modernization in the name of the values of homogeneity and 'authoritarian egalitarianism' – a significant trait of the political culture of post-Communist societies that consistently gives preference to state-guaranteed equality of conditions over market-generated insecurity and vertical differentiation. In retrospect they sometimes declare[21] their own or their country's devotion to the ideology of Marxism-Leninism as having been nothing but a tactical move to achieve national protection, which to an extent was granted, in return, by the Soviet Union. As this protection is no longer provided, national purity, security and cohesion must be advocated as such, without the veil of Marxism-Leninism.

The use of ethnic nationalism by elites of the old regime wishing to keep themselves in power and to stem the tide of pluralist democracy can be observed, together with all its atrocious consequences, in the case of Serbia. In response to the events of 1989 Serbian conservatives moved to build a 'Greater Serbia', using 'an image of threatened Serbdom to slow or halt the shift toward pluralism sweeping the region ... Conflict along ethnic lines was ... actively created and provoked by ... political actors in order to forestall native trends toward democratization' (Gagnon 1994: 118). Gagnon describes the strategy of the proponents of the old regime as the 'purposeful creation and exploitation of [ethnic] hatred as a means of stopping or slowing shifts in the locus and structure of power in Serbia' by 'diverting attention from the [dismal results of] economic policy' and 'raising the specter of Croatia's wartime fascists, relying on images of massacres and mutilations of Serbian children and civilians' (pp. 119, 121, 123).

'Proletarian internationalism' and 'the socialist commonwealth' have not only failed; they never took root in the first place. Nationalist sentiments and ethnic aspirations were muted and repressed by the Communist regimes, but never obliterated (Linden 1991: 30). Internationalism just served as an official ideology avowed by elites in order to avoid hostile reactions from Moscow. It never played the role of a widely accepted value, and it was prevented from becoming accepted as such both because national and sub-national differences between the people of the Comecon countries remained highly visible in terms of levels of prosperity (cf. Zaslavsky 1992: 104) and because 'internationalism' in practice often meant 'Russification', as in the Baltic states. Given all these facts and experiences, the resurgence of nationalism and of ethnic aspirations hardly comes as a surprise. More precisely, 'nationalism is neither "returning", "rising" nor "reappearing". It never left Eastern Europe' (Brown 1991: 35). 'Nationalism and national minority grievances in East Europe are not so much new as newly heard' (Linden 1991: 33). It is the 'disintegration of the coercive system of checks and controls', together with the newly won political resources of 'greater freedom of expression and access to information generated by *perestroika*' (Zaslavsky 1992: 106) that 'inevitably leads to ethnic flare-ups' (Prazauskas 1991: 582).

The economic need for boundaries As the prospects for a rapid improvement of the economic situation are bleak, and as reasonably evenly distributed returns from a positive-sum game based on large-scale economic cooperation and division of labour are not to be anticipated for the near future, the overwhelming economic premium is upon protection rather than production. The economic crisis makes it imperative to 'keep and defend what we have'. This means a state must do two things. First, prevent the outward flow of valued and extremely scarce resources (such as fiscal revenues, goods, investment, jobs, territories, weapons that could be used for either military or economic purposes, the latter, for instance, in the context of international disarmament deals) which 'we' do not want to share. Secondly, prevent the inward flow of problems (such as inflation, the burdens of the military-industrial complex, administrative chaos, migrant surplus populations, refugees and alien elements that might threaten the linguistic and cultural homogeneity of the nation). The Baltic republics and the Ukraine, by cutting themselves loose from the Russian empire, have sought to facilitate the process of their modernization and to further their eligibility to join the common European home of the EC or EFTA. Moreover, the adoption of negative beliefs about other ethnic groups – and the role attributed to them of causing the current conditions of economic misery – may provide a kind of psychic comfort and relief that makes it easier to endure economic distress and uncertainty.[22] Under conditions of a pessimistic assessment of the economic future and strong political hostilities stemming from the past, the 'normal' preference for maximizing 'our' gain may turn into a more aggressive preference for maximizing the difference between 'our' and 'everyone else's' gain. And, in the absence of both strong political centres of authority and developed socio-economic divisions, the only units between which this type of game can be carried out are ethnically defined ones.

The weakness of state power In principle, this imperative of being protected by strong boundaries could also be complied with by having a strong state enforcing strict internal and external distributional rules. As the power of the state to establish and enforce such rules is widely and rightly seen to be absent, a primordial, or ethnic, pattern of inclusion and exclusion is rationally resorted to.[23] As the Communist states 'failed to gain loyalty and identification through the provision of goods a modern state was supposed to be able to deliver' (Linden 1991: 31), East Europeans had little reason to identify with their states even while these states seemed stable and secure. After the actual breakdown of much of the 'state capacity' of East European states, the state was further discredited as a reference point of identification and loyalty. The 'whole' of which people feel part is no longer the state, but the national or ethnic collectivity. As a consequence people code each other not according to the identity card they carry, but to the language they speak.[24] The breakdown of an effective monopoly of state violence has exposed minorities without any (nearby) patron state, in particular, to sometimes extreme forms of 'civic' violence and discrimination (for example, Gypsies in Romania and most of the other Central East European post-Communist states).

Internal minorities as external minorities of neighbour states Many of the internal minorities of East European states are – and are seen as being – at the same time external minorities of neighbouring states, which are also seen as foreign patron states of these minorities. Such foreign adjacent patron states of internal minorities are Turkey for Bulgaria, Hungary for Slovakia, Serbia and Romania, Poland for Lithuania, Albania for Serbia and Germany for Czechoslovakia, to name just some of the cases of potential irredentist movements. Sometimes minorities are reciprocal, as with Slovakia and Hungary, or Greece and Albania. With the dissolution of the transnational regime of the Warsaw Pact and its peace-keeping function, each of the states with ethnic minorities has reason to anticipate that the minority's neighbouring patron state will 'protect' its minority, which may, in the extreme case, take the form of annexation of the territory inhabited by the minority. With just a subtle twist of logic, the anticipation of this kind of event can be used as an excuse for ethnic exclusivism and pre-emptive repression. In Bratislava one can hear the relationship of Slovaks to the Hungarian minority described in the following words: 'We have nothing against the Hungarians, but it would be foolish not to realize that they are the fifth column of a potentially hostile state.' As a consequence, and in order to protect themselves from discrimination and hostile activities, minorities might be trapped into seeking the help of patron states (as ethnic Hungarians in Romania, Serbia and Slovakia have done, and Turks in Bulgaria), which in turn is of course interpreted by the respective majority as unmistakable proof of the validity of the original suspicion. The problem is particularly tricky in the 'reciprocal' cases, where a downward spiral of mutual hostage taking will easily set in, following the logic: 'What they are doing to our people, we are entitled to do to their people.' Another complication occurs if there is more than one ethnicity conflict in one country. In such cases minorities can gain an obvious strategic premium by joining forces and seeking mutual support; examples include Poles and Russians in Lithuania as well as Gagauz and Russians in Moldavia, and also the Hungarians in Slovakia who have expressed a strong preference for continued Czech predominance in a preserved federal state. Also, if separation or secession occurs, this process is likely to set off a chain reaction into a second round of separation, or at least of demands for autonomy. For instance, after the Slovaks seceded from the federation with the Czechs, the Hungarians in

Slovakia had every good reason to try to secede (or win strong guarantees for regional autonomy) from the Slovaks in response (Lendvai 1992), and to organize as Hungarians in anticipation of such an event.

Memories feed anticipation Post-Communist societies discover and rewrite their own national histories, including the hitherto largely distorted and repressed history of civil and international wars. This reappropriation of history serves not only to celebrate the greatness of the nation to be reborn, but also to revive inter-ethnic tensions. On both sides of an ethnic divide what 'they' (for example, the Croats) have done to 'us' (the Serbs) is rediscovered; in response reciprocal hostilities and cruelties are (re)discovered; and each of the two sides is aware that the other side is aware of those incidents in the past. In many of these countries stories are now being told for the first time in public of how ethnic groups served as collaborators or became victims of the collaboration of others in the war and other crimes of the Nazi regime, as well as victims of the secret Hitler–Stalin agreements. In this cognitive state and in compliance with the respective 'lessons of history' the party that has been the victim of past oppression may feel encouraged to take revenge, or at least to make sure that such oppression will never be repeated; and the former perpetrators of oppression are likely to turn to preventive repression[25] in order to avoid just this. In a way, whoever remembers history seems condemned to repeat it.

Ethnicity as a collective resource As in some Western countries, ethnic (and regionalist) politics on the part of some peripheral, economically underdeveloped minority is a powerful instrument with which to extract concessions and subsidies from the centre. The threat of non-cooperation and eventual secession and/or territorial fusion with the adjacent patron state is a particularly effective bargaining tool when vital raw materials are involved, or the control over the military means of violence, such as in the new states formed out of the old Soviet Union – Byelorussia being the most obvious case in point as there is no tradition of struggle for ethnic independence in this former republic. It is a bargaining situation of blackmail in which the obstructive potential, or 'nuisance value', of one party is brought to bear: 'I' can get 'you' to do something favourable to me in exchange for my refraining from doing something hostile to you. This is an instance of the 'perverse'[26] kind of exchange in which action is traded for inaction, and threats are typically disguised as warnings.

Similarly, ethnicity can serve as a resource for rich minorities (or majorities) unwilling to share what they have with their less fortunate neighbours within the same state. The first republics to secede were

Estonia, Latvia and Lithuania in the case of what was the Soviet Union, and Slovenia and Croatia in Yugoslavia. All these ethnic new states occupied top positions, in terms of GNP per capita, within the federative union from which they separated, which also explains the respective federal governments' desperate and violent resistance to the separation. An extreme example of this sort is the attempted separation of Katanga from the Republic of Congo in 1961, which was seen at the time as being instigated through bribes by foreign companies. An equivalent or complement to the secession of a comparatively 'rich' province is to take measures to force minority members to emigrate and to confiscate what they have to leave behind; this can be done through depriving the minority of its civil rights – including the right to participate in the incipient privatization process, as is widely supported in Latvia (where the resident Russian population amounts to 48 per cent according to Wolkow 1991: 41–2) and the other Baltic states. External minorities can also be used as a strategic resource. For instance, intellectuals in Tirana feel that Albania can never be reconstructed without the cooperation – and the property and other resources – of ethnic Albanians living in Kosovo. In fact Albanians living abroad are seen as virtually the only asset the country can look to in the process of its economic reconstruction.

In addition to being used as a positive economic resource, xenophobic mobilization and hostilities can also be employed as a political weapon that need not primarily or exclusively be turned against its immediate objects, a group of 'foreigners'. This speculation is at least invited by the experience of flares of ethnic violence against asylum seekers and other low-status foreigners (of widely diverse ethnic backgrounds) that have recently occurred in the East German (and, to a lesser extent, also West German) *Länder*. Given their frustrating situation of absolute and relative economic deprivation, many East Germans feel alienated and betrayed by the (West) German government, which had promised them rapid economic recovery and, in the eyes of many East Germans, failed so blatantly to deliver. Now, given the genocidal crimes that have been committed by Germans and the fact that they are remembered as such both abroad and domestically, the commission of acts that betray racist attitudes and are even remotely reminiscent of such crimes is bound to inflict substantial damage not only upon the victims, but upon the international credibility and reputation of everything the united German state has so far rather successfully pretended to stand for. There is simply no more 'cost-efficient' way to demolish parts of these precious – as well as precarious – resources of reputation, credibility and respectability than throwing firebombs at buildings inhabited by foreigners or destroying Jewish graves; nor can it escape the understanding of even the most uneducated youth that committing such acts will surely determine the content of the front pages of tomorrow's international newspapers. In the special circumstances of the united German state this kind of instrumental use of ethnic violence may well be interpreted as a particularly vicious tactic of political protest being directed against people other than its immediate victims.

Furthermore, electronic mass media that operate in minority languages provide a collective status increase to these minorities less by bridging physical distance between its members than by their exclusion effect. Particularly if languages are being used that are linguistically as removed from the majority language as Hungarian is from the Slovakian, Turkish from the Bulgarian or Albanian from the Serbian language, and given that minority bilingualism tends to be more widespread than majority bilingualism, it becomes very costly to the majority to share and control the contents of what is being transmitted. Thus the minority is virtually endowed with the power resources provided by a secret code.

Ethnicity as a resource of status groups Ethnic politics as a pretext for status interests is another case of 'unauthentic' use of ethnicity. Its beneficiary is first and foremost the political class itself.[27] An aggressive politics of minority rights can also serve to promote the interests of minority professional, intellectual and cultural elites. If the minority is granted the right to have courts, administrations, regional parliaments, media, schools, universities and theatres operating in the minority language, this implies a virtually exclusive labour market domain for native speakers, who will occupy the positions of journalists, judges and so on. At the same time aspiring occupants of these labour market segments are well positioned to advocate and promote ethnic politics, thereby furthering their own status interests.[28] In the Soviet Union as elsewhere the 'indigenous intelligentsia, ... ethnic political elites and middle classes were the groups most prone to use nationalism as an instrument of competition against other ethnic groups for economic and political privileges' (Zaslavsky 1992: 103).

Associational wasteland Post-Communist societies are atomized societies. Communism has destroyed all institutions of autonomous collective action (with the limited exceptions of the Catholic Church in Poland and the Protestant Church in the former GDR) and replaced them with state-dependent organs of authoritarian mobilization, which are falling apart with the end of the regime. As a consequence people have no cognitive, ideological or organizational patterns that would help them to code the social universe and guide their decisions as to whom to trust and with whom to cooperate.[29] 'In a situation of growing social disintegration, nationality remains a major means of individual psychological defense and a seemingly natural bond uniting otherwise atomized members of a decayed society into meaningful groups' (Zaslavsky 1992: 107). The sheer absence of imagined as well as institutionalized collectivities, such as classes, status groups, professional or sectoral associations and constituted religious groups, moves the ethnic code into a prominent position.[30] In this associational wasteland ethnicity and nationalism are virtually the only categories thought capable of providing guidance for collective action, while the newly formed political parties, trade unions and business, professional and other associations are often viewed with contempt, cynicism and apathy by voters and constituencies. Siklova (1991: 771) reports a joke from Prague which captures the populist logic of nationalism: 'Here, the left has no ideology and the right has no money. What remains is nationalism.'

No equilibrium The politics of ethnification and chauvinism may paradoxically not be contained but on the contrary propelled by the rational expectation that no fair and stable solution of ethnic conflict will be possible as long as ethnic identifications are not marginalized and relativized. At the same time it is well understood by the ethnic groups in Eastern Europe that this is the decisive moment: a new game is being started and the 'original endowment' of territorial and legal resources which will determine the relative position of those involved for the indefinite future is being distributed. Both of these assessments, the absence of a stable equilibrium and the urgency of the issues involved, are apt to inflame ethnic and chauvinist sentiments and to provoke unilateral pre-emptive strikes.

Indeterminacy and irreconcilability of conflict is typical of a situation in which no compromise is easily found. This need not be due to the psychological fact that individuals and groups attach high and hence uncompromising value to questions of identity,[31] as Schöpflin (1991b: 54) claims. If the minimum demand of one side exceeds the maximum concession that the other side is prepared to grant, compromise is impossible. Still worse, if one side expects that the concessions it makes to the other side will serve as a stepping-stone enabling them to launch further demands more effectively and to extract more far-reaching concessions in the future, a slippery slope[32] emerges that provides some apparent legitimacy to intransigence. 'Neither side can make concessions for fear that the other side would take unfair advantage of it' (Schöpflin 1991b: 55). Since the values of pluralism, tolerance, and compromise are absent from the political culture, and given the expectation that the economy will remain (at best) a zero-sum game anyway and thus will not provide much space for bargaining about material issues instead of identity issues, ethnocratic rigidity appears to be a rational strategy of elites, particularly as it appeals to their constituencies and makes their power more secure. After having committed themselves to the highest priority of ethnic issues, elites are locked into the logic of 'ethnic reductionism', according to which everything is viewed through the prism of ethnic identity and power.

Nationalism as a source of solidarity? Nationalism and ethnic politics may be activated by the rational consideration of political elites that they can serve as a moral and political resource in overcoming the extreme and highly divisive difficulties posed by the process of transition to a market economy. 'Nationalism can and does have extraordinarily effective energizing results and can mobilize somnolent communities into responding to external and internal challenges' (Schöpflin 1991a: 10). The feelings of primordial, even quasi-familial communal bonds and the spirit of sacrifice and solidarity that can be induced by appeals to the common fate of the nation or the ethnic group may be expected to help to encourage the much needed attitudes of endurance, wage restraint, cooperativeness and patience. 'Nationalism has the potential to breathe life into the new democracies by mobilizing dispirited and apathetic electorates, but at the same time relieving the pressure of popular material demands which the economy cannot satisfy' (Batt 1991b: 8). Such virtues may be particularly called for in the areas of social security and welfare. As the Communist version of the welfare state has broken down and a successor has not yet been installed in most of the post-Communist societies, and as increasing numbers of people fall victim to joblessness and losses in real income as a consequence of privatization and marketization, the appeal to ethnically based solidarity, and the invocation of duties inherent in such solidarity, may succeed in motivating people to share their resources with those in need. After all, there is a striking positive correlation in the West between the level of and support for social policy spending on the one hand and the degree of ethnic homogeneity of the respective societies on the other, as, for instance, a comparative glance at Sweden and the United States reveals.

Given the mostly undesirable and highly dangerous consequences that all these 'rational' considerations of resorting to ethnic politics will entail, a question that is obviously of the greatest interest is what cures can be offered that might prevent these dangers from becoming

real or spreading even further. Such cures can be subdivided into purposive 'therapies' that emerge from legal-constitutional designs inten-
tionally imposed (or self-imposed) by strategic protagonists and those
that evolve, in the way of a spontaneous healing process, as a by-
product of societal modernization without intentional action playing a
major role. The following review explores both of these alternatives.

Institutional cures

The problem that designers of institutional cures to the ills of ethnic
politics would have to face is clear enough. The task is to reconstruct
by legal and constitutional means the measure of unity, integration,
coherence and peace that has prevailed in the area under Communist
rule and that has been due in the past, to a shocking extent that we
have only now become aware of, to repression and military force. The
puzzle that any design of a stable and peaceful new order would have
to resolve is the following: those forces that significantly contributed
to the upheavals in East Central Europe and eventually to the defeat
of Communism itself, namely the political forces of ethnic nationalism, turned into a major threat to peace, prosperity and progress
towards democratic stability soon after Communism's demise. The
damage, loss and suffering already exceeds – and will conceivably
exceed to a much greater degree in the future – the worst experiences
of the irreversibly disintegrated Communist regime. Is there any constitutional equivalent to the peace-making function of Communist dictatorship?

If rational people, both on the elite and mass levels of post-
Communist politics, are likely to converge on strategies of ethnification for all the reasons given so far, we are confronted with a serious
dilemma. I wish to review the major ways out of the dilemma of ethnic politics that have been proposed and recommended. Schematically
speaking, the problem of institutional cures can be subdivided into
two steps. First, a procedure must be designed through which the parties involved can come to agree on principles by which ethnic conflict
is to be resolved. Secondly, these substantive rules, rights and principles must themselves be instituted.

Procedures leading to a new regime of civic and international peace The
famous question 'What is to be done?' presupposes that the logically
preceding question has been answered already: 'Is there anyone, that
is, a sufficiently powerful centre of agency and governance, who
could do it?' The problem of coming to terms with or containing

ethnic conflict can be summed up in the following paradox. Before disunity can be processed and eventually dissolved, there is a need for unity concerning rights, rules and agency. But given the intensity of disunity, such unity about agency and procedures is unlikely to emerge. This constitutes a particularly thorny problem in the case of political rights of ethnic groups. The question then assumes the form 'Who has the right to decide about who has the right to participate in collective decisions?' If the unity of 'the people', including the rights of minorities, is a constitutional construct, who is its constructor?

The choice of answers to this question is limited. Five options concerning procedures can be distinguished, and to some extent combined in practice. Effective rule-making can proceed through arguing in public, bargaining behind closed doors, presidential prerogative, the intervention of transnational bodies and unilateral action of territorial units claiming the right to secede.

First, arguing in public. This alternative is typically conducted in the form of round-table talks. In 1990 Nikolay Kolev-Bosiya, the chairman of the Bulgarian Independent Association for the Defence of Human Rights, proposed that all the main political parties should hold a series of public round-table discussions in order to arrive at a set of clear and detailed principles, later to be worked into a coherent legislation by parliament (Engelbrekt 1991: 5). The problem with this procedure is that not all parties may be willing to be part of such discussions, and that those who are willing may fail to reach an agreement.

Secondly, bargaining behind closed doors. This was the choice made in the Czech and Slovak case, where members of the two national parliaments met for six rounds of negotiations to determine the constitutional rules according to which Czechs and Slovaks should coexist in the future. When the last of these talks, held at the Slovak nomenklatura hotel at Papiernicky on 12 November 1991, failed to produce a result, President Havel suggested proceeding that same day to the third of our four conceivable options, namely presidential prerogative. He demanded the right to call a referendum on the future constitutional set-up of the country before the general elections held in June 1992. The problem with this solution, however, is that such a prerogative, including the all-important right to formulate the question or questions that are to be answered in the referendum as well as to pick a date, must first be granted to the presidency. In Havel's case the federal parliament denied him this right[33] in a vote taken on 21 January 1992, as 'many deputies viewed [Havel's initiative] as an attempt to curtail the parliament's powers' (Pehe 1992: 27). Many similarly well-intentioned initiatives, among them ingenious and complex proposals for electoral law reform (Chapman 1991), are trapped in the same logical loop.[34]

Fourthly, transnational bodies can determine from the outside – through monitoring the minority rights situation and administering the sanctions of diplomatic recognition or non-recognition, through the granting or denial of economic aid and ultimately through military intervention – the constitutional design and the conduct of ethnic relations. This method of establishing rules includes bilateral agreements between independent states aiming at the mutual protection of their minorities and possibly also the rather promising instrument of dual citizenship arrangements (Wolkow 1991: 43). One problem with this rule-making approach, the external imposition of rules, consists in the possible and in fact likely disunity among those who are to play the role of designers and enforcers of rules. Both bilateral action (for example, the treaties that have been made between the Federal Republic of Germany and all its East European neighbours) and unilateral action of a single hegemonic superpower appear to be less vulnerable to defection and opportunism than rule-making through multinational bodies such as the European Community or the Western European Union. For in the last case two cooperation problems are enmeshed within each other: the cooperation among conflicting ethnic groups and the cooperation among those external bodies who have to enforce cooperation in the restoration and the durable keeping of peace.[35]

Much hope has been invested in this type of solution to ethnic strife (cf., for example, Linden 1991: 34). But, as the protracted Yugoslav crisis illustrates, its difficulties are also manifest. First, transnational organizations (such as the Conference on Security and Cooperation in Europe, the North Atlantic Treaty Organization, the European Community, the Council of Europe or the European Bank for Reconstruction and Development) are composed of the governments of member states and thus do not themselves have a fast, easy and reliable mechanism for achieving consensus as to how and when to perform their supervisory function. Secondly, the anticipation of the role of these transnational organizations may encourage ethnic separatism rather than overcoming its consequences. Thirdly, even if the peace-keeping function is successfully performed, this is more likely to be accomplished through external threats and rewards than through a constitutional act of 'self-binding' and the lasting moral and political commitment that supposedly flows from it. As a consequence suspicions concerning the 'imperialist' intent (or, at least, consequences) of the imposed settlement of ethnic conflict will be raised, and hostile ethnic sentiments will be heightened rather than appeased.[36]

Fifthly and finally, unilateral action of an ethnic group can be resorted to, either in the version of changing borders (through either secession or conquest) or changing the location of people. If borders are redefined and resistance is encountered, civil or international war will result, the stable outcome of which will, however, be determined by – and be contingent upon the recognition of – other states and transnational bodies. The other, even more dangerous variant of unilateral action, of which genocide is the most extreme form, includes the open expulsion of ethnic minorities or the use of repression, forced assimilation and discrimination with the goal of forcing the minority either to leave or to give up its claim to its identity and to the individual and collective rights attached to it. Thus proponents of unilateral action aim at creating a congruence of territories and ethnic groups. They can accomplish this by treating borders as constant and people as variable or, inversely, by treating borders as variable and people as constant.

Substantive principles In contrast to the five variants of the political process through which a settlement of ethnic conflict can be achieved, I now wish to come to a review of types of outcomes or 'products'. Among individual citizens conflict can be resolved in any of three ways: we agree on common and binding principles, we bargain with the aim of reaching a compromise or we rely on and grant each other the use of our private resources. The respective collective analogies are constitutions, bargaining systems and privatization of (for example, economic, religious) issues, including the devolution of issues to forms of local and regional autonomy or self-government. In interethnic relations the corresponding outcomes are inalienable legal guarantees, participatory rights and boundaries defining functional or territorial autonomy (of which secession is the extreme case).

First, a human rights approach (as an instance of collectively binding guarantees) is unlikely to solve the problem, be it focused on individual rights (for example, of free movement across borders) or rights of collectivities (language, self-government). For it is extremely difficult and often plainly impossible to draw a line at which all the rights of a minority are fulfilled, but at the same time none of the rights of the majority is violated. If the perception prevails (as it does in societies with strong primordial bonds and poor economic performance and without a democratic political culture) that 'your acquisition of rights is equivalent to my (potential) loss of rights', this imagined impact of human rights upon the allocation of material wealth and/or physical security will stand in the way of the recognition of, and *a fortiori* the implementation of, human rights. Granting rights always means some loss of control over those to whom these rights are granted. In view of the zero-sum situation of economic activity, as well as the recent history of ethnic repression, many ethnic majority elites are rationally extremely reluctant to accept this loss of control over minorities.

Even such apparently harmless issues as minority language rights are embedded in strategic considerations, rather than being resolved on the basis of shared principles or the lofty notion that 'the existence of regional or minority languages [is] an expression of cultural wealth' (as proclaimed in article 5 of the Council of Europe's Draft European Charter for Regional and Minority Languages, 1991). Once the right to speak and write the language in public is granted, a predictable sequence of further demands[37] will be raised by the minority, as the 1991 Bulgarian conflicts over the use of the Turkish language illustrate; and each concession along this sequence will encourage and strengthen the demand for more.

Secondly, an unequivocal participatory method of deciding ethnic conflict is not available, as participation can start only after the relevant universe of those entitled to vote or to be represented has been established, and the universe itself cannot be defined through the will of the (which?) people. More specifically, there are two questions that cannot be decided by democratic voting: who is entitled to participate in elections and what is the question that is to be decided on? Concerning the latter problem, it is, for instance, by no means obvious that the Czechoslovak problem of territorial reorganization is in fact to be framed as unity or confederation of Slovakia and the Czech Lands. It might as well be framed as a question concerning the division of the state into four (such as Czech, Moravian-Silesian, Slovak, Hungarian) or even more ethnic sub-units. A way out of these problems might be sought through ethnic quota to be enforced in legislatures or the public administration, in which case, however, the minority would have to be granted, in order to provide it with a relevant weight, a share of seats that is greater than its actual share of the population. Consociational bodies or ombudsman-type arrangements share the same characteristics. Again the paradox emerges that the problem must already be solved (that is, the majority must be willing to grant some form of more than proportional representation) in order to become solvable (Williams 1991).

Finally, territorial boundaries drawn around homogeneous populations will not do, given the mixed and dispersed pattern of settlement of ethnic groups in Eastern Europe, which is also often not even stable over time. These peculiarities preclude the Spanish solution of granting the ethnic minorities inhabiting the Basque Lands, Galicia and Catalonia (and subsequently fourteen more) a statute of limited autonomy which is defined in territorial and functional terms. Also, the

Spanish minorities, in contrast to their East European counterparts, do not have adjacent ethnic patron states to which they might be tempted to turn for help in dealing with the Spanish central government. As the failed attempt to form ethnically homogeneous 'cantons' as autonomous administrative units in Bosnia-Herzegovina ('departmentalization') indicates, dispersed and mixed patterns of settlement do not lend themselves to this technique of peace-making – partly because the resulting units are too small and thus involve heavy diseconomies of scale, and partly because an agreement on the functional division of authorities between regional and central governments is not easily reached in a context of a history of intense and violent hostilities. What needs to be in place in order for a territorial autonomy solution to become operative is a consensus as to what, as 'local' affairs, can be left to the territorial sub-unit and its autonomy (for example, education and culture) and what needs to be decided by the central government (for example, monetary and defence issues). Again in order to reach consensus, consensus on this sort of vertical differentiation of issues and domains must already be firmly established, as it is in fact established in Switzerland. In the absence of a reasonably clear horizontal territorial division, a consensus on this kind of vertical functional division is unlikely to come forth. In particular, dispersed patterns of settlement will lead the minorities within minorities to claim military defence functions for themselves. The fear of ethnic majorities (among them Bulgarians, Slovaks, Serbs) in Eastern Europe remains that, in some parts of the country, they are made minorities within minorities – and as such are hostages to the minority of Turks, Hungarians or Croats.

Linz and Stepan (1992) have claimed that the temporal sequence of founding elections can make an important difference, as illustrated in the contrasting cases of Spain, Yugoslavia and the Soviet Union. 'If all-union elections are held first, there are strong incentives . . . to create all-union parties, and an all-union agenda . . . If in multi-national polities the first elections are regional, . . . there will be strong incentives for political contestation to focus on antistate ethnic issues' (pp. 124–5). But this interesting observation does not escape the problem of circularity, for the adoption of the appropriate temporal pattern of 'all-union elections first' presupposes not only prudence, but power, support and the presence of an all-union party system which would prevail over ethnic and regional concerns. To achieve trans-ethnic integration of the state, important elements of such integration must already be in place.

Thus all three classical methods of resolving conflict (human rights, participatory rights, boundaries) seem to hold little promise for a stable solution and, given the stakes involved, the overwhelming premium is upon creating a *fait accompli* and letting the argument of greater force decide, as in the Yugoslav civil war. Unfortunately, political theory, as well as the practices of international law and diplomacy, seem to have little to offer to counter this logic of rational political nihilism.

Evolutionary cures?

But cures do not need to be 'designed'. In the most fortunate of cases they occur in an evolutionary process of spontaneous self-healing. Whatever the value of such medical metaphors, they help to direct our attention to possibilities of emergent solutions whose virtue resides precisely in the fact that they are not premeditated and administered as solutions. In conclusion, I would like to speculate briefly on three routes which might bring about such emergent solutions. My three labels are 'learning from experience', 'class politics' and 'multiplication of identities'.

Learning from experience The horrors of ethnic conflict and civil wars, or fear of civil wars, may be pervasive enough to effectively discredit nationalist elites in the eyes of their constituencies. Mass resistance against the destruction and suffering may give rise to a common interethnic desire for peace and security. Such a benevolent scenario would unfold due to the widespread anticipation that present conflict, war and repression will provide future historical justifications for its indefinite continuation and escalation. But it would be unrealistic to expect such a learning process to come easily. As the experience of virtually all modern peace movements demonstrates, any appeal to making concessions and engaging in compromise will be rejected by elites as possibly well intentioned, but certainly counter-productive, as it is depicted as encouraging or facilitating the hostile activities of the other side. It is probably only the visible temporal coincidence of peace initiatives on both sides of an ethnic divide that provides credibility to the call for 'bilateral unilateral disarmament'.

The formation of class politics Another evolutionary path leading out of the apparent impasse of ethnic politics may consist in a gradual change of the political agenda that is brought about through successful capitalist transformation of East European economies. Such transformation would consist in privatization of property, liberalization of prices, the marketization of labour power and eventually economic growth. The essential precondition is that the 'limited good' image prevailing in agrarian societies (Jowitt 1992: 67) gives way to the positive-sum self-perception of industrial society. The gains to be made along this route by some and the relative losses and conditions of insecurity to be experienced by many may help to change the patterns of conflict, as it becomes both more urgent and more promising to organize along occupational, sectorial and class lines, rather than ethnic divisions. At least, these various divisions would gradually begin to cross-cut and thus neutralize each other (Prazauskas 1991: 583). As a consequence ethnic issues would gradually be displaced by material ones, namely issues of rights and distribution. To be sure, this path of structural modernization and its concomitant agenda alteration is unlikely to be a smooth one, for in order for ethnic politics to give way to class politics the obsession with the former must already be sufficiently weakened to allow the dynamic of market-driven economic growth to take hold. Most importantly, the reliance on ethnic or other primordial association, distribution and discrimination must not be allowed to stand in the way of socio-economic modernization.

Multiple identities In addition to the political and economic civilizing processes just mentioned, a further evolutionary path can be envisaged that leads away from a condition of 'ethnic reductionism', where people's belonging to a particular ethnic group is held to be the essence of their identity, to a condition of multiple identities, where, depending on the context, sometimes their properties and qualities as human beings and sometimes their identity as members of national, occupational, ethnic or religious collectivities are treated as prominent, both by themselves and by relevant others. But this cultural modernization is contingent upon the prior steps of political and economic modernization, in the absence of which radical parochialism and ethnic reductionism is likely to prevail. 'Under conditions of security, I will acquire a more complex identity than the idea of tribalism suggests ... Imagine a multiplication of identities, and the world begins to look like a less dangerous place. When identities are multiplied, passions are divided' (Walzer 1992: 171). Perhaps even more is required than an internal plurality and division of the self, namely a hierarchical ordering of the various identities that are available to people. Such a hierarchical ordering would allow the 'higher', more inclusive and more universalist identity to contain and limit the expression of the more particular one. The various identities would thus relate to each other in the way of a modern federation (rather than a postmodern confederation). Only if the self of the citizen reliably takes precedence over the self that belongs to local or primordial communities or to economic groupings of interests will a relapse into reductionism be safely precluded.

5

Disqualification, Retribution, Restitution: Dilemmas of Justice in Post-Communist Transitions

Any regime change involves the forward-looking task of building a new political and economic order out of the ruins of the old. But it also involves the backward-looking task of removing these ruins, where they are not usable as construction materials of the new, but rather stand in the way of what is conceived as a smooth transition. The two tasks interact: it is only to the extent that a credible break with the past is implemented that the effort of a 'new beginning' becomes credible. But the way in which this break is carried out must be consistent with the principles of the new order, and not tainted by those of the old, as the latter would amount to the prolongation rather than the abolition of the old order. Furthermore, the clearing away of the rubble of the old regime is a task that can never fully be accomplished, given the limitation of resources at the beginning of the new regime. Still worse, some of the traces of the old regime cannot be removed or compensated for at all, as one cannot 'undo' the past. These problems of retroactive justice need to be disentangled by the new elites.

Is something to be done?

In all post-Communist regimes detailed evidence has emerged which shows that those in charge under the old regime have committed acts which are punishable, as well as morally and politically strongly objectionable, under the new regime and, to an extent, also according to the letter of the laws of the old regime. Large numbers of relevant cases of the illegal exercise of power and the violation of the rights of citizens are to be found in the following areas:

the violation of international law through the military intervention of Warsaw Pact troops in Czechoslovakia in August 1968;

the dictatorial interference of the party leadership with the orderly functioning of the media, the judiciary, other political parties, the churches, academic life, the arts and other organizations, including branches of the state administration itself;

the repressive violation of the rights and liberties of individuals through the police and other security organs of the state, including border guards, as well as rights violations that occurred in total institutions such as prisons, camps and also, in some countries, psychiatric hospitals;

the illicit appropriation of material wealth by members of the ruling elite.

A general amnesty for these people and their acts would not appear acceptable to the new political elites. It would probably also be rejected by the mass of the people of post-Communist societies, who would hate to see those who have assisted in the acts of repression and criminal mismanagement of the previous regime having a chance to return to positions of power and privilege. If they were granted this chance, it might mean that people moved into leadership positions whose involvement in the former regime, where such involvement is not fully known and clear to the general public, makes them liable to blackmail through the threat of exposure. For all these reasons the relevance of such acts and their perpetrators, whatever the lines of demarcation chosen, must be defined and processed in ways that stand up to the standards of the new regime of liberal democracy and rule of law. At any rate, something must be done, and retroactive justice administered.

Or must it? There are five arguments, or at least intuitions, in the light of which administering formal justice to the acts and protagonists of the old regime appears ill-advised.[1]

First, informal justice must do the job. People know their oppressors, and they will – and should be given a chance to, for at least a short period of time – take revenge, perhaps even through selective killings, or death sentences issued by special courts.[2] After that supposedly cathartic moment silence should return, and incriminating documents should perhaps even be burnt. Alternatively, non-formal and extra-juridical methods, such as personal,[3] educational, historical, political and moral discourses, should be used to assess guilt, which can also be done not instead of, but in addition to, formal legal procedures.

Secondly, after the demise of the old regime, and confronted with the chaos it has left behind, we have more important things to care about than retroactive justice. Formal court procedures are costly, and the professional manpower used in them is more urgently needed for other purposes. And, after all, almost all of us have somehow been implicated in and contributed to the functioning of the old regime, albeit perhaps only through cowardice and opportunism; it might be unfair to punish just those who have been implicated in official functions.

Thirdly, retroactive justice is of necessity both unfair and misleading because it focuses on just one category of the destructive legacy the old regime has bequeathed to the present and future. This category is the violation of rights – but what about the categorically 'systemic' effects which nobody can possibly be punished for, such as the ruined economy, the spoiled environment or broken and alienated personalities? Furthermore, corrective justice applied to the past and the drawing of a sharp line between the old and the new regimes may be an act of dishonest symbolic politics, as it may help to cover up the continuities that remain in the holders of power and privilege in the old and new regimes. A ritual of severance may conceal the solid ties that connect the past with the present and future (cf. Ackerman, forthcoming, chapter 5).

Fourthly, retroactive justice might in fact be called for when it cannot be implemented in unobjectionable ways, and it should therefore not be attempted. If standard criminal law is to be applied, it is applied to a situation which is basically different from the standard situation to which it should be applied. This standard situation is one in which one or more of three things are called for, and supposedly fulfilled by the administration of criminal law: the perpetrator must be prevented from committing the same acts again; others must be prevented from doing so; or the public in general (in whose name the law is being administered) needs to be reminded, and its awareness sharpened, of the validity of the values (such as life, liberty, property) that are being protected by criminal law. As none of these three functions of criminal law, which are the only ones legitimating it, is in need of being fulfilled in the post-1989 situation,[4] it can only be for less respectable functions – politics, revenge, retaliation – that criminal law is being employed. As a consequence more new wounds will be opened than old ones healed, and misguided as well as dishonest attempts to do justice in this impenetrable field will only grant an undeserved afterlife to the old regime, for instance by providing its proponents opportunities to defend themselves in court and inciting moral conflict in families and between generations.[5]

Fifthly, while justice can be done by sentencing key protagonists to prison or even death, pragmatic considerations speak against doing it as it is likely to provoke revenge on the part of those punished.[6] They may still control sufficient power, organizational strength, means of violence and means of military or civilian intelligence to strike back and punish the prosecutors, which is why parts of the military apparatus, after an attempted coup, were respectfully referred to as *poderes facticos* in post-Franco Spain. The repeated *carapintada* military revolts in Argentina have effectively prevented criminal sanctions from being applied against known mass murderers and torturers. The analogous arguments are being heard in Russia and Romania in the mid-1990s.

A thick layer of fog, consisting of traces of all the intuitions and considerations summarized above, both pro retroactive justice and con, has been lying over the post-Communist world since 1989. Neither clear, universally accepted and consistent principles nor legislative and judicial practices have emerged from this fog. A persistent sense of 'something must be done, but nothing can really be done in good conscience' dominates the scene. My ambition in this chapter is limited to explaining why it is so hard[7] to come up with a consistent and clear-cut solution, and why at the same time it would be so desirable to have one. My task is thus to provide an overview of problems, solutions of problems and the attendant problems of solutions.

Needless to say, all the above arguments have their specific social base. As could be demonstrated by a comparative analysis of justice in regime changes,[8] the inescapably political conflict over how justice is to be administered after democratic regime changes involves at least the following types of groups: the elite of the former regime; the elite of the new regime; the direct victims of the repressive acts and human rights violations of the old regime, including their families and relatives; and the resistance or dissident movements who have (successfully) fought the old regime. Finally, the agents of those institutional sectors that fall under the label of 'absolute spirit' in Hegel's terminology, namely the churches, the arts and scholarly institutions, have an often ambiguous role to play in the process of coming to terms with the past.

I shall concentrate on the dilemmas of post-Communist retroactive justice as they appear in the German case, with occasional glances at others. This is obviously due to the trivial fact that this is the one I know best and have had opportunity to study continuously since 1989. But the German case has also an interesting systematic relevance. If a solution to the problem of retroactive justice can be designed and implemented anywhere, it should be in Germany. It goes without saying that my reason for believing so has nothing to do with national character or the like. Rather, it has to do with the two German particularities. For one thing, Germany is the country with the greatest experience in addressing – and debating the proper way to address – the crimes of its recent past, due to the unique nature and volume of these crimes.

My second reason for believing that Germany is of special interest requires a lengthier elaboration. The German case of post-Communist retroactive justice is unique, if compared with all other post-Communist transitions, in that the state by which and in which these crimes have been committed, namely the German Democratic Republic, has ceased to exist. Its component parts have become part of the new Federal Republic of Germany, and as such are largely governed by the legal and institutional structure (as well as most of the political elite) that had evolved in the former West German state. Thus it comes at least close to the truth to state that, seen from the point of view of the old GDR and its population, a 'foreign' regime has been imposed upon its territory, while in all other post-Communist states the regime change amounts to a giant bootstrapping act of self-extrication. This peculiarity had the predictable, in fact intended, consequence of shaping and implementing a much more abrupt, rapid and comprehensive regime change, which was made feasible because the former West German state offered itself as the 'Archimedean point' at which the required leverage could be generated. This state, since its size and resources were much greater than that of the old GDR, came to play the role of the functional equivalent of the occupation regimes after the Second World War, which were also able to impose upon the defeated territories virtually any concept of social and political order they saw fit. Yet one may ascribe the structural problem of the other post-Communist states to the very fact that there is no 'occupation regime' or equivalent, and they hence do not have – or are merely at the beginning of a long and slow process of forming – intermediary bodies exercising the kind of 'governing capacity' that is needed, among other things, to come to terms with the past according to strictly imposed rules and procedures.[9]

Hence it is only Germany that is in command of the political resources to effectively enforce whatever rules and principles have been derived from the intense theoretical and moral debate about how to come to terms with the past, a debate that has been, for good reasons and with relentless force, prominent in the German public sphere since 1945. No other country has seen an equally intense debate, and none has a measure of autonomous political control over the remnants of the past comparable to that of the new German state that came into being after the inclusion of the former GDR. From all this it is safe to draw the conclusion that if even the Germans do not find a consistent and practicable solution to the problem and if even the Germans fail to implement it, no other country will be capable of coming even close to a satisfactory way out of the dilemmas of coming to terms with its Communist past. Germany must therefore be the case chosen for a 'most favourable case analysis'.[10]

Saying that the German public has developed a sharp awareness of the problems of retrospective justice through being exposed, for more than a generation, to the experience of the Nazi regime and its repercussions in time and space does not amount to saying that the two pasts to be dealt with are similar or analogous. We probably cannot draw definite lessons from the past about which lessons to draw from the past. The only general lesson that can be drawn is the need for – and the practice of – fair deliberation. Treating the former GDR elites and their criminal elements with the same kind of benign neglect that many Nazi leaders and activists enjoyed in the early years of the West German state would raise the objection that the German elites are unwilling or unable to learn from their past failures to face the past. But treating them differently, that is, more severely, and prosecuting their acts more thoroughly would raise the objection that by implication the SED regime is taken as more criminal and objectionable than the Nazi regime – an obvious absurdity. The three most important differences that exist between the situations after 1945 and after 1989 are clear enough. First, the earlier case involves unparalleled charges of genocide, war crimes and crimes against international law, none of which applies to the latter case. Secondly, the earlier case was processed by the victorious powers after a total military defeat of the German Reich, whereas the second case must be seen in the context of a relatively robust liberal democracy being established in the now unified Federal Republic of Germany, which has the legitimate authority to deal with the injustices perpetrated in the former German Democratic Republic. Thirdly, the task is made somewhat easier by the fact that the former GDR, in stark contrast to the Nazi regime, had at least nominally[11] adopted (through legislation, in its constitution and through the ratification of international laws and agreement such as the Helsinki documents) certain principles against which the acts that its political elites committed, ordered, condoned or tolerated can and must be measured.

As a consequence of these vast differences both the option of 'adopting the same approach as before' and the option of 'doing better this time' are out of the question. The only remaining option[12] is to approach the new case on its own terms and in independent ways, keeping in mind that the only thing it has in common with the earlier case is that it again poses a formidable challenge to our moral, political and legal capacities. The challenge is that 'something must be done' – even if, to the extent the above five negative arguments have any validity, this 'something' may eventually consist of a well-reasoned decision to limit the kind and scope of action taken, up to the point of 'doing nothing'.

The options available

If something must be done, three principal options are available, as well as any number of combinations thereof. There are supposedly perpetrators and victims, and there are both the means of civil law (regulating the allocation of property rights, income and status) and the means of criminal law (dispensing negative sanctions, such as fines and imprisonment). Combining these two distinctions yields three options: disqualification, retribution, restitution.

1 Disqualification (or proscription) refers to acts, mandated by law, designed to deprive categories of perpetrators, be they natural or legal persons, of (some measure of) their material possessions and civic status, which are deemed to have been either unrightfully obtained under the old regime or acquired due to the function they performed under (and in active support of) the old regime, in which case they are not liable to criminal prosecution. This type of measure can also be aimed at the property of corporate bodies such as the Communist Party or parties, state-controlled trade unions, newspapers, publishing houses and so on.
2 By retribution I mean the dispensing of criminal sanctions against individual perpetrators of criminal acts, proven in a formal court proceeding and on the basis of a criminal code.
3 Restitution refers to acts, mandated by law, which are designed to compensate victims, in cash or kind, for what the old regime has deprived them of.

I shall concentrate in this chapter on the first two problems, disqualification and retribution, and save the discussion of restitution (of property) for chapter 6.

There is obviously a fourth theoretical possibility of compensating the victims by means of criminal justice. This option, however, plays just a marginal role and is therefore excluded from the present discussion: such criminal justice is as a rule restricted to negative sanctions.[13]

The first empirical generalization[14] I wish to make is that none of the post-Communist regimes can rely on any one of the three main options to the exclusion of the other two. Probably all three strategies will be used in all cases. Disqualification cannot be excluded because there are many functionaries whose acts made up the old regime and whose further presence in, or access to, important positions in society is therefore unlikely to be tolerated by the elites and masses under the new regime, even though they have not committed criminal acts according to the laws of the old regime and are thus protected from criminal prosecution by *nulla poena sine lege*. These individuals, categories of individuals and corporate bodies must be deprived of some of their material and civic status through appropriate laws – unless, that is, one wishes to stretch the arm of criminal justice by applying standards of natural law, international law or 'general principles of law recognized by civilized nations'[15] and to base criminal prosecutions on these and similar constructs. The type of 'punishment' to which these people are liable is thus not of a strictly 'criminal' nature. They are deprived of parts of their rights as a collectivity[16] not on the basis of individual trials, but usually (and controversially) on the basis of documentary evidence alone (as well as occasionally an additional 'expertise report' on individual cases issued by the Federal Agency for the Administration of Stasi Files) and at any rate without the benefit of an oral hearing, and thus on the assumption of the collective guilt of the holders of certain positions. And the law states both a limitation on the time up to which the disqualification can be imposed and a limitation of the duration of the disqualification itself. If the disqualification consists in making the accused's connections with and role in the old regime known to the victims, as well as to selected authorities and institutions ('disclosure', as is the case with the Stasi[17] informers in the former GDR), such exposure may subsequently lead to further informal, civilian or criminal sanctions and the loss of status and rights that is associated with each of these.

Retribution also cannot be excluded, as key protagonists in the old regime seem to have regularly violated their own legality in the service of the regime, and there is widely held prima facie evidence that at least these cases must be brought before a regular criminal court. And nor can restitution be excluded, as victims of the old regime will generate pressure for re-privatization and compensation. After all, expropriated property must somehow be returned to legitimate hands, and re-privatization is the method most favoured, certainly by the former owners and their heirs.

Civil and criminal sanctions applied to perpetrators and victims all serve to accomplish what I will term first-order effects. They consist in the allocation of positive or negative sanctions. From these, second-order effects of judicial strategies can be distinguished. Such effects condition, in a much less determinate fashion than first-order effects, the attitudes and dispositions for future action on the part of third parties and the public in general. To illustrate, sentencing someone to X years in prison will do something very predictable and determinate to that particular person. But it will also meet with approval or disapproval among the wider public, make people trust or distrust the judicial system, deter an unknown number of potential perpetrators of the same criminal act and have other rather diffuse and long-term effects of various sorts. Often the effects of restitution and retribution are not only uncertain, but even ambiguous. One measure of restitution may generate a general satisfaction that justice is done. It can also incite permanent conflict over who has been unfairly privileged by the kind of justice that has been implemented and whom this justice has left out or discriminated against. Similarly, a scheme of retribution can either put to rest or alternatively stimulate the thirst for revenge.[18] Whether a sense of catharsis or of escalating conflict will prevail is likely to be determined by the psychological need for scapegoats or for whitewashing.

While the careful assessments of juridical truth (that is, guilt) may help the growth of civil peace, there is no short cut. We would be reluctant to speak of justice if punitive acts against presumed perpetrators of the old regime were advocated for the sake of achieving those cathartic second-order effects alone. Ritual sacrifices may placate the gods. They may even help to elevate those who perform them to the heroic status of moral greatness and intransigence. But they can hardly be justified by civilized standards of criminal justice (Jakobs 1992). To Karl Heinz Bohrer (1992) this seems to be a negligible defect, for he castigates the moral weakness shown by the 'peaceful' behaviour of the agents of the GDR transition. 'There weren't enough deaths.' 'The demand ought to have been: give [the criminals] and their sympathizers the boot.' But for that, the elites in charge had too much 'fear of a tough political decision' and lacked 'a sense of being in their death throes' as well as 'political morality of the most fundamental sort'.

Whether or not any chosen combination of the three types of measures will eventually, in spite of much popular demand and support for these measures, contribute to such overall political goals, namely 'coming to terms' with the past and uniting society on the basis of the new liberal-democratic institutions, is a question that evades any juridical calculus. The reconciliatory effect of retroactive justice is particularly questionable where suspicions are well founded that the true motives of the proponents of retroactive justice are to deal not with past injustices, but with present political enemies,[19] for instance by construing a case of 'guilt by association' against the democratic Left. Nor is it self-evident that retroactive justice can accomplish much in the service of the political integration of society, or that there is much need to accomplish it, as the demise of the old regime appears irreversible anyway.

The overall outcome in terms of political integration and reconciliation may also be determined by synergetic effects which make the second-order effects of juridical strategies contingent upon favourable political or economic developments. For instance, some modes of dealing with past injustices (such as the restitution of property that is residential housing) may meet with widespread disapproval under conditions of continued economic stagnation and insecurity, while they are experienced as quite harmless if the economy works well. Unsystematic evidence would also, and perhaps counter-intuitively, suggest that people who have been active in the struggle against the old regime, and hence perceived and experienced its harshness most directly, will normally[20] advocate more moderate modes of punishment than those who have lived in conformity and acquiescence to the old regime. An explanation might be that dissident activists feel an overwhelming gratification and relief from the very demise of the old regime, and their own role in this demise and in the shaping of the new regime, while other less activist groups give priority to settling old scores.

The methods of disqualification, retribution and restitution must all be applied within a temporal frame. This frame consists of answers to two questions. First, from when onwards are acts that occurred in the past liable to corrective action? In particular, will acts of expropriation that occurred in the years 1945 to 1949 be considered as reversible, or only those after 1949? Secondly, up to which future point in time is legal action to be taken? This involves the deadline for registering claims in restitution cases, as well as the statute of limitation in criminal prosecution or a deadline for disqualification measures (it is five years in the Czechoslovak case, for example, but fifteen years in the German case). In answering these questions the following dilemma must be resolved. On the one hand pragmatic considerations may speak in favour of applying a narrow horizon to both directions of the time axis. This would lead to focusing on the relatively recent past and to adopting some rule such as 'the sooner we get this behind us, the better'. On the other hand, and in view of the enormous case-load the judicial system and the administration will have to process, the adoption of an extended time horizon may be preferable. This is also suggested by the principle of equality before the law: no one should go uncompensated – or, for that matter, unpunished – just because the expropriation he or she has suffered, or the acts committed, occurred in the distant past, or because gathering the necessary evidence takes so long or because the courts are so overburdened.

It goes without saying that the past cannot be changed or undone. Nor can the cultural values, attitudes and behavioural patterns that were cultivated under the old regime be undone – or at best they can be undone only in the medium or long run – because these remnants are largely beyond the reach of legal and political intervention. What can be done is to neutralize the other kinds of impacts the past can have on the present and the future by eliminating some of the reasons for the feelings of injustice, resentment, fear, envy, hatred, cynicism and frustration. The question as to what kind of potential impact of the past must be avoided is perhaps more easily answered than the subsequent question of how to avoid it. Ideally, all relics, memories and conflicts should be eliminated which might hinder the emergence and consolidation of certain qualities of public life, such as a viable political culture, the unity of the nation, a peaceful civic life, trust in political institutions and loyalty to the law. The ways and rules by which post-Communist societies deal with their past are likely to have weighty consequences for their own future developments in all of these dimensions, and these consequences will in part depend upon which popularly held principles are credibly being followed and adhered to in the process of coming to terms with past action and past suffering. How much punishment, rehabilitation, compensation, restitution and deprivation of illegitimately appropriated property and status is called for, and in which combination and over what distance of time? I shall be concerned, in each of the subsequent sections, with the respective dilemmas that are to be encountered in pursuing the disqualification, punishment and restitution strategies.

Disqualification: civil law applied to the perpetrators

The legal instruments being applied for the purposes of disqualification are to be found, regarding the German case, in the *Stasi-Unterlagengesetz* (Stasi Files Act),[21] passed by the Bundestag on 20 December 1991, and in relevant sections of the *Einigungsvertrag* (Unity Treaty)[22] of 31 August 1990, which was worked out between the governments of the Federal Republic and the German Democratic

Republic during the summer of 1990 and became effective the second after the GDR ceased to exist according to the stipulations of this treaty, which was at midnight on 2 October 1990. In Czechoslovakia the legal instrument for disqualification is the Lustration Act, which was passed by the federal assembly of the Czech and Slovak Federal Republic (CSFR) on 4 October 1991 (cf. Pehe 1991; Laber 1992).[23]

The method of disqualification can be applied, in contrast to most criminal law, to both individual persons and corporate bodies. On the basis of appropriate legislation their property can be confiscated, their income (including pensions) can be reduced, their access to private sector and, in particular, public sector jobs can be restricted or denied on either a permanent or a temporary basis and their civic respect and esteem can be undermined by publicly denouncing denunciators and making their acts and role in the old regime public through exposure. It is not always easy to draw the line between disqualification on the one hand and actual punishment under penal law on the other in substantive terms. As I use it here, disqualification consists either of the withdrawal of special status rights or privileges[24] or of some curtailment of general status rights of categories of people or corporate entities, while punishment connotes the outcome of a formal legal trial resulting in the individual defendant's loss of liberty or (rightfully acquired) property or income. In the case of disqualification individualized inquiries into guilt and innocence play at best a subsidiary role, while the formal proof of individual guilt and, pending that, the assumption of innocence are the *sine qua non* of criminal proceedings.

Two types of justifications are provided for these practices of civil disqualification. One is based on the backward-looking notion that the status and privilege of which categories of people are to be deprived (such as luxury weekend houses or professorial positions) were undeserved in the first place, as they were acquired as a reward for loyalty to or complicity with the regime. The other is the forward-looking justification that the people in question, their attitudes and competence, and the networks of solidarity existing among them, would constitute a threat to the orderly functioning of the new democratic regime if they were allowed access to important political, administrative or professional positions.

The most easily implemented forms of disqualification of tangible goods are probably dismissals from jobs, non-admission to jobs and the taking away of privileges, such as special pension benefits and occupancy of houses. All of this must be done on the basis of plausible indicators, to be used as the independent variable of some legal formula, of the kind and degree of active involvement with the regime (for example membership of the party, the government and managerial bureaucracy, the Academy of Sciences, the military leadership, the apparatus of the secret police, with its tens of thousands of unofficial informers – or also regular police forces and paramilitary units?).

In the months following German unification and in accordance with the *Einigungsvertrag* (p. 470) a total of 250,000 state sector employees of the former GDR (administration and state services) were transferred to a status of 'pending'.[25] The terms of their further employment were to be determined for a period of (mostly) six months, during which time they received 70 per cent of their previous pay, the implication being that if they were not notified about their further employment within that time, they were automatically dismissed. Allowable reasons for dismissal are of different kinds. In the absence of plausible indicators of objectionable acts in the past (or instead of them), indicators of the technical incompetence of individuals or the lack of need for their services can be used to disqualify people and deny their eligibility for public sector re-employment.[26] Similarly, most social science departments of East German universities were first dismantled[27] and then re-opened; those staff members who did not successfully pass first an individual examination of their academic competence[28] and then an examination of their past political behaviour were automatically dismissed by not being re-hired.

In the German case the abrupt introduction of the West German currency and economic trade and production regulations in the summer of 1990 devalued much of the physical and human resources, thus generating a rate of overall unemployment in the territory of the former GDR which even as late as 1995 was still realistically estimated at about 30 per cent, a figure that is probably unprecedented and unparalleled in any industrial society. On top of this mainly 'economic' cause of disqualification, the introduction of the legal, administrative and educational systems through the *Einigungsvertrag* rendered the knowledge, skills and experience of large numbers of people working in these public service sectors obsolete, as they would have had to operate within an institutional environment that they were often 'technically' incompetent to handle. The dismissal of such 'incompetent' staff, as expressly authorized by the *Einigungsvertrag* (p. 471), helped to take care of many of those cases in an implicit way which in other countries would have had to be processed on the basis of explicit charges of involvement with the previous regime and its political police. This explains why violations of rights of others is just listed as an inconspicuous supplementary criterion making dismissals lawful (p. 472). Much of the 'political' purge is camouflaged and mixed up with 'economic' and 'technical' disqualification.

Disqualification practices, if applied to a more than trivial extent, soon began to raise doubts which concern both their consequences and their legitimating principles. Let me start with the consequences.

Countries which rely extensively on disqualification may deprive themselves of significant portions of the managerial and administrative manpower and talent that they depend upon in the process of economic reconstruction. Again East Germany is special in this regard, as it can afford the replacement of large numbers of former officials, administrators and professionals, given the supply of such personnel of at least equal – and, in view of the newly imposed legal and institutional structure, often better – skills that can be imported from West Germany.[29] At any rate, in any other post-Communist country it would appear neither feasible nor desirable to dismiss and replace a full 50 per cent of all judges and prosecutors, as in fact happened in the former GDR (*Frankfurter Allgemeine Zeitung*, 11 April 1992).

Moreover, dismissals may provoke hostile attitudes on the part of those affected, or potentially affected, by such measures, leading to acts of sabotage, revenge, obstruction, resentment and conspiracies on their part. They may even create martyrs, which is even more likely with criminal sanctions against key protagonists of the old regime.[30]

Such practices may set, as liberals and socialists have some reason to fear, an undesirable precedent whereby future acts of government serve to eliminate opposition elements from the public sector or violate civil liberties in other ways. The inclination to adopt the view that, for the sake of fighting the traces of the old regime and its former supporters, virtually anything should be allowed is quite perceptible among post-Communist elites. Governments may become addicted to witch-hunting or scapegoating, and may resort to ever more indiscriminate use of such practices as a solution to all kinds of political problems. The call for stiffer measures of disqualification may turn from a weapon directed at the elites of the old regime into a weapon against the more liberal forces within the new, thus creating what I have called above (note 19) 'third-order effects'. An example is the reading of the names of alleged collaborators among the members of parliament to parliament and on television that occurred in the Federal Chamber in Prague in 1991.

The practice of disqualification may also provide individuals with opportunities to exploit the sanctioning potential of the state as a private weapon or means of blackmail. The greater the scope of disqualification measures at hand, the greater the opportunity for individuals to give – false or accurate – testimony as to some fellow citizen's role in the old regime, or to withhold accurate testimony and thereby

extract some profit through blackmail. On a collective level such practices may also be used to incite and encourage politically motivated
campaigns for revenge directed against broad strata of the population
or highly visible members of the elite. It has therefore been the stated
purpose of the German *Stasi-Unterlagengesetz* to regulate access to
these documents and prevent them from being used for illegitimate
purposes. As knowledge, however, cannot be expropriated, and as the
possession of documents and their use for selective leakages is exceedingly difficult to police, the effect may be quite the contrary.

The practice of disqualifying agents of the old regime may also give
rise to a thoughtless habit – or, alternatively, a consciously designed
hidden agenda – of personalizing the nature of the regime itself, and
by implication of whitewashing all those whose names are not listed
in the official files on members, office holders or informers – all of
which might amount to an obstacle to coming to terms with the past
in an adequate, fair and critical way.

Political conflicts may be exacerbated rather than reconciled since it
does not often make sense to portray broad categories of members of
various organizations as self-evidently burdened, due to some notion of
'guilt by association', by collective wrongdoing in the past. Against such
practices of categorical disqualification the case can virtually always be
made that either 'not all of them' were guilty in a meaningful way or
that in fact members of other organizations (or even individuals that did
not belong to any incriminated organization) were equally guilty.
Similarly, the practice of disqualification leads to the elimination from
(or future non-admission to) public sector jobs (including, for instance,
driving public buses), but by no means all positions of power and influence. A former dissident has rightly complained that something must be
wrong with disqualification if it does not stand in the way of a former
Stasi functionary's becoming president of the board of directors of a
major company (Jens Reich, *Frankfurter Allgemeine Zeitung*, 11 July 1992).

Concerning principles rather than consequences, the following
objections are being raised.

This practice of sanctioning the perpetrators will involve some violation of the principle of equality before the law, as some of the active
supporters and functionaries of the old regime will find it much easier
to conceal their role in it than others, and thus escape disqualification
more easily.

Another rule-of-law principle appears to be violated in that disqualification, the impact of which may in many cases be at least as severe
as a formal criminal fine, is executed retroactively, and without the
people in question having had a chance of knowing the consequences
of what they did at the point of doing it.

If all members of an organizational, professional or status group are automatically liable to some loss of property and status, they are not – or only marginally – given a legal chance to invoke excuses that might exonerate them individually. To the extent that they are given this chance, the burden of proof is reversed, as appears to be the case with the Lustration Law.

Categories of people who are to be prosecuted or disqualified can be formed according to what they have done (and what they received as reward for doing it) or according to the kind of position they occupied (including the membership status they held). In the latter case position is taken as a proxy for acts, or the act of accepting a position is itself what the disqualification sanction is attached to, which presupposes that the person in question was aware that he or she was in the position. The first alternative, acts as a criterion, has been applied in Germany, whereas the second alternative (position, including transitory positions such as that of a student at a party academy) is adopted in Czechoslovakia.

The first alternative appears to be more consistent with rule-of-law principles, though not entirely so. The newly formed Federal Agency for the Administration of Stasi Files, popularly called the Gauck Agency after its chairman and eventually equipped with a staff of more than 3,000, serves to illustrate the problems. This agency's work is based upon a huge quantity of files of the former state security, reportedly measuring more than 100 miles in length. Each of these files contains two kinds of information: data on individuals and groups under observation and data on the informers who provided this information. While the original purpose of the files was to make available information of the first kind, they now serve as an inventory of the latter. Data on groups and individuals do not matter any longer,[31] except to individuals interested in finding out what the security apparatus knew about them, and as a database for future political and historical research. Even where they contain materials relevant to civil law or criminal proceedings, courts would have to reject them, with the exception mentioned in note 31, as inadmissible evidence, as they have been gathered in ways that violate civil rights. What matters as a basis for disqualification is the second type of data, on informers (both 'official' and 'unofficial', the combined number of which is estimated at over 200,000 in the case of the GDR) and their methods of observation.

Several doubts are in order concerning the quality of this database as it is to be used for this purpose.[32] First, is the database complete? The answer is clearly negative as some of it has been destroyed, it was not complete even before parts of it were destroyed because some sources (such as leading party members, members of parliament) were serving as informers without being registered as such, and some files have been removed from the official archives and are suspected of being in private hands, where they may serve as ammunition for future political and private conflicts and campaigns. As a consequence the category of those to be disqualified on the basis of existing and available files is substantially smaller than the 'intended' total. Moreover, and due to other features of the security apparatus, it may also be larger than the intended total as it may contain false positive identifications. Just as it was common practice to report false output figures in production, and understandably so given the pattern of incentives in a state-managed economy, it may have been in the interests of individual state security officials to falsely inflate their accomplishments and to report to their superiors that certain people (for example, lawyers, well-placed activists of parties, churches and citizen groups) had committed themselves to serve as unofficial informers. These people would then appear in the files as informers without ever having agreed, orally or in writing, to play that role. Another variant of how the population documented in the files can become 'too large' is recruitment of informers through blackmail. If the kind of threats attached to that blackmail are sufficiently significant, this could serve, in a formal criminal trial, as a legal excuse or partial exoneration for cooperation with the security apparatus. But the conditions of recruitment, ranging from voluntary cooperation to extreme forms of blackmail, are obviously not documented in the files. If anything, the creators of the files tend to emphasize voluntariness – an image that is being endorsed by the current use of the files for the purpose of categorical disqualification. This issue is therefore open to controversies that often cannot be resolved by clear evidence, which is equally the case with informers who have been falsely identified as such by the apparatus itself.

An ordinary rule-of-law rule follows the logic 'if . . ., then . . .', with both of these terms being reasonably precisely defined. I have argued so far that in the case of disqualification on the basis of acts committed in the old regime the 'if' is fuzzy due to the deficiencies of the database. Although the procedural problem is greater with 'false positive' than with 'missing accurate' identifications, the latter is in no way negligible. While no criminal can rely on the argument that other criminals, having committed the same act, get away with it unpunished, the matter is different if a systematic bias can be held to operate. Such bias prevails if those who get away were in fact never in danger of being prosecuted, or if they had a chance to have the evidence against them destroyed. A further problem with the database is that its contents are being made available in ways that distinguish three classes of cases: first, higher-ranking public sector position holders and applicants in whose cases the agency must make available data on the person's Stasi involvement to the hiring agency; secondly, other personnel within and outside the public sector whose data can be released contingent upon the consent of those affected by the data (this will obviously lead to strong pressure to grant such consent, and to suspicion in cases where consent is not granted); thirdly, a residual category of persons whose data are released and used just because they happen to be available to interested third parties, without a mandate of the agency or the consent of those affected.

Moreover, the 'then' (in our case the consequences of 'disqualification') is also fuzzy. This is less true if the consequence is defined as a 'ban from public sector employment for X number of years', though this could be said to be unfair as it punishes older people (who have more restricted chances of finding alternative jobs) more severely than younger ones. But such a ban is not the only consequence of being identified as an informer. Other consequences concern private sector employment. How will a private employer respond to the information (supplied voluntarily by the worker, acquired through the employer's own investigation or provided by the agency as part of its legal mandate) that the employee to be hired has served as an informer? The answer to this question, confirmed by an interview I conducted with the personnel manager of a large West Berlin company, is that anything can happen, meaning anything from treating that piece of information as strictly irrelevant, to strict discrimination in hiring, or blackmail after hiring. But this does not exhaust the consequences. Former informers will also have to face the indefinite uncertainty that some of their victims will find out about their activities and respond by private means of revenge and/or public denunciation, which in turn may motivate informers to form protective networks among themselves and to put their inside knowledge to some strategic use. It would be only a slight exaggeration to say that the logic of the law is something like this: if the 'if' is satisfied, almost anything can be done to you by anyone. All of this works against the clear purpose of legal sanctions to restore civic peace through the allocation of precise and exclusively state-administered sanctions.

Retribution: criminal proceedings against perpetrators

One might be tempted to think that outright criminal punishment is preferable to disqualification because the proceedings themselves are more dramatic, draw more public attention and are therefore likely to have more of a 'cathartic' effect.[33] This effect, however, may also be, as I said, misleading in that it depicts the past exclusively as the outcome of criminal machinations of a bunch of criminal individuals on whom society is now taking revenge. In a similar vein, one might argue that punishing some culprits uses up far fewer resources and processes than the third alternative, namely restitution and compensation. Taking both of these considerations together, one would be led to conclude that criminal proceedings are the most cost-effective way to deal with the past. That would presuppose that the use of criminal law is without its own serious dilemmas, which it certainly is not.

Retribution is applying negative sanctions to individuals for specified acts, within a formal procedure and on the basis of substantive legal rules. I will thus proceed by exploring the types of acts being punished, the forms in which they are punished and the justification that is being offered for punishing them.

The acts that make people candidates for criminal prosecution are basically those listed at the beginning of this chapter. They range from crimes against humanity to the active support for and execution of the routine functions of the regime.

The forms of sanctions are distributed over an equally broad range. At one extreme there is 'revolutionary' violence, of which the only example among our cases is the summary execution of Ceaușescu and his wife on television in Romania in December 1989.[34] Next we have military tribunals and highly politicized special courts as sanctioning agencies. Thirdly, and in a more civilized as well as more civilian way, the sanctioning power of the state can be used in regular criminal prosecutions in ordinary courts. Disqualification, in spite of all the problems mentioned before, may be considered as a still milder form of punishment, but it is ambiguous in many cases, and does not take place within the system of criminal justice. Finally, and short of blanket amnesty, we find (proposals for) forms of sanctioning that again operate outside the court system and involve, with the help of lawyers, professional historians and economists, determining and declaring publicly the guilt of individuals (with or without a formal appeal to those found guilty to acknowledge their guilt).[35]

Lastly, we come to the justifications for the choice of punishable acts and forms of punishment. These range from 'revolutionary' to 'opportunist'. In between these extremes we find first justification through natural law constructs, which are held to provide a sufficient basis for criminal prosecution even in the absence of adequate positive law. I will not discuss the vast problems of revolutionary and natural law types of justification at this point. Next, international conventions, international law and standards adhered to by 'civilized nations' are invoked. A further justification is the standard rule-of-law principle that only those acts and all those acts must be brought to trial that were declared punishable by positive law at the time of commission.[36] Finally, punishment can be justified with a consequentialist eye to the achievement of desirable and the avoidance of undesirable effects. The latter, namely arbitrary non-prosecution, was practised on the occasion when political leaders of the former German Democratic Republic (who were nominally liable to the West German law and actually within the reach of its powers) were paying official visits to the West German government in Bonn.

Whatever acts are chosen for criminal prosecution, and whatever justification is invoked, a further difficulty is that the conditions and events that made the old regime so harsh for its citizens are not easily causally attributed to acts of specific individuals. This rule also applies vice versa: those (criminal) acts that can clearly be attributed to decision-makers are often of a trivial quality. Consequently, if put on trial and sentenced, it would look as if the right people were being tried for the wrong reasons.[37] It would look, to borrow a phrase that Noam Chomsky coined for Watergate, as if the company 'Murder Inc.' were being prosecuted for a tax fraud.

This apparent unrelatedness of people and conditions is, in a sense, paradoxical. For it is part of the very nature of 'real socialist' societies that everything that happens is decided upon, and nothing happens through such impersonal mechanisms as the market or an autonomous legal system. The solution to the puzzle may be this: as everything is being decided upon, there are not even impersonal formal rules as to who may or must decide in a given situation, because the competence to make decisions is also continuously being decided upon. In that sense it is seriously misleading to describe the regime as 'bureaucratic', thereby invoking Weberian notions such as calculability, formal rationality or predictability (cf. Engler 1992). Hence the power structure becomes opaque to itself, and everything becomes contingent upon cliques, connections, clans and informal channels of communication. What happens is not ordered by those nominally in charge, and official orders remain unenforced.[38] It is notoriously and discouragingly difficult for criminal prosecutors to bring any light into a jungle of this kind by establishing robust causal links between people and events, to say nothing of conditions and aggregate outcomes.

As far as the gravity of sanctions is concerned, there is clearly a broad overlap between what I have called 'disqualification' and criminal punishment in the proper sense, and some of the objections mentioned before apply *a fortiori* to the latter, which involves criminal prosecution of individual cases with the potential consequence of imprisonment. I limit myself to some additional ones.

1 If tried in a criminal court, the defendants may – sometimes rightly – argue that they were 'just following orders' and that a refusal to do so on their part would have had consequences that they could not justly be required to accept. Instead of receiving positive sanctions (remuneration) for their services, they may have acted for the sole purpose of avoiding negative ones. Quite regularly, informers for the state security apparatus seem to have been recruited through blackmail. The standard defence argument is that, instead of the informers, the ultimate authors of such orders (and of the threats attached to them) should be tried; and if they could not be tried legally (or, in the German case, had even been respected as legitimate statesmen by the very same elites who were not putting lower-ranking defendants on trial), the defendants should also be acquitted. At any rate, 'it seems wrong to expose and punish the intermediaries of terror without also exposing the leaders' (Cepl 1992). 'A systematic tendency to punish the less guilty simply because they are easier to catch is abhorrent' (Elster 1992b: 10).

2 The defendants could also argue, and sometimes equally rightly, that they did not in fact give any information, or any information with the potential of harming any fellow citizens, by performing the role they were performing in the service of the regime. Given the density of the network of surveillance, individual informers can claim that they were just passing on information the security apparatus had already obtained from other sources, or that they were led to believe this was the case. In this situation the harm caused by any individual informer would have been negligible. Moreover, Stasi informers could argue that by informing the state security service they were helping the subjects on which they were spying. Similarly, they might be able to demonstrate that they were both informers and the victims of illegal surveillance carried out by others (including parallel informers checking on the reliability of their reporting), which would exclude the possibility of treating them as unequivocal 'perpetrators'.[39]

3 Furthermore, they might argue, relying on vulgarized milieu theory, that they were unaware of the now alleged criminal nature of the acts of which they are accused; given that they had been brought up in a regime that pardons, and in fact sometimes mandates, criminal acts for the sake of higher political purposes, they had no reason to doubt the rightness of what they were doing – even if they had not been forced to do it (as in 1).

4 Finally, another standard excuse of lower-rank administrators and informers is to argue that they were unaware of their role and

ignorant about the damaging consequences their action might have had for others.

5 In order to invalidate such standard excuses (of being forced, of having done nothing objectively or subjectively wrong, of having themselves been victims or of having been ignorant) the court would need evidence and testimony that is sufficiently immune from the suspicion that it is incomplete, unreliable, biased, manipulated or selective. For instance, even if there is clear evidence in the files of the security apparatus that person X has been on its payroll for voluntarily serving as an informer, it is still an open question as to whether this evidence can be trusted since it might also have been fabricated in order to impress higher officers within the apparatus or, during the last months or weeks of the old regime, to discredit the person with the prospective new post-Communist authorities. Similarly, documents that might have been used to clear the defendants might have been destroyed or might be impossible to locate in the huge system of 'information pollution' that the old regime has left behind. In the absence of trustworthy evidence and given the ubiquity and partial credibility of the above defence arguments, and also given the immense number of cases and the limited capacity of the criminal court system, its verdicts may be seen to suffer from an unacceptably strong element of chance, arbitrariness and social bias that either reproduces the power hierarchy of the old regime or involves the danger of 'creating martyrs'. Both of these outcomes would clearly not strengthen, but undermine the trust in the new democratic system and its rule-of-law principles.

6 A significant procedural problem in criminal prosecution has to do with retroactivity, which is excluded by the rule-of-law principle. Here three variants of the problem must be distinguished. (1) Substantive retroactivity concerns the use of norms which were not part of positive law at the time the act in question was committed. Norms of international law or supra-positive law may be invoked to bypass *nullum crimen sine lege*. Procedural retroactivity can take the form of (2) extending the temporal limitation for legitimate prosecution and (3) suspending a limitation that has already become effective.[40] The two types, of which the latter is more problematic than the former from a rule-of-law point of view, can be distinguished by locating different points on a time axis, as in the following diagrams, in which:

(a) = point of commission of punishable act;
(a') = end of old regime;
(b) = 'now';

(c) = point of criminal prosecution;
(d) = legal limitation of possible prosecution, as it was valid at (a);
(d') = new limitation, retroactively adopted in (b).

'Extension' follows the rule: push (d) into the more distant future, so as to leave sufficient time for (c), given the case-load at (b)

|–(a)——————(b)——————(c)–(d)——————(d')→

'Suspension of limitation points' follows the rule: suspend (d), because no prosecution could take place between (a) and (a'), and allow for a trial at (c), with or without a new limitation at (d').[41]

|–(a)————(a')—(d)————(b)————(c)————(d')→

Restitution: compensating victims

A strong preference for this option may result from the consideration that it is generally much easier to identify victims than to identify those who deprived them unrightfully of their lives, health, property, income, career or freedom. This priority might also do more to heal wounds and to further political integration.[42] Upon closer inspection, however, it turns out that being a 'victim' is not a self-evident and easily recognized fact, but a thoroughly political construct. And even after the quality of being a 'victim' is established, it depends upon which legal doctrine legislators wish to follow whether compensation is granted at all, and, if so, on the basis of rights, needs or desirable consequences. These questions, together with their moral, political and economic evaluation, will be further explored in the following chapter.

6

The Morality of Restitution: Reflections on Some Normative Questions Raised by the Transition to a Private Economy

This chapter consists of three parts. The first describes in a systematic fashion the choices that can – and in fact must – be made when the transformation of the state-administered into a predominantly 'private' economy is to be accomplished. The second part presents the normative arguments for preferring restitution to other strategic options for the creation of a predominantly private economy. The third part subjects these arguments in favour of restitution, and by implication the action based on these arguments, to one version of a test of their morality.

The conceptual framework: restitution within a hierarchy of choices

Unlike the emergence of capitalism in the West, the creation of a new economic system in Eastern Europe is to a large extent a 'political project' (cf. chapter 3). Transformers have to make deliberate (and, as such, highly visible) choices concerning the whole economic structure and fabric of society. In doing so they face a number of possible

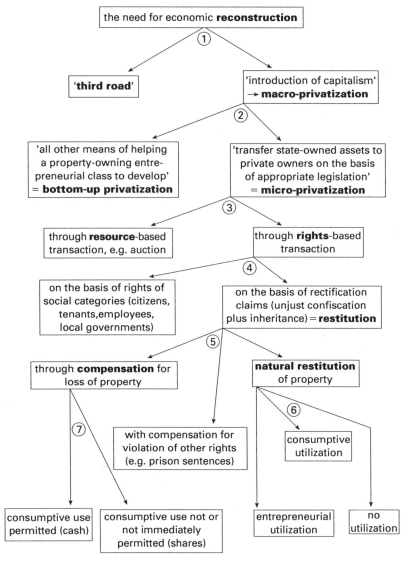

Figure 6.1 Strategic Choices in the Process of Economic Transition

options. Figure 6.1, which also introduces the terminology to be used here, lists the major options available in the field of property reform. With the exception of the fundamental choice of the favoured economic system, these options are not necessarily mutually exclusive, but can be combined.

In contrast to the situation that prevailed during the Prague Spring in 1968, the programmatic notion of a 'third road', or of a different, more democratic and at the same time more efficient variety of 'socialism' that might replace the Soviet-style economic regime, was conspicuously absent in the post-1989 events (junction 1). As a consequence 'mixed' modes of economic organization, such as market socialism, played at best a marginal and ephemeral role in the search for a way out of the post-1989 economic morass.[1] Instead a wide consensus on the need for and the desirability of 'introducing capitalism' had emerged, with the remaining controversies boiling down to issues of timing, sequencing and methods. To be sure, post-Communist economies will have to maintain a state-operated, state-subsidized and state-managed industrial and perhaps also agricultural sector for some time to come. But this results from political and economic necessities, not from strategic choice or design; the variations in the length of this transitory period among national economies are due to preferences for a 'slow' versus a 'rapid' pace of transformation. Nowhere, however, do we find a project being officially proclaimed and implemented that would in the long run foresee something different from 'capitalism', that is, an open economy with private property and market determination of prices.

The introduction of capitalism, first of all, comprises a change in property relations leading to an economy with a dominant private sector. In one of its several meanings the term 'privatization' is used to describe the intentional creation of such an economic order. In this meaning 'privatization' refers to everything that is thought to be conducive to the creation of a macro steady state characterized by a dominant private sector. Hence the term 'macro-privatization' can be used. The desired outcome can be achieved in two different ways (junction 2), either by the legal transfer of productive assets from state ownership to private holders of property titles or by actively supporting what has been called 'bottom-up privatization' (Sachs 1992: 44), namely the political facilitation and encouragement of a 'spontaneous' development of a 'new' private sector 'from below'. Public discussion concentrates on the first strategy. Yet 'micro-privatization', as it will be called here, is only one of two roads to macro-privatization, which can be accomplished even if major parts of the formerly state-owned assets turn out to be impossible to transfer to private owners. This is clearly illustrated by an interesting back-of-the-envelope calculation by Bolton and Roland (1992: 285f), which reveals that only about 30 per cent of all employees in Eastern Europe are to be immediately affected by the privatization of previously state-owned enterprises, assuming that the post-Communist economies adopt the enterprise size patterns and the sectoral composition of the OECD countries and that both the new small enterprises and the new enterprises in the service sector emerge 'from below'.

Roughly speaking, resources or rights may be used as the 'currency' of micro-privatization, or the transfer of state-owned assets into private hands (junction 3). Again both options can be combined, for instance if only national citizens, and not foreigners, are entitled to enter bids for the purchase of state property. Rights-based transfers can rely either on rights of citizenship, employee status and tenant status or on the right of former ownership (and inheritance) (junction 4). If the latter method is adopted, we speak of restitution. It should be noted that the restitution of property concentrated on here is only one form of restitution, as this term also refers to other kinds of unlawful damages inflicted by the old regime (junction 5), such as the loss of a job, of a home or of freedom through imprisonment. A combination of 'economic' and 'non-economic' restitution occurs when property is being returned that has been confiscated by the old regime in connection with a conviction for alleged (political) crimes, such as the actively pursued desire to leave the country. Restitution can take the form of natural restitution, that is, the giving back of the identical or an equivalent piece of property, or of compensation for the (definitive) loss of property (financial restitution). Compensation may be earmarked for (micro-)privatization, for instance if privatization vouchers are issued, or alternatively recipients may spend compensatory payments according to their private preferences (junction 7).

While both forms of restitution may be intended to be a form of micro-privatization, they do not necessarily turn out to perform this function. This, first of all, applies to compensation payments which are not earmarked for privatization. Such payments may be used for the purchase of state-owned assets or for investing in a new private enterprise, but can also be spent by recipients for purely consumptive purposes. A discrepancy between intention and outcome is also conceivable in the case of natural restitution, as restored productive assets may be used for consumptive purposes (former farmhouses are turned into weekend homes), resold to the state (for instance to agricultural cooperatives) or entirely withdrawn from any economic utilization if the restored owners lack the talent or taste for assuming an entrepreneurial function and thus for employing the newly acquired assets for productive purposes (junction 6).

Testing morality

'Morality', as the term is used here, is a quality that pertains to the reasons with which someone justifies and defends his or her action, not to the action itself. A course of action becomes morally respectable if its author is able to provide strong and compelling moral arguments for that course of action, and if the action appears to be motivated by these reasons, rather than by reasons other than those stated. There are two large classes of such reasons: reasons of duty and reasons derived from the desirability of the known consequences of action. Assessments of the morality of such reasons, that is, their moral validity, come in a thick and a thin version. In a thick version we need to determine whether the arguments on which the perpetrator bases the action's justification are 'in fact' valid, that is, whether a duty to follow a certain course of action really exists or whether, respectively, the consequences someone stresses are actually desirable ones. Such a substantive test of moral arguments will not be undertaken here.

Instead this discussion relies on a 'thin' assessment of the morality of arguments given as reason for action. Such an assessment boils down to a test of the consistency, authenticity or honesty of the person involved. The question is whether or not arguments are invoked only opportunistically, selectively and idiosyncratically, thus raising the suspicion that the person in fact makes an immoral use of moral arguments, employing them as a pretext for the pursuit of selfish or otherwise morally less respectable courses of action.

In the case of arguments of duty the morality test would be whether or not the arguments a person advanced to justify a particular mode of action are always invoked and appear to be held universally valid by that person.[2] Yet such a test can easily become sterile and uninformative as it is taken as axiomatic that no abstract principle of justice and morality exists that can possibly apply to all cases. It might even be immoral to overextend arguments of duty beyond the proper boundaries within which duties apply, and beyond which they lose their compelling quality. Strict and universal compliance with principles often comes at the cost of highly undesirable consequences[3] and outright moral absurdities – the well-known problem of *Gesinnungsethik*, or fundamentalist ethics of conviction. People in modern societies can be morally expected to acquire some awareness of the fact that any single principle of morality will soon turn out to be insufficiently complex and hence inoperative, as its simplistic misconstruction will force them to violate in practice what they state as moral precept. Being aware of this fact and still failing to provide for the requisite complexity of moral rules is a characteristic feature of ideological thinking. Ideologists adopt a moral norm which they know cannot be implemented in all the cases for which it is claimed to be valid. As moral dilemmas are ubiquitous, and as a perfectly moral behaviour may (and does as a rule) consist in following one moral norm up to a limit at which the shift to another moral norm is made, the test of morality would have to focus upon the demarcation line between different moral norms. The test of morality concerns the morality of coping with moral dilemmas, the prevalence of which only naïvety or, for that matter, calculated hypocrisy can ignore. The decisive question then becomes: do people provide an explicit moral meta-rule[4] that specifies and qualifies the scope of validity of moral norms, or do they simply invoke one norm as universally valid, with a view to violating it for what appear to be opportunistic, arbitrary, capricious, contingent and anyway unstated reasons. If this is so, the question of morality turns into the question not so much of the substantive rules that are being followed, but of the fairness of the stopping point at which we limit the scope of validity of any single substantive moral norm and balance it against competing norms.

Similarly, in the case of utilitarian arguments based on generally desirable consequences the test would be whether or not the person concerned has made a reasonable effort to assess the actual or likely consequences of the action, whether he or she has compared them with the foreseeable consequences of all alternative options available and whether all consequences of action, and not just the more appealing ones, have been taken into account, where such knowledge can be acquired, with due effort, on the basis of available experience and theory. Again the negative case would be one in which the consequences that are invoked in defence of the action are both highly uncertain and incompletely assessed, even though information is in fact available that would lead a more conscientious or less preoccupied person to anticipate the dubious nature of the outcome. Similarly, even if there is some evidence that the desired outcome will be brought about by the chosen strategy, the utilitarian moral argument for its choice would be weakened if it could be shown (and the person can reasonably be expected to be aware of the fact) that an alternative strategy is known which would generate the same outcome faster or more reliably or at lesser cost.

In practice arguments of duty and arguments of desired consequences are usually combined into moral hybrids. What we find, as a rule, is the more or less muddled claim that following a certain course of action is both mandated by moral principles of duty and at the same time prudent in view of the feasible options and the desirable consequences that are likely to result. Combinations of deontological and consequentialist arguments may take different forms. Three types of hybrids can be distinguished.

1 At one extreme assorted reasons of duty and of consequences are piled upon each other in order to appeal to various segments of a

political coalition that is to be formed by this tactical use of various kinds of moral arguments. If the hybrid combination survives the test of having its component parts scrutinized separately, we have a case of 'moral luck', as arguments of duties and arguments of consequences simply converge in suggesting the same rule should be followed. Outside this happy coincidence, it appears that arguments which are not strong enough to stand on their own feet are pasted together in the service of some political tactic of coalition building and in order to make up for each other's inherent deficiencies. Given such a constellation, an ideological hybrid may turn out to be less[5] effective in moral terms than the sum of its deficient component arguments as the presentation of one flawed moral argument tends to cast doubt on the validity of all other arguments.[6]

2 In another variant of hybrid arguments the components are more consistently connected. Deontological arguments for restitution may be accepted, but at the same time explicitly qualified by consequentialist ones. In such cases an attempt is being made to do, as it were, justice to different criteria of justice. In such morally perfectly respectable cases people refer to arguments of consequences in order to avoid the immoral overstretching of deontological arguments mentioned above. This qualification may strengthen the moral validity of a claim.

3 Sometimes compliance with moral norms leads to side-effects which are desirable on their own, for example facilitating a kind of catharsis, allowing groups to build a 'corporate identity' which sets them apart from others, or winning some moral 'beauty contest'. One of the consequences when a person acts morally is often (though certainly not always) that he or she is perceived by others as moral, the (intended) consequence of which is that he or she 'does well by doing good'. It must be questioned, however, whether reputation building and the striving for moral prestige can serve as a consequentialist argument (as opposed to a welcome by-product) that is fit for public use.

Arguments for restitution

There is an interesting asymmetry between deontological arguments for and against restitution. Any deontological argument for restitution faces a threefold burden of proof. Proponents must demonstrate that Communist expropriations were invalid due to their unlawful or illegitimate character, that there exists something like a duty of post-Communist governments to rectify injustices of the *ancien régime*[7] and that this duty takes precedence over other, conflicting duties. In contrast, a case against restitution can be made by invalidating just one of these three claims. Opponents of restitution will try to exploit this situation. For political reasons, it seems that their optimal strategy is to deny (presumably by the use of duty-based arguments) the validity of Communist seizures and the existence of a moral obligation of the present government to rectify past injustices. This mixed strategy allows the combination of the plea against restitution with the condemnation of (or of display of regret over) past confiscations.

First, were Communist expropriations invalid? The bulk of these seizures were lawful by Communist legal standards. Questioning the validity of the expropriations under Communism, therefore, demands the reliance on an external normative standard. Western political and constitutional thought, as embodied in the expropriation clauses of most Western constitutions, may provide for such a standard. These clauses normally stress two legal conditions pertaining to state seizures of private property, namely that expropriations must be in the public interest and that they must be adequately compensated for (see, for example, Ackerman 1977; v. Brünneck 1984; Epstein 1985). Applying these two criteria clearly renders most of the Communist seizures illegitimate. As a rule no (or only symbolic) compensation was granted. In addition, one might also argue that these expropriations could not possibly have been in the public interest as the Communist systems were run by a monopolistic elite and were not legitimized by democratic means. The use of such an external standard can be justified in, at least, two ways. One may assume the existence of something like a natural right to property. Moreover, one may argue that Western norms had been part of a communal order that survived under the surface of Communism and that the Communist law, like the colonialists' law in former colonies, has hence never truly been valid (for this kind of argument, see also Klingsberg 1992: 96–101).

Secondly, have post-Communist governments a duty to rectify eventual injustices which had been committed by the old regime? In order to arrive at an affirmative answer one can construe a general obligation of governments to correct injustices of their predecessors even after the upheaval of a basic regime change, or even an obligation of the living generation to correct past injustices. A less sweeping justification follows from whether the events of 1989 are read as revolution or restoration (Preuss 1993a). Did they in fact amount to a 'true' revolution that led to the constitution of a new polity, or were they just the outcome of the people's resort to its right of resistance? If the latter, what was aimed at (and what needs to be completed through restitution) was the restoration of the (presumably) better and more dignified pre-Communist conditions. It is thus this second interpretation which provides for a clear case for the restitution of property which has been illegitimately taken by the state. Had, in contrast, the breakdown of the old regime been a truly revolutionary process, two arguments against restitution would arise. First, given the revolutionary nature of the process, the new regime would have no reason to assume responsibility for the wrongdoings of the old. Secondly, it would be even less inclined to do so because restitution would involve the new regime in just another round of 'expropriating from the expropriators', and hence in the quandary of living up to its claims of 'we are not like them' and putting an ultimate end to economic authoritarianism.[8]

Thirdly, does the conceivable duty to rectify past wrongdoings take precedence over other, conflicting duties of the government? In many respects the duty of rectification conflicts with other duties of the government. To begin with, what about the non-negligible rights of third parties affected by the eventual restitution of property, for example the rights of people who bought confiscated property from the state? As Bence (1992: 14) states the general problem, along Burkean lines: 'With time any situation in life, even one grounded on some form of injustice, will become the basis of new forms of human relationships. The unjust nature of the relationship at the beginning of this process will not, or only partially, be carried over to the new relationship. As a consequence of this, any attempt to put right a particular injustice will inevitably lead to further injustices.'

Another case of conflicting duties is this. If (at the decision point of junction 3) a productive asset is auctioned by the privatization agency, the state will at least receive a revenue that can be used for, say, highway construction or the balancing of the state budget. If an equivalent piece of machinery, building or land is restored to the heirs of its previous owner, no such revenue will result, and no such (let us assume) collectively beneficial purpose can be served. To stress the point, one might say that restitution, if compared with other forms of privatization, is a scheme designed to deprive society of that portion of public goods that is equivalent to the hypothetical revenue from sale. If rectifying past injustices is a moral duty, it can also be held to be a moral duty of political elites to care for the collective needs of citizens.

How can we measure and compare the relative weight of such conflicting duties? One way to proceed is to look for temporal hierarchies. The duty to correct an injustice dates from the point in time at which the injustice was committed, whereas the belief that it is a duty of governments to care for collective needs of citizens and to provide for high levels of authoritarian and paternalist security is (arguably) a belief that has been inculcated in citizens by the practices and ideologies of the old regime and thus dates from a later point in time. One conclusion would be that the 'older' duty takes precedence. But exactly the opposite conclusion makes more sense.[9] The argument leading to the latter conclusion is the following. While temporal distance does not turn an unjust decision into a just one, the perceived damage inflicted by the injustice declines over time.[10] In most cases most people will develop a pattern of adjustment to injustice that involves forgetting, 'getting used to' the unjust condition, fatalism, reliance upon substitute means and tactics of getting compensation and the gradual loss of hope that justice could ever be restored since it has not been for such a long time. Several of these mechanisms of adjustment will certainly apply when injustices (and the rectification claims based upon them) are inherited. The next generation will develop less intense feelings of deprivation than the parents who were immediately affected, particularly as they do not anticipate the opportunity of having those injustices corrected.[11] Therefore the 'demoralization costs' (Michelman 1966/67) of a lack of restitution of ancient losses appear to be rather low. In contrast, more recently developed notions of social justice, and the views on the moral duties of the state and government corresponding to them, tend to give rise to intense feelings of frustration and moral indignation.

Concerning the balance of feelings of injustice, it would seem to be safe to make the following generalization. The demand for restitution of confiscated property has played but a negligible role in the opposition to and eventual breakdown of the old regime, and the possibility of getting that property back from the state was subjectively even more remote than the entirely unexpected breakdown of the regime itself. From this it would follow that as the demand for restitution has not played a significant role in the demise of the old regime, satisfying this demand should not be taken as a priority of the new regime whenever such redemption would involve a conflict of duties.

Turning now to arguments concerning collective utility, the utilitarian argument for restitution most often cited in the literature is that restitution enhances the credibility of economic reform by demonstrating the government's belief in the virtues of private property.[12] According to this argument, restitution is primarily a means of building up a certain stock of reputation and what was earlier called 'moral prestige'.[13] This may well imply the acceptance of immense economic and social costs in the short run, since it is the fact that restitution is adopted in spite of these costs which can help governments to gain credibility, and since bearing these costs can therefore be interpreted as a form of long-term investment.[14] Because of these costs, restitution is clearly a second-best option which one would not choose in a world without credibility problems.

The problem of demonstrating honesty and determination can be elaborated with regard to two fairly typical constellations. Credibility problems may arise if the government has difficulties in binding itself or its successors to decisions and preventing itself or them from committing certain future actions (Rodrik and Zeckhauser 1987/88), or if important economic agents (for example, foreign investors) lack trust in the present government, that is, find themselves unable to tell whether an ostensibly reform-minded government is truly reform-minded or just engaged in reformist rhetoric in order to conceal its intentions to the contrary (Rodrik 1989). In the first case a future change of action must be excluded. In the second case relevant non-governmental agencies must be assured that the currently stated preferences of the government are its true preferences. Obviously both of these problems are abundant in Eastern Europe.

To begin with the former, theoretical speculation and empirical evidence suggest that political support for market-oriented reforms tends to weaken in the course of the reform process (Przeworski 1991: 167–71). Rational economic agents observing the process may thus expect a future slow-down of economic reforms and may be led to disbelieve the government's proclaimed commitments to continued reform. One way for the government to tackle this problem is to commit itself irrevocably (as well as its successors)[15] by burning the bridges and by manipulating future incentives. Restitution may be a way of doing so as it will be difficult or, at least, politically costly to change a restitution law once adopted. In contrast, a case-by-case approach to privatization gives the government much more scope for discretionary action and thereby increases the probability that the government will accommodate rising anti-reformist pressures by slowing down the process. Hence restitution can be seen to have the virtue of credibility-enhancing irreversibility.

The second type of credibility problem is also prevalent in Eastern Europe in the 1990s. As the overwhelming majority of political forces proclaim their recognition of the need for as well as the desirability of a transition to capitalism, economic agents, both at home and abroad, face severe difficulties in identifying the true preferences of the government and in distinguishing between 'authentic believers' and 'strategic pretenders'. These problems are aggravated by the peculiarities of government formation in the post-Communist countries, such as the appearance of 'new faces' without an established political record, the weak ties between the political elites and social interests, the still limited consolidation of political parties, and also the prevalence of coalition governments which are often themselves based upon very broad 'forum' parties. As, for all these reasons, economic agents have little cause to trust official announcements, a genuinely reform-minded government will feel the need to build trust by adopting strong and unambiguous measures and to set itself clearly apart from political forces hostile to economic reform. Restitution may act as a signal serving exactly this purpose. Let us again consider a case-by-case approach to privatization as a conceivable alternative. There may well be economic grounds for such an alternative privatization procedure. Yet for domestic as well as international observers it is difficult to assess whether case-by-case privatization has been chosen for efficiency reasons or solely because it leaves some leeway for 'nomenklatura privatization' and increases the government's leverage on the pace of the privatization process. In contrast, reliance upon restitution (and upon keeping silent on its negative distributional, fiscal and other effects) may allow a reform-oriented government to set itself apart from its opponents and to convince economic agents that it 'truly' means what it says.[16]

Turning to a different argument from consequences, restitution may also be advocated because it is thought to be the best way to overcome the absorption problems which are endemic to the East European privatization process. The sale of former state-owned assets is complicated by the large discrepancy between the low amount of domestic savings, reserves as well as incoming funds, and the huge stock of state assets. As a consequence reliance on asset sales will either slow down the privatization process or lead to discount sales due to the law of supply. In the latter case problems of distributive justice arise as current capital owners, be they foreigners, members of the former nomenklatura or possessors of 'dirty money' such as black-marketeers, benefit from being able to outbid ordinary (and properly deserving) citizens of present and future generations. In addition, too large a foreign ownership may be undesirable for both political and economic reasons (Kornai 1992: 173f). Restitution can be treated as a way of tackling the absorption problem since it makes parts of the overall assets to be privatized unavailable to monetary purchasing power, hence allowing for both the speeding up of the privatization process and a partial exclusion of foreigners and the former nomenklatura. This applies to restitution in kind as well as to compensation by privatization vouchers.

Any concluded act of restitution generates three known facts. First, the previous owner does not control the asset any more. Secondly, a former non-owner does. Thirdly, other potential owners are excluded from control over the asset. Restitution can thus be looked at – and justified – in terms of all three of these angles: giving it away, receiving it and preventing others from receiving it. Deontological justifications for restitution clearly stress the second point by focusing on the recipients of the assets and their entitlements. In contrast, the consequentialist arguments clearly take a different perspective. What matters from the point of view of both the credibility and the absorption arguments is primarily that the state and certain other groups (foreigners, nomenklatura members) do not have, keep or acquire the assets.[17]

These differences hint at the fact that deontological and consequentialist justifications for restitution rest on different normative theories of private property. Deontological arguments are based on natural law theories (both Christian and Lockian), which claim that private property is rightful (and must be returned) because it is a divine endowment or deserved through the owner's own labour. Hence justice calls for the original property rights to be returned to the identical owner (or the heirs). The functionalist theories on which consequentialist justifications for restitution rest insist that private property is an indispensable element of a viable and prosperous economic order, provided that it is competently and competitively managed. According to this theory, it does not matter by whom state-controlled assets are privatized as long as they are privatized by someone – and presumably this someone should be qualified by 'functional' characteristics rather than family or ethnic descent.

Moral justifications for restitution are often seen to serve – and at the same time to cover up – interest politics and strategies of coalition building. This comes as no surprise since, from the point of view of politicians, restitution may be an attractive means of expanding their electoral base. This applies in particular to the natural restitution of land, which may allow for the creation of a significant and relatively homogeneous constituency of smallholders. Such political considerations are part of the normal and perfectly legitimate process of interest politics and clientelistic political exchange. As such, they are not directly relevant to our discussion of morality, unless moral justifications are in fact invoked in the pursuit of political strategies and unless political goals are presented not as part and parcel of political programmes, but as generally binding moral precepts.

A 'thin' test of morality

Although this chapter does not engage in a 'thick' test of deontological justifications for restitution, outlining some of the questions such a test would have to deal with might be helpful in order to highlight the differences between the two types of tests. As mentioned before, deontological arguments against restitution can refer either to the validity and legitimacy of the Communist expropriations or to the obligation of the state to correct past injustices. A conceivable argument against the illegitimacy of the Communist seizures which draws on the classic discussion about the abolition of serfdom (Preuss 1993a; Winter 1986) would be that no compensation has to be paid if expropriations aim not at the isolated confiscation of a certain piece of property, but at a fundamental change of the property order as such. Yet even if one accepts the illegitimacy of the Communist seizures, one might question the moral obligation of the post-Communist governments to rectify these injustices.

Roughly speaking, three kinds of arguments against such an obligation can be mustered. First, one may interpret the 'events of 1989' as 'true' revolution leading to a fundamental break with the past by constituting an entirely new polity (Preuss 1993a). Secondly, one may draw a parallel to losses of property that occur as a consequence of theft or war. Governments are not normally held responsible for such losses, though they may well be causally attributed to the state's previous action or inaction. Thirdly, one may refer to the new injustices which would result from restitution and which have to be balanced against the injustices that result from a failure to restore. A 'thick' test on morality would then have to assess the validity and the relative merits of all these considerations.

A further consideration that would be called for in the context of a 'thick' test is the following. If it is just confiscated property (as opposed to the loss of freedom, careers or health) that is to be restored or compensated for, the question must be asked as to what justifies this practice of differential treatment. But even if no such difference is made, it is not clear why restitution, even if generalized, should take place. After all, Communism was no natural disaster, but a disaster that the entire society has both 'caused' and suffered from. Could not the suffering inflicted by it be seen as a collectively self-inflicted suffering – and therefore accepted as a kind of fair historical 'punishment'? To be sure, the inflicting was carried out and the suffering was endured, at least in their extreme forms, by very different categories of individuals. But as only (some of) those who were personally most clearly responsible for the suffering of others can be sanctioned, only some of those who suffered most extremely from the consequences should be compensated. If this is so, it is in no way evident that the heirs of former owners of confiscated property should be given priority as candidates for the latter category, as Communism caused damage to individuals that was much worse than the loss of property. Arguably, one might therefore follow the rule of limiting retroactive justice to the worst cases by punishing only the most guilty and compensating only the most severely affected innocent victims, while relegating the huge remainder to a sphere that cannot possibly be dealt with through formal procedures of retroactive justice (cf. chapter 5). Moreover, some collective compensation for the collectively suffered damages of the past can be seen in the opportunities and intrinsic qualities that the new economic and political order offers to all. But again these are questions involving criteria of substantive justice that cannot be dealt with here.

In contrast, a 'thin' test of morality does not attempt to deduce substantively just rules, but rather takes at face value the empirically adopted provisions which govern restitution in Eastern Europe. It is then decided whether those rules, whatever their content may be, are of a sufficiently precise, explicit and complex nature to allow them to cope with the dilemmas that are to be expected in their implementation. What are thus of interest here as criteria of morality are stated second-order rules that define the scope of the applicability of the substantive rules. Given the wealth of options available in the process of building a predominantly private economy, and given the conflicts of interest that are bound to emerge, there is no simple universal principle that is self-evidently 'right' and applicable in all cases. Claiming such a principle and leaving the rest to the contingencies of empirical constraints, political interests and practical feasibility would be opportunistic, hypocritical and thus immoral. Even after both substantive positions, that Communist confiscations have been unjust and that the new regime has a duty to rectify these injustices, have been assumed there are still many decisions to be taken that define the scope of the injustices to be rectified, the way in which this is to be done and how conflicting principles of justice are to be weighed and balanced against each other. These decisions themselves must be argued for in terms of principles of justice, rather than left to 'pragmatic' *ad hoc* considerations. It is the presence, explicit moral justification and consistent use of such implementation rules which serve as the criteria of the 'moral' quality of restitution. Among other things, the implementation rules of restitution schemes – their 'fine print' – must provide answers to the following questions.

1 Which injustices are to be covered by restitution?
2 From what time onward must property have been confiscated in order to qualify for restitution or compensation?
3 What kind of property is to be restored?
4 Who is to be entitled to restitution?
5 To what extent is property to be restored?
6 What are the conditions and duties attached to restored property upon the acceptance of which restitution is made contingent?

1   Confiscation versus other injustices There is a discrepancy between
the treatment of property confiscations and that of other injustices
committed by the old regime. The laws intended to tackle the latter
problem provide only for limited compensation in a small number of
cases (see Bohata 1991: 326–31 for Czechoslovakia; Knerer 1992: 326f
and Okolicsanyi 1993: 49f for Hungary) and hence sharply contrast
with the more generous provisions on the restitution of property
losses. Obviously no argument of duty exists which would justify the
preferential treatment of dispossessed property owners (Ackerman
1992: 90f). As Elster (1992b: 16) has argued, 'in an ideal scheme of rectification, [other] forms of suffering, no less than material deprivation
or loss, would provide valid grounds for compensation. It would be
arbitrary and wrong to single out one group of victims – the owners of
tangible property – for compensation.' Preferential treatment for former property owners has been justified by the practical difficulties in
assessing and compensating non-property losses and the presumed
moral imperative of 'doing what one can'. Yet it would be morally
wrong to let the choice of rectifying strategies be guided and distorted
by the morally irrelevant fact that property can be given back, while
years lost in prison cannot. Hence the concentration on property
losses primarily reflects the strategic importance attached to property
reform and the higher political leverage of property owners compared
with other victims of Communist regimes.

2   Cut-off points The determination of cut-off dates is complicated by
the complex history of Eastern Europe. Communist seizures were pre-
ceded by earlier uncompensated expropriations, be it by the Nazis or
their allied or satellite governments, under Soviet occupation or by the
democratic post-war governments. In Czechoslovakia and Hungary,
for example, the great majority of large industrial enterprises had
been nationalized even before the Communist seizure of power. All
this invites a number of delicate questions. To quote but a few: what
about the restitution of Germans who had suffered expropriation?
How should the confiscation of property which had previously been
taken from Jewish owners be dealt with? What about seizures under
the Soviet occupation regime, in the case of Germany, before the foundation of the GDR?

    The post-Communist governments have, as a rule, tried to confine
restitution to expropriations after the Communist seizure of power. In
Czechoslovakia the cut-off date is 25 February 1948, so the expropriations under the Benes government are not covered (Cepl 1992: 209). In
Germany the Unity Treaty explicitly exempts confiscations between
1945 and the foundation of the GDR in 1949 from restitution (Badura

1990; Doyle 1992), though the constitutionality of this stipulation was later appealed before the Constitutional Court. In Hungary the compensation law originally covered the period from 1949 to 1987. It was the Constitutional Court which forced the government to adopt a second law providing for the restitution of property confiscated between 1939 and 1949 (Paczolay 1992: 824; Pajor-Bytomski 1992: 57f).

In the German case both the Soviet government and the democratic GDR government that was constituted in 1990 insisted upon the continued validity of the expropriations which were carried out during the period of Soviet administration, in particular the land reform. In 1990 this permitted the West German federal government to interpret the respective provisions of the Unity Treaty as inevitable concessions and a price to be paid for unification. In Czechoslovakia the definition of the cut-off date has been justified by both the democratic legitimation of the Benes government and the fact that many of those affected by confiscation were held to be Nazi collaborators or traitors or illegitimate beneficiaries of 'Aryanization' of Jewish property (Cepl 1992: 209; Franklin 1991: 8–11). This does not appear to be the whole story, however, as strategic considerations also played a role. They would have to be argued for in terms of collective utility. Ignoring the seizures before 1948 was considered advisable because otherwise the can of worms of both domestic and international (that is, Czech–German) conflicts over the expropriation and expulsion of more than three million Sudeten Germans between 1945 and 1948 would have been opened.[18] In Hungary the original cut-off date aimed primarily at the exclusion from restitution of German Hungarians who suffered expropriation and expatriation. As no persuasive moral arguments were presented, the Constitutional Court criticized the corresponding provisions as arbitrary and inconsistent with the principle of equality and declared them unconstitutional (Paczolay 1992: 824).

3   *What kind of property is to be restored?* Several restitution laws provide for preferential treatment for land. In Romania, to take an extreme case, restitution applies only to land (Leonhardt 1992). Hungary is another interesting case. Here restitution was supported mainly by the Independent Smallholders Party, whose strategic position in the coalition government under its prime minister, Antall, enabled it to commit its coalition partners to the goal of restitution (for the politics of restitution in Hungary, see Bartlett 1992: 112–17; Fischer 1992; Klingsberg 1992: 81–119; Paczolay 1992). It took three decisions of the Hungarian Constitutional Court to limit the preferential treatment for land. According to a first draft of the Compensation Law,

expropriated land would have been given back, whereas other kinds of confiscated property would have been only compensated for. Asked for an advisory option by the prime minister, the Constitutional Court held such a differential treatment of forms of property unconstitutional. The draft of the Compensation Law which was adopted by the parliament in April 1991 favoured landowners in a more subtle way as it provided significantly higher maximum compensation for those who made their claims with regard to arable land. In a third decision on the compensation issue the Constitutional Court rejected the respective provisions as arbitrary and contrary to the constitution's equal protection clause. Even the final version of the Compensation Law, in force in effect from 10 August 1991, privileges former landowners by granting them the exclusive right to make use of compensation vouchers in land auctions.

In the case of land the physical character of the property, as a rule, has remained unaltered since the expropriation, and relatively good records exist, so that restitution is relatively easy. Again such 'pragmatic' reasons cannot be adduced to justify the differential treatment of different kinds of property from a moral point of view. In order to justify the higher maximum compensation for which the April draft of the Compensation Law provided, the Hungarian government argued that there are additional costs and burdens pertaining exclusively to land. The Constitutional Court, however, convincingly showed that only a very small group of former landowners would have benefited from this provision. Having undermined the government's official justification, the Constitutional Court then criticized the respective provision as arbitrary and incompatible with the Hungarian constitution's equal protection clause because of the lack of any other justification (Paczolay 1992: 825). With regard to Hungary it is thus easy to suspect the different attempts to privilege landowners of being driven by political interests, primarily that of the Independent Smallholders Party, which hoped to nurture a political constituency of smallholders and to benefit from the prevalent fears of speculative land purchases by foreigners and possessors of 'dirty money', as well as from the fact that land, especially if cultivated without wage labour, is widely considered as a particularly 'worthy' form of property.

4   *Who is entitled to restitution?*   Most restitution laws exclude foreigners from restitution. In Czechoslovakia the laws on large-scale and on land restitution, unlike the Law on Small-scale Restitution, restrict the right to claim to current citizens and permanent residents of the country (Bohata 1992; Burger 1992/93: 488). The same is true of most of the Polish drafts of a restitution law (Gralla 1992: 329). In contrast, the

Hungarian compensation laws also permit claims by people who were Hungarian at the time of confiscation or had lost their property in connection with their expatriation (Knerer 1992; Pajor-Bytomski 1992). In order to justify the exclusion of foreigners it has been argued that only those people who had to live under the Communist regime should benefit from restitution. Yet this justification sharply contrasts with the clause of the Czechoslovak Law on Large-scale Restitution which permits foreigners to make claims if they re-adopt Czechoslovak citizenship and residency. This hints at the true motives behind the exclusion of foreigners, namely a mixture of consequentialist arguments against too large a foreign involvement and political interests catering to chauvinist sentiments.

A second issue is the treatment of legal persons (corporate owners) who are, in general, excluded from restitution. Yet this does not apply to the churches, as specific laws governing the restitution of church property were adopted in most East European countries (see Gralla 1992: 330 for Poland; Obrman and Mates 1993 for Czechoslovakia; Oltay 1993 for Hungary). From a comparative perspective, preferential treatment for churches is particularly drastic in Hungary and Poland. In Hungary the church is the only property owner eligible for natural restitution. In Poland a striking contrast prevails between, on the one hand, the early adoption as well as the unproblematic amendment of provisions regarding the restitution of church property and, on the other, the delayed decision on a general restitution law. It is hard to find a justifiable principle supporting the privilege assigned to one sort of corporate owner. As, according to Hungarian law, church property is restored only if it is to be used for the original purposes (religious, educational, charitable and so on), one might argue that the commitment to a specific future use of the property is such a criterion. This criterion is, however, ambiguous for two reasons. First, other corporate owners are obviously not allowed to reclaim confiscated property even if they are in fact willing to make similar commitments. Secondly, it is not clear what the legitimate reason (as opposed to the ruling party's interest in assigning to the church a strong role in education and social services) is for making an exception in favour of the church.

A further demarcation problem concerning recipients has to do with the legal definition of 'inheritance'. In this regard Czechoslovak and Hungarian legislations differ. The former provides for an extremely inclusive solution by making testamentary heirs and distant relatives such as grand-nieces eligible for restitution (Cepl 1992: 210). In its definition of intestate heirs the Law on Large-scale Restitution is much more generous than the original Civil Code.[19] No reasonable demarcation rule can be detected, other than the government's strategic consideration of spreading benefits as widely as possible in order both to keep property out of the control of the former economic elite and to earn broad political support in the process. It is not only that restitution comes to most of its eventual beneficiaries as a pleasant surprise or windfall profit, much like winning in a lottery, as they had adjusted to the definitive loss of their parents', grandparents' or uncles' farms and factories. Due to the expansion of the category of eligible claimants many beneficiaries may not even be aware of the existence of the property that is now being 'returned' to them. In contrast, the Hungarian provisions are much more restrictive as they narrow the circle of entitled persons and their claims in comparison with the inheritance rules of the Civil Code, for example by not granting restitution claims to testamentary heirs (Pajor-Bytomski 1992: 59f). In order to justify these deviations from the law of inheritance, legislators have referred to the consequences of a more inclusive solution by arguing that such a solution would impose too heavy a burden on the public finances and would also slow down the settlement of restitution claims.

5   *To what extent is property to be restored?* Restitution laws often link the amount of compensation to the size of the property loss or limit the size of property to which restitution claims can be made. The Hungarian Compensation Law, for instance, provides for a compensation ceiling and relates the amount of compensation to be paid in a steeply regressive way to the size of property loss (Pajor-Bytomski 1992: 66f). Similarly, the original Czechoslovak laws included a maximum limit on the size of land to be restored, which was later abolished. In general, limitations on compensation payments can be justified in terms of budgetary reasons. Yet the design of the Hungarian compensation system suggests that distributive considerations also played a certain role as the limitations affect the (relatively small number of) more wealthy owners. In the case of natural restitution budgetary reasons do not apply to the same extent. The amendment of the original Czechoslovak provisions might hence be interpreted as an indicator of the dominance of strategic reasoning. Whereas ceilings were initially introduced in order to deal with widespread sentiment against the restoration of land, later landowners succeeded in asserting their interests.

6   *Property rights relative to duties* Several restitution laws make restitution or, at least, the form of restitution contingent upon the current or future use of the property. As mentioned before, churches in

Hungary are entitled to the restitution of only those parts of their confiscated former property that they are ready to commit to the original purposes. In Germany former owners lose their claim for natural restitution and must accept compensation instead if the transfer of the respective assets to a third party facilitates investment (for details, see Preuss 1993b: 6–9). In Czechoslovakia compensation is paid only in the case of land which is used in the public interest, such as sports grounds, cemeteries and so on (Bohata 1992: 324). Provisions which encourage or protect a specific use of property can be justified as attempts to take into account the eventual negative economic or social effects of natural restitution. In general, they are legitimate ways to reconcile deontological and consequentialist considerations and to avoid an overstretching of duty-based arguments. Moral doubts arise, however, if such provisions apply selectively. This is clearly the case in Hungary, where only the churches are allowed to apply for natural restitution by promising a specific use of the property.

In all the above questions and in all the countries under consideration there is thus an abundance of ambiguities and fuzzy demarcation lines. If restitution is a duty, it must be a duty applying in all cases. As it cannot possibly apply in all cases, limitations must be established which define the scope of restitution. The sum of these limitations gives the property titles that result an artificial and somehow denatured quality. Property is not something that 'I' own, due to my effort, luck or family ties; it is something that 'someone else' has bestowed upon me due to a political decision that has visibly been crafted under all kinds of situational and strategic constraints. Furthermore, the limitations must themselves be argued for in terms of duty. If they are not, the suspicion arises that underneath the proclamation of lofty principles of justice all kinds of arbitrary interests, privileges and resentments govern the actual practice of restitution. Our review has shown that strong reasons for such a suspicion are present in all the above cases and issues.

Let us now apply our 'thin' test to consequentialist justifications for restitution. Here two points need to be scrutinized. First, in addition to the alleged positive consequences, a large number of negative effects also have to be taken into account to make a consistent and complete utilitarian argument. Moreover, and in order to arrive at a robust argument, specific probabilities would have to be attached to both the desired and the undesired consequences. In the process of this intellectual exercise it might, rather disappointingly, turn out that the realization of these negative effects is more likely than that of the positive effects and that the negative consequences will clearly outweigh the desired ones in terms of overall utility, even if respective probabilities were taken to be equal. Secondly, a consistent overall utility maximizer would have to engage in the further consideration that there are alternative ways to achieve the desired outcome, some of which may be less costly, less time-consuming or more reliably effective.

Our 'thin' morality test is now concerned with whether there is conclusive evidence, or at least some indication to the effect, that the proponents of restitution have undertaken these causal and comparative considerations and have arrived, on the basis of the empirical and theoretical knowledge available, at a valid conclusion that yields a utilitarian argument in favour of restitution, or whether they have allowed themselves to be guided by preoccupations, faulty analogies, undeclared interests and other opportunistic considerations while just pretending (or irresponsibly postulating on the basis of shaky evidence) that restitution is mandated by utilitarian morality alone.[20] The latter kind of suspicion would be cumulatively supported by the proponents' failure to take into account and effectively deal with the following consequentialist objections to restitution, particularly as negative consequences of restitution have often been put forward by critics (see, for example, Kornai 1992: 157f) and can thus be assumed to be widely known.

Restitution causes certain injustices and undesired distributional consequences. First of all, restitution does not correspond in any sense to criteria of need, past or future achievement, or to standards of equal citizenship rights. Instead it usually implies a redistribution at the expense of those members of the present generation who receive no compensation, and also at the expense of future generations who are deprived of either the privatization proceeds or access to restored pieces of private property.[21] Thus, in extreme cases, people who have suffered under Communism for forty years may end up paying (either in taxes or in terms of missed opportunities) for well-to-do people abroad. Further undesirable distributional consequences, especially in the form of unemployment, also arise if the beneficiaries of restitution practise a particularly unscrupulous pattern of entrepreneurial behaviour or if they are uninterested in or incapable of the productive use of their new property, none of which can be excluded by the restitution statutes *per se* and is sometimes positively caused by them. Other aspects add to the perceived unfairness of restitution. For instance, feelings of indignation, envy and moral outrage may result if restitution comes as a pleasant surprise to beneficiaries who had already 'written off' their (or their parents') property. At the same time the very process of restitution tends to lead to new injustices. For a number of reasons obstacles to verifying title are ubiquitous in Eastern

Europe. As a consequence the documents necessary to prove former ownership and inheritance rights may be easy to locate in one case and difficult in others, thus making for contingent inequalities among those entitled to restitution.

Restitution 'perpetuates the tendency of people to direct their energies into claiming resources from the state rather than to work hard to earn such resources' (Batt 1991a: 78). On the one hand it nurtures exactly the 'old' economic attitudes and styles of behaviour that are to be overcome. On the other it tends to induce people to direct their activities at influencing the political parameters of restitution by lobbying or bribery ('rent-seeking').[22]

Restitution implies either the giving away of potential sources of state revenue (restitution in kind, restitution by vouchers) or extra public expenditure (compensation in cash). In both cases it aggravates the notorious fiscal problems of post-Communist states (Campbell 1992) and causes deadweight losses because of the need for higher taxes.

The former owners and their heirs may not necessarily be the most suitable owners and entrepreneurs. Thus restitution may lead to a certain misallocation of assets. To be sure, this will be a temporary phenomenon if trading is not restricted and if transaction costs are low.

Natural restitution makes property rights uncertain until restitution claims are filed and resolved, thus increasing the risk of private investment and positively delaying the privatization process. The valley of uncertainty concerning rightful property titles through which the economy as a whole must pass widens the more the deadline for registering claims is extended into the future, but also the more the court and administrative capacities assigned to the processing of these cases are limited. Restitution tends to be a slow process in which valuable time and other resources are wasted.

If it leads to the restoration of the smallholdings which temporarily existed after the post-war land reforms, natural restitution may imply the creation of highly inefficient family farms which have difficulties in obtaining the necessary funding and are hardly viable as agricultural producers unless they are permanently subsidized. A good example is Romania. Here 'the application of the Land Law resulted in excessive fragmentation of land, incompatible with agricultural equipment designed for large surfaces. This . . . caused a huge decline in agricultural output, resulting in the necessity to import grain' (Frydman et al. 1993: 255f).

If eventual beneficiaries prefer a consumptive use of the compensation and if such a use is not prevented by the design of compensation, restitution via compensation will fuel inflation.

As 'systemic stability will rest, in the long run, on the perceived legitimacy of the privatization process' (Stark 1990: 385), there is a certain danger that restitution may put into jeopardy the general success of the 'great transformation'. It is not only that the distributive effects of restitution may prevent the emergence of the social consensus which is needed for the lasting establishment of a new polity (Ackerman 1992: 90). In addition, the political character of restitution provides for arguments and interpretative frames that may play a role for an indefinite future.[23] For viewed in retrospect from any future point in time, those who may have become wealthy by making good economic use of their restored property are likely to be denounced for owing their wealth not to their entrepreneurial efforts and skills, but to an entirely undeserved lucky chance that an arbitrary political decision is seen to have bestowed upon them. In that sense private property created through restitution or compensation is different from private property created through Lockian 'original appropriation'. The distribution of property will be remembered and continuously judged as one originating from a particular process. This modality of acquisition may in turn affect economic and political outcomes. 'It is the form and modality of the process itself rather than the objectives followed in transferring property rights which will determine the outcome' (Pedersen 1992: 9).

Taken together, these points seem to suggest that favourable outcomes of restitution must be balanced against possible and even probable negative ones. Failure to account for the latter and to take measures designed to minimize or neutralize them may substantiate a moral verdict even according to our 'thin' test. Considering the costs of restitution, one should perhaps consider less costly functional equivalents to restitution which would generate the same amount of beneficial effects while avoiding some of the economic and political damage involved in restitution.

Strictly speaking, the consequentialist arguments cited in favour of restitution hardly add up to justifications for restitution proper, but only to a justification for the partial giving away of state assets. Neither the functioning of the two credibility-building effects mentioned before nor the partial overcoming of the absorption problem depends on the transfer of property to its previous owners. A lottery, for instance, would accomplish the same effect, as would handing out privatization vouchers to all citizens. This is not the place for discussing the general merits and problems of a voucher solution (see, for example, Blanchard and Layard 1992; Bolton and Roland 1992: 287–9; Kornai 1992: 172f), but just for pointing out the proper distribution of burdens of proof. Allocating state assets to the citizenry as a whole is at least a superior alternative to restitution as it provides the benefits that are expected from restitution at lower costs, namely without risking the provocation of tensions within the population and with a higher degree of fairness in the distribution. In response to this proponents of restitution would have to provide some evidence concerning the differential advantages of their preferred method over vouchers or lotteries, and it is hard to see that they could.

The expected or, at any rate, publicly predicted outcomes of privatization in general and restitution (as one of its methods) in particular are largely those outcomes that are seen to be achieved in West European capitalist countries, namely growth, broad prosperity and political stability. This analogy may or may not be valid. In fact much speaks against its validity and, by implication, against the usefulness of consequentialist arguments in the building of institutions in Eastern Europe. The intuition that building a replica of the institutional machinery that has been so successful in Western countries will generate the same outcomes as those observed in the West is analytically too deficient to carry much weight. The analytical defects are the following. It may well be the case that it is not the institutions alone, but the institutions together with certain cultural patterns and traditions, that are the causes of the desired outcomes, while only the formal rules that make up the institutions, and not those supportive behavioural habits, can be 'imported' (cf. Offe 1995). It may even be the case that institutions cannot be copied because their 'spirit', or the shared context of meaning and (for example, religious) beliefs in which they are embedded and on which their viability hinges, cannot be copied. Another defect of this intuitive analogy lies in its failure to cope with the question of the historical origin of institutions. Speaking very roughly, in the West the institutional order of capitalism was not introduced in an instrumental mode, that is, in order to promote growth and prosperity (which were only later discovered and understood to be welcome by-products of an order based upon private property and free markets), but 'for their own sake' and in the pursuit of the moral and political (or, for that matter, religious) duties and principles incorporated in that order. The desired consequences may need a very long and uncertain gestation period to materialize, and underestimating this may cause frustrations to emerge in the meantime which in turn will positively preclude the hoped-for result. Needless to say, all of these disappointing courses of events need not come about. We simply do not know and, given our ignorance, it would appear to be irresponsibly risky, perhaps even morally objectionable, to transplant institutions on the basis of any consequentialist reasoning whatsoever in the context of post-Communist transformations. An argument derived from consequences requires reasonably robust knowledge of these consequences. If this is so, and if such knowledge is missing, arguments of duty may be the only ones that count.

7

A 'Special Path' of Transformation? The German 'Accession Territory' Compared with its East European Neighbours

In this chapter I shall compare and distinguish three 'families' of Central and East European societies in transformation. I shall, as in chapter 2, be using a conceptual schema that is meant to distinguish three modes of macro-social integration at the level of national societies, namely the economic, the political and the national-cultural modes. This conceptual frame also proves its worth when addressing the phenomenon of rapid social change such as is occurring in such unprecedented manner in Central and East European societies. Unlike other processes of transformation, such as took place in Central Europe after the Second World War, or in Southern Europe and in Latin America in the seventies and eighties, this change is being unleashed at all three levels at once (see chapter 3). At first glance this simultaneity and the fact that the transformation itself (and perhaps also its ultimate vision of a European and Western market economy, democratic constitution and 'modern' culture) is not oriented towards a theoretical conception, a revolutionary strategy or a proven model make it appear by no means obvious that the result will indeed be economic, political or cultural 'integration'.

In sociology we associate notions of durability, stability, reliable action coordination and inclusion with the notion of 'integration'. In an operationalized understanding of the term the concept is perhaps less suited to measure the degree to which a society approximates an ideal state (irrespective of its form or foundations) and better deployed to estimate how far it has advanced from a state of nature in which, according to Hobbes, life is 'nasty, brutish and short'.

The integration of post-Communist societies is far from stable because the old mechanisms of action coordination are no longer in force and new mechanisms have not yet or have only fragmentarily taken their place. The major sociological questions are therefore: which of the post-Communist societies in the process of transformation have attained what degree of integration in the course of changing their national culture, their economy and the institutionalization of a constitutional order, as well as how we can best account for the differences in level and mode of integration, especially the integration processes that have failed.

In this context I shall again assume that societies accomplish macro-integration predominantly (although certainly not exclusively) at the political, economic and cultural levels and predominantly prioritize one of these levels for attempts at (re)integration. By choosing such a conceptual strategy I do not wish to contend that societies which can in some discerning sense or other be described as 'well ordered' must possess mechanisms of coordination at all three levels. It is precisely under conditions of unstable integration, however, that it will be possible to ascertain whether it is the political, the economic or the cultural factors which primarily come into consideration as a society's 'lifeline' and maintain that minimum measure of action coordination necessary for the society to endure. I shall distinguish between the three modes of integration only in this sense of prioritization.

Accordingly, we can regard a (potentially quite chauvinist) notion of the unity of the particular society – a unity its members believe is justified in terms of history, language, tradition and religion – as a hallmark of the cultural integration mode. The political mode of integration would be marked by the strong emphasis on constitutional norms and on strong and under certain conditions highly repressive political institutions, as well as by the latters' ability to suppress, regulate and centralize political conflicts. And, last of the three, the economic mode of integration rests on an awareness of a spatio-temporally constant complex of investment, production and consumption which extends to all areas of society and holds at least the prospect of the fulfilment of valid claims to prosperity and security. In this context conflicts over distribution, even those of a sharp nature, do not pose an obstacle, but they can instead, as a glance at Scandinavian conditions shows, contribute to economic integration, for they position all the sectors of society in one and the same structure of divisions and involve them in the same class-bound game of collective economic rights and advantages. Conflicts *per se* are not a sign of disintegration, but rather only 'second-order conflicts', that is, conflicts over which conflicts are important and according to what procedures they should be fought out.

This tripartite scheme is also reflected at the meso-level, where we find it in the common political subdivisions. First, there are the Christian/denominational and national ideologies and parties which place corresponding cultural values at the heart of their attempts at social or political integration. Secondly, there are the workers', farmers' and economic parties, which interpret their identities and manifestos in economic categories. And, thirdly, there are the liberal, radical, republican and revolutionary parties, which focus primarily on certain principles and institutions of the legal and constitutional order.

Moreover, we re-encounter the tripartite division at the micro-level, namely in the categories engendering integration at the level of the anthropological capacities for social action which the respective modes of integration are meant to address and activate. In the case of economic integration what are involved are the rationally pursued interests of buyers and welfare state clients. In the case of political integration it is reflected in the ability of citizens who wish to ensure that their rights are protected and that they are guaranteed rights of participation to act in line with reason and in a manner regulated by institutions. And in the case of cultural integration we are dealing with that human ability which older political theory termed 'passions' and which we would today describe as that cultural tradition of the members of a nation which serves to engender identity.[1]

In other words I am assuming that we can discuss in sociological terms whether and to what degree given societies describe themselves primarily as a positive-sum game of interested parties or as a just and rational constitutional order or as a homogeneous community based on common values and traditions and draw their cohesion from this prevailing self-description. Conversely, it must be possible to state whether the macro-level disintegration of societies has its roots in the failure of the economic system of production and distribution, of the political-institutional system of rulership and conflict regulation, or of cultural cohesion and the mutual recognition of members of the 'social community' that is based on it.

The question as to the mode and level of shortcomings of social integration in the post-Communist societies is clearly the proper concern of a long-term research agenda. I shall therefore focus here solely on some of the points of comparison between the factors determining the mode of integration in the post-Communist society that was formerly the German Democratic Republic as opposed to the mode and level of integration of some of its former Comecon 'brother countries'. I shall concentrate on whether and for what reasons the former GDR is taking a 'special path' in post-Communist development. To pre-empt my findings, the answer is intrinsically contradictory. We shall see that the answer to this leading question can plausibly be made in a weak negative, a weak affirmative, a strong negative or a strong affirmative mode.

In view of the relatively underdeveloped materials available in comparative research on the transition in Eastern Europe,[2] this project can only amount to presumptions illustrated by empirical matter, assumptions, as it were, based on the future 'hard' findings which historians and social scientists will come up with.

I

The comparison will involve those countries under the sway of Communist rule that belonged to the Comecon and the Warsaw Pact, but not the Soviet Union itself: the GDR, Czechoslovakia, Hungary, Poland, Bulgaria and Romania. I shall start by mentioning a series of features that the 'revolutions' in Eastern Europe had in common.

The upheaval that started in 1989 is to be distinguished from the classical modern revolutions (namely the French, Russian and Chinese revolutions) in that it was not informed by a theory of revolutionary progress and then implemented by a revolutionary elite which had gained power by non-institutional means. This 'untheoretical' pattern was, incidentally, similar to that which had caused these countries to fall under Soviet power in the first place. In other words the change of power occurred as a consequence of external control following the Second World War and not of upheaval from within. Whereas the theoretical cartography for the route from 'capitalism to socialism' has existed since the mid nineteenth century, and in vivid practical form since 1917, before 1989 there was no such map for the opposite path from socialism to a democratic market economy. At any rate, the verdict of no confidence in the regime of the state socialist monopoly parties which history declared was by no means a constructive vote of no confidence, for the defeat of the old regime was neither radical nor manifest enough, from an economic, political, military or moral point of view. It underwent no endogenous 'collapse', but rather simply 'rotted away', as Lenin termed it, during which process relatively contingent conditions related to foreign policy succeeded in making it impossible for the regime to persist. It was not an already existing revolutionary avant-garde which took the helm in this situation, but instead an ideologically multi-coloured alliance of 'forum parties' which was soon to prove unsteady and which had a low and rapidly contracting capacity for government.

The mass demise of the Communist regimes in the region had been anticipated neither within the system nor without, nor had there been sufficient reflection on the possibility of its happening. The notion, proven in observing other revolutionary processes, that contradictions 'mature', 'come to a head' and gradually enter people's consciousness, can be applied only to a limited extent here. All the observers and probably the strategic protagonists themselves were taken by surprise by the breadth and consistency of the events. This fact lends credence to the interpretation that, despite all the problems of control and integration which the state socialist regimes were struggling with, what was involved was not a process of crisis and conflict that had long been on the cards and in the final instance was intrinsically ineluctable, but rather a configuration of economic, political and international affairs related to specific persons that appears improbable retrospectively, and at best to have had a certain inevitability about it.[3]

The collapse of the national Communist regimes in 1989, and in its wake that of the economic and military bloc structures, were determined by a cross-border causality. This causality functioned as a sort of knock-on effect that impacted at the level both of the elites and of the masses. In this context the most important causal factor was the unmistakable refusal of the Soviet leadership to assume the role of re-insurers of the state socialist order, with the backing of their military clout, as in 1953, 1956, 1968 and 1981, or even, after the deterring example of events in China on 4 June 1989, to allow member countries to take a path of their own that involved violent repression.

Because of the decision not to rely on the military option of violently suppressing the oppositional movements, and also as a result of the strategic acumen and political maturity of the oppositional movements themselves, the upheaval in the countries considered occurred mainly without the use of violence – with the exception of Romania.

The changes in national regimes in Central and Eastern Europe are all defined by the same feature: if only because of the lack of economic resources, they were not informed by the vision of a 'third' path or even a path of 'their own'. Instead they were influenced by the wish to take over and emulate West European models of political, economic and cultural modernization in the long term.

They were all, moreover, embedded in the socio-spatial organization of Central and Eastern Europe, with the deep historical roots this pattern had. This pattern involved a degree of ethnic, religious and linguistic 'mixed settlement' in a manner quite uncommon in Western Europe and, furthermore, was informed by the fact that all these countries were tied into the overarching structure of a decrease in modernization the further east one went. The 'East' always started on the eastern limits of one's own territory – with all the usual negative connotations of the notion, such as cultural, political and economic backwardness (Kadritzke 1992: 181). A clear feeling of superiority thus emerged in dealings with the respective eastern neighbour: the Baltic states felt themselves superior to the Russians, the latter believed themselves superior to the members of the Asian republics in the Soviet Union, the Croats felt superior to the Serbs, the Serbs to the Bulgarians, the Bulgarians to the Turks, the Hungarians[4] felt superior to the Romanians (Stölting 1992) and, most pronounced of all, the Germans (who were themselves 'East') felt superior to the other Comecon countries.

Economically and politically those countries have no choice other than to attempt to copy the institutional frame of the capitalist democracies. They are therefore all jointly dependent (and not just ideally) on the highly industrialized democracies. This dependency encourages an unbalanced view of what is good. Only the setbacks along the road to economic and political modernization are ascribed to the intrinsic abilities, conditions and problematic heritage of the countries themselves. Progress, by contrast, depends – or so a widespread view in East and West alike would have it – on the assistance and support that is forthcoming from outside. Quite understandably, the volume of direct investment from the West is taken as the yardstick of how far the post-socialist societies have already undergone 'normalization'. Seen thus, asking what the future prospects of the post-Communist societies are is tantamount to asking whether it is possible to emulate capitalist democracies in cultural and historical terrain which lies outside the spatial sphere in which 'occidental rationalism' developed. (The latter issue has clearly not been tested to date, and in the case of the South Asian and Latin American newly industrializing countries has more or less been shown to be impossible.) At any rate, the post-Communist regimes are all objects of 'paternalistic' Western strategies in the political, economic and military domain and share a belief that the prospects for their future development are by and large defined by this status as objects. In this connection the German case is paradigmatic for post-Communist social development as a whole, if on a small scale.[5]

Despite the important features which they have in common, it is questionable whether the properties of an 'identity based on membership of a bloc' shared by all six countries are of any real significance for forecasts or explanations of the course these societies will take and the mode and level of integration they exhibit. For these common features – thus the first objection I make to my own hypothesis – exist in the face of differences which derive from the great difference in resources on which the individual countries can draw when coping with by no means identical but at most similar problems. Should this be the case, the generalizing designation of the Central and Eastern European countries as 'post-Communist' would be relatively uninformative, for it pinpoints only common features (of the problems) and does not highlight the characteristic differences in the potential for solving the problems.

We can distinguish three basic theoretical approaches to the investigation of post-socialist transitional processes. They can be summarized under the headings 'theory of modernization', 'genesis environment' and 'path dependency'.

Theories of modernization consider as essentially the same both the problems and those possible solutions which are privileged in evolutionary terms. This similarity is found to obtain between the different countries and with regard to the transitional process from authoritarian to liberal democratic regimes in the West and in South America (see Müller 1992). What is involved is a paradigm of 'designer capitalism' which is preferred above all by economists (Stark 1992b: 299) and potentially encompasses over-schematization and abstraction away from 'local particularities'. There is a danger here of a post-socialist repetition of the structural problem or 'rationalist fallacy' of state socialism. Stark suggests 'the failure of socialism rested precisely in the attempt to organize all economic processes according to a grand design' (1992b: 301), which could equally be said of the consultants from elite US universities and the World Bank who were swiftly flown in after 1989. There is a certain elective affinity between this group of theories and the pragmatist orientation of external elites; in fact one could be forgiven for thinking that those people who are bent on implementing only fixed prescriptions possess an activist approach to administration and problem solving.

Ken Jowitt (1992) formulated a diametrically opposed position under the heading of 'genesis environment'. He describes the situation in post-Communist countries as a state of perfect destructuration comparable to the situation when 'the earth was deserted and empty'. Everything is possible and nothing can be excluded; there is no privileged path into the future, no evolutionary regularity and no recognizable creative will. This gloomy scenario involves the violence unleashed by wars between gangs and tribal rivalries and an institutional vacuum in which the decisive role will be played by individual charismatic persons. In this conception what is expected is a situation in which people are only passively involved and are not able to control the course of events. This impotence is exhibited both by the internal masses and by that section of the external elites which possesses neither the means nor the ambition to foster modernization, but instead attempts simply to limit the damage and avoid disasters.

Following this pointed juxtaposition, it will hardly come as a surprise that I wish to prioritize a third, median position, namely one that accords the post-Communist constellation of social problems the status of an unprecedented special case of rapid social change, but at the same time keeps in focus the similarity of problems in the individual countries as well as the presence of social and cultural traditions, not to mention institutional and economic resources, typical only for particular nations. This leads us to expect a constrained plurality of nationally specific transitional paths taken, the course of which will be determined not only by the Communist history of the individual countries over the last fifty years, but, over and beyond this, by the economic, political and cultural preconditions created in the individual countries by their respective histories over the last five hundred years. Stark (1992b: 300) states: 'Instead of institutional vacuum, we find routines and practices, organizational forms and social ties, that can become assets, resources, and the basis for credible commitments and coordinated actions.' Such expectations refer pragmatically to the position of internal elites and emphasize primarily the conditions and potential they have in their national context.

I wish in the following sections to describe and contrast some of the differences between the paths taken by the post-Communist countries under discussion. I will then go on to draw some conclusions on the mode and level of integration of these societies and the specificities of East German society in transition.

II

First of all, I wish to present a typology of six East and Central European societies in transition (see table 7.1). They were formally

Table 7.1 A classification of (post-)Communist states

	CSR and GDR	Hungary and Poland	Bulgaria and Romania
Duration of transition or breakdown	short	long	very short
Mode of transition	capitulation of old regime	party competition/ election[a]	compromise[b]
Geo-strategic location	'front-line states'	intermediate	remote from Western Europe
Industrial output per capita before 1989	high	intermediate	low
Level of 'nationalist' integration	precarious to non-existent	high	fragmented
Level of repressiveness	intermediate	low	high
Elite continuity before/after 1989	low	intermediate	high
Institutional change of economic system	rapid (*tabula rasa*)	slow (*transición pactada*)	delayed exchange of elites
Prospects for integration into EC	favourable[c]	remote	very remote
Nature of ethnic minority conflict	non-existent	external minorities in neighbour countries	internal minority with ethnic ties to neighbour country[d]
Record of economic reforms	extensive up to 1968, thereafter discontinued	continuous, increasing after 1968	no significant reforms
Record of internal opposition	weak and late	strong[e] and continuously increasing	very weak due to repression
Constitutional development after 1989	only after territorial reorganization	gradual revision of old constitution	rapid adoption of new constitution through referendum
Size of private sector	small and decreasing	big and increasing	non-existent
Religious structure	strongly Protestant[f]	Roman Catholic majority[g]	Orthodox Catholicism
International crises	dramatic (1953, 1961, 1968)	intermediate[h]	non-existent
Prevailing mode of societal integration	economic success	national identity	political repression

[a] Poland since 1990.
[b] Also Poland up to 1989.
[c] Accomplished in the case of the GDR.
[d] Also Slovakia after 1992.
[e] Hungary: elite level, party; Poland: mass level.
[f] Protestant majority in the GDR and Czech Republic.
[g] Strong Protestant minority in Hungary.
[h] Hungary: since 1956 and Austria Treaty; Poland: martial law 1981.

independent 'brother countries' in the Comecon and Warsaw Pact[6] and the change in their regimes occurred between the summer of 1989 and the dissolution of the Soviet Union.[7] On the basis of all seventeen variables used, the typology provides a surprisingly stable form of classification in which in each case the same two countries exhibit greater similarities to each other than to the other four. In each instance there are two cases in the category of societies integrated primarily through economic success, namely the GDR and the CSR; then there are Poland and Hungary, which are integrated predominantly through national identity; and lastly we have Romania and Bulgaria, which are above all integrated by means of (repressive) political rule.

The GDR and the CSR, the 'state socialist success stories', are integrated primarily economically and, for all the notable differences between them, in the following ways they have more in common with each other than with any of the other countries. The change in regime between 1989 and 1990 took place relatively quickly, measured from its beginning to its domestically and externally recognized irreversibility. This change was the result of a swift break with the past[8] and not of ongoing conflicts, reform movements and negotiations, such as set the scene in Poland and Hungary in the eighties. In respect of their strategic military position both the GDR and the CSR are clearly front-line states; in 1953, 1961 and 1968 this position (and the danger to world peace imputed to it) was used to justify spectacular acts of military repression. Their industrial potential was well established and constantly expanded owing to wide-scale pre-war industrialization, and per capita industrial output was correspondingly high. In addition, the fact that they are the only two of the six countries in which a strong labour movement existed before the Communists seized power also has to do with their pre-war history as industrialized societies. Both countries exhibit a low degree of national integration, if for opposite reasons. What was involved in the case of the GDR was less than a nation and in the CSR more than one nation, namely the coexistence of two titular nations, the Czechs and the Slovaks. This coexistence had been far from stable throughout the seventy-year history of that country and had been solved on a stop-gap basis with the federal form instituted in the 1968 constitution – the only such structure in the Warsaw Pact outside the Soviet Union itself. Political repression in both the GDR and the CSR was of a medium level. The internal organization of rule in both countries owed more to the ideal type of a 'cadre bureaucracy' than was the case in the other four. After the Wall came down in 1989 the economic elites and, above all, the disgraced political[9] elites were more or less replaced, a move that went substantially further in the GDR than in the CSFR. In both countries the change in regime took the shape of the old elites capitulating and did not involve either a compromise between old and new elites as in Bulgaria and Romania or electoral competition between political parties as in Hungary and, since 1990, Poland too (see Bruszt and Stark 1991). The prospects of integration into the European Union have already come true for the GDR owing to German unification and are more likely for the Czech Republic than for the other four countries. In both the former GDR and at least in the Czech part of the CSFR internal or external minorities do not form the basis of conflicts addressed by domestic or foreign policy. Thus ethnic conflicts do not obey some bilateral, ethnocentric logic of 'us against particular (always hated) others', but instead the situational, historically unfounded logic of a chauvinism of affluence of 'us against all the others' – be they Russians, Vietnamese or Gypsies. In both countries the history of the attempts to reform economic policy comes to an end in the late sixties because an adequate economic output and an immunity to crises[10] meant there was no compelling need for initiatives in favour of greater market control or decentralization, measures that were felt to be politically risky. This feature of the history behind the change in regime sets the stage for the further course it took.[11] In both countries the history of domestic opposition is short and not particularly dramatic.[12] Until a relatively late point it did not extend beyond the circle of intellectual dissidents and oppositional church circles – both of which had been sealed off from the rest of society. One reason for this was that the regime was able to afford to pay[13] the mass of the working population 'hush money' for remaining loyal to it and to guarantee relative prosperity. Another joint characteristic is that both countries developed their own constitutions only after the establishment of the new (in the case of the GDR, territorial) order. Under the old regime in both countries the private sector was small and contracted continually; not only industry, but also agriculture and the service sector were almost totally nationalized. Both countries traditionally had strong ties with West Europe, but these were rigorously prevented from developing any further by repressive cultural policies and sharp limitations on travel.

The properties shared by Poland and Hungary, the two countries of conflict featuring national integration, are quite different, and they have decidedly different values in all the fields mentioned thus far. The most important differences are as follows. The change in regime required almost a decade and occurred in the form of repeated confrontation between the governing elites and social movements (in

Poland) or via negotiations between rival elites (in Hungary). In both countries calls for civil rights and rights of participation were heard at an earlier date than in the two 'front-line states' and had a greater impact.[14] Minority conflicts referred predominantly to Hungarian minorities abroad;[15] this is far more pronounced for Hungary, with minorities in Slovakia, Serbia, the Ukraine and, above all, Romania, than for Poland, with the strong and concentrated Polish minority settlements in Lithuania. The strategists of the Warsaw Pact regarded Poland and Hungary as militarily less sensitive countries owing to their geographical location, or at least after the Hungarian uprising of 1956 and the effective neutralization of Austria within the East–West conflict. Hungary bore the weight of an ongoing grievance in terms of national policy, in the shape of the Trianon Agreements and the Soviets' military intervention in 1956, while in the case of the Poles the fusion of national and Roman Catholic symbolizations of collective identity predominated. In Poland too, however, the collective self-identity of the Poles was formed around the role of victim, as in the course of its history the Polish nation was repeatedly forced into this role by the two major powers bordering on it. In other words the population of each country has ample historical reasons for complaining that as a nation it has borne the brunt of injustice. This engenders a strong measure of integration through the agency of the nation (Sitzler 1992), which has led to a specific 'national Communist' system of rule. In both countries the new constitutional order has been generated from within, that is, along the lines of a piecemeal and correspondingly arduous revision and rejuvenation of the old constitution. The private sector has remained large in both countries, or rather grown continuously – in Poland it has, above all, been the agricultural sector that has blossomed, and in Hungary the 'second-tier economy' of commerce and service industries. Roughly 70 per cent of the production companies in both countries run themselves, which will no doubt facilitate the transition to a market economy (Fischer and Gelb 1991: 93).

For all their differences, the joint profile of the 'agrarian countries integrated primarily through repression', Bulgaria and Romania, is again quite unlike those described above. (Following the division of Czechoslovakia which took effect in 1993, Slovakia should increasingly be considered in this category as industrialization did not occur there until after the Second World War.) In both cases the abrupt[16] and comparatively violent collapse of the rather more patrimonial or, as Juan Linz terms it, 'sultanist' old regime, something that had quite manifestly not been prepared by internal opposition, was triggered by conflicts involving domestic minorities, namely the Turks in Bulgaria and the Hungarians in Romania. Interestingly enough, the state religion in both countries is the Russian Orthodox Church. As in Serbia and Albania, at the first free elections[17] members of the elite in the old regime were returned to positions of power and, conversely, both countries were the first in which the completely new constitutions were approved by plebiscite and in which a great deal of continuity has been maintained in the elites. Bulgaria is the only Eastern bloc country which at no point after the war attracted attention owing to deviant positions among either the masses or the elites, partly because of the historically rooted, unswerving loyalty to the Russian leaders, as well as the solid backing for the regime among the agrarian section of the population. The Romanian Ceauşescu regime, by contrast, leaving aside its independent foreign and foreign economic policy, neutralized all deviation on the domestic policy front by means of extremely repressive measures. This is one reason why the history of both countries is somewhat undramatic as regards events involving military repression or confrontation. Romania, despite its independent foreign policy, and Bulgaria, despite the minority problems there and the fact that it bordered on two NATO member states, never took the stage as the acute focus of international crises.

The above typological portrayal of some of the important socio-political variables behind the change in regime and the history leading up to it shows that, together with the CSR, the GDR represents one of a number of types of state socialist countries. Indeed it must not be rated as some rank outsider, but instead more as a special case, so that talk of a 'special German path' or of the German 'exception', to use Wiesenthal's term (1992: 164), is not justified. Moreover, we have seen in the case of all the variables[18] discussed here that the internal similarities between the three types are so pronounced that there is cause to expect considerable deviations and possibly further diverging trends and patterns to emerge in the course of further developments in the three groups, but not necessarily between the individual countries. Retrospectively, we could perhaps assume that the state and mode of transformation in the 1990s has been shaped more by the specific history of the last five hundred years than by the far-reaching joint 'bloc membership' of the last fifty years, as is often and superficially inferred.

III

This first finding immediately becomes questionable[19] if we cast a glance at the specific features of the initial conditions, the transformation process and the results thus far of the upheaval in the GDR. This change in perspective, which I intend to adopt now, is well suited to the task of defining the GDR as a type of its own and it would suggest that, instead of the straightforward '2–2–2' grouping outlined above, we should opt for a '1–5' division according to which the GDR is a clearly emphasized exceptional case.

Initial conditions for the transformation of the GDR

The GDR was a state, but, unlike other countries, it was not a nation or even a state association of several nations. Despite all the political and educational attempts by the regime to eradicate any orientation towards a unified German national history, after the Wall came down public opinion researchers ascertained that at least in the first years following 1989 citizens of the former GDR identified far more strongly with the 'German nation' than did citizens of former West Germany. Even the sovereignty of the GDR was far from stable and was recognized only at a late date by the international community. Certainly the concept of a sovereign state must include its effective monopoly on issuing passports to its citizens, and it was precisely this feature of sovereignty that was disputed by West Germany. The GDR was, according to the famous remark by Otto Reinhold, as 'a workers' and farmers' state' a society integrated quite predominantly by its government-ordained economic constitution, and not by political institutions or national identity. From the very outset the pledge to reunification contained in the West German Basic Law questioned the GDR's claim to being a state in its own right, a claim that was itself fragile. The special role of all citizens of the GDR – one made the norm by the Federal Republic, which virtually regarded them as West German citizens – and the points of identification for a joint history, culture and language, areas that extended beyond the GDR's territory, finally led to the failure of the attempt to constitute GDR society solely on the basis of a constitution of the economy backed up by the use of repression. Was there a specific mode of social integration in the GDR, an essentially petit bourgeois, conservative, productivist, modest and egalitarian 'form of life' in the 'socialist human community' with its 'niches' and solidarity? Such did indeed exist, and not just in the minds of people nostalgically harking back to state socialism. This syndrome of social norms and independent traditions collapsed the moment it came into contact with Western consumer culture, however, and is today discredited as a fictitious mode of social integration. This state of affairs will not be changed by the indignation of those who are retrospectively starting to cultivate their 'GDR identity'.

It was the mass exodus of the GDR population, which commenced, prompted by these two legal-political facts, following the collapse of the GDR regime and the Wall, that rendered developments in the rest of Central and Eastern Europe from August to December 1989 both definitive and irreversible. And it was this endeavour to restore national unity, as laid down in the Basic Law, which inevitably led in swift succession to the Four-plus-Two negotiations, then to the economic, currency and social union on 1 July 1990 and, finally, to the contractual self-dissolution of the GDR, which acceded to the territory governed by the Basic Law. This process revealed that the attempt to forge the identity of a society and to justify its difference from all other societies solely in terms of the economic mechanism it had installed was a hyper-materialist error. There was no parallel for such an attempt in any comparable country. The failure of this endeavour is instructive, above all, because the mode of purely economic integration and constitution typical of GDR society was remarkably successful as such. The GDR experienced its only severe economic crisis, as opposed to the phenomenon of stagnation that became apparent to a comparatively great degree from the beginning of the eighties, in the closing months of its existence, namely as a consequence of the economic and currency union. The GDR was the richest and most productive Comecon country, owing to, among other things, its pre-socialist industrial structure, its *de facto* EC membership and the credit resources it was able to tap in the FRG. It is, to say the least, uncertain and quite doubtful whether, in circumstances unlike those that then simply happened, the internal management problems and potential for conflict would, in view of the external assistance granted for survival, in fact have given the regime the *coup de grâce*.

The GDR was the only regime to have emerged in the Eastern bloc as a consequence of the Second World War that, in the overall historical continuum, was not a victim but a primary aggressor. 'Whereas the peoples on both sides of the Oder and Neisse rivers had to digest their collaboration, the Germans were on the side of the aggressors' (Habermas 1992: 247). As a consequence the liberation by the Red Army and the Soviet occupying forces formed not only the military and political starting point of the GDR's history, but also the source of a stylized legitimation (of the state as a whole and especially of its leaders, who had been shaped by their experiences in concentration camps or in exile) which was proclaimed as a moral catharsis and change. The GDR founded itself as an 'anti-fascist' state and praised itself as the 'better' Germany (Meuschel 1992: ch. I), and until the late fifties this rigorous attack on its own most recent history (which ostensibly rendered it unnecessary to 'work through' those events explicitly) did indeed serve as a political and moral substitute for the national forces of integration on which the new regimes in the other East European countries were able to rely. This additional reason for legitimation, the antithesis of the Nazi past and the purging of that past by means of subjection to the Soviet regime, made the GDR one of the most loyal members of the Soviet bloc up until the eighties, as did its geographical and military position in the front line and its open linguistic border. Between 1953 and the middle of the 1980s there were no positions inimical to the regime which struck a chord at the level of either the elites or the masses. In all the other Central and East European countries people remembered the Red Army of 1944 to 1948/9 as the army that liberated them from foreign rule, whereas in the Soviet occupation zone it was experienced as the liberator and as the victor over that area's own criminal regime – a regime which had seized power – and thus as the agent meting out deserved and, for purgatorial reasons, welcome punishment. At an early date the GDR forwent any attempt at using a national mode of social integration, something that may have also occurred because the GDR was the only country in the Eastern bloc in which problems with internal ethnic minorities or nationalities or worries for a minority of fellow countrymen abroad played no role as a potential for conflict. In all the other five countries these themes of conflict served to keep alive a consciousness of national identity, history and culture and give it a keener form.

It is in this context that we must see the fact that the GDR's pre-Communist past could not function as a conceivable link for an alternative, pluralistic and democratic political perspective or a dominant source of inspiration for oppositional groups there, whereas in Poland, Hungary and Czechoslovakia the respective pasts were indeed used to this end. This was the case not only for temporal reasons – in the GDR the experience of liberal-democratic political institutions was more remote than in the other countries discussed here, and dated back to before 1933 – but also for the objective reason that the Nazi regime retrospectively cast a shadow on political and social conditions during the Weimar Republic, the constitution and social conditions of which did not succeed in preventing the Nazis' rise to power. In the years after 1949 it was from this vantage point, which the party elite used strategically, that the second German state was given its fundamental legitimacy as an anti-fascist entity: something that did not need to have recourse to a 'German' identity, but, and thus on a tack confrontational to the FRG and at best drawing at the same time on the history of the Communist Party (KPD) during Weimar and the Spartakus League, was conjured up as a point of identification. The GDR thus invoked the moral construct of a 'better Germany'.

The absence of its own integration mode based on a nation state, the daily immigration offerings the FRG disseminated via the electronic media and the rapid erosion of this moral construct of an 'anti-fascist' republic were the reasons why throughout its history the GDR was threatened with the attraction of emigration the economic prosperity of the FRG exerted on its population. And only the GDR had to cope with these factors. No other country needed to resort to such a spectacular means of repelling such a threat as the GDR did in August 1961 with the erection of the Berlin Wall.

For many years the costs of this support – and at the time it was probably in fact truly the last resort – were on the one hand that the regime that had built the Wall fell into extreme international disrepute and on the other, and perhaps more disastrously, that the GDR forthwith believed it could save itself the serious[20] trouble of providing its own legitimation or identity because physically shutting its population off from the 'exit option' functioned as a substitute for legitimation and political integration. The regime, which damaged itself in the process, grew addicted to this purportedly permanent state of affairs in which contradiction from an oppositional quarter could be treated as unworthy of attention simply because after 1961 it could not lead to emigration. The permission to leave the country selectively granted some 'inimical' forces within the intellectual opposition and the occasional enforced emigration of members of the opposition served to fine-tune the level of domestic conflict; moreover, such persons could also be used as objects of exchange in political relations with the FRG.

The opposition in the GDR was weak and could be kept weak; the line taken by the governing monopoly party was correspondingly tough and doctrinaire. In the GDR all systems of mass protest (such as that of 17 June 1953) or of opposition within the elites to the Soviet leadership or their proxy governors were, right up until the Gorbachev era, far more underdeveloped than in the other Central European countries.[21] The GDR leadership was able to afford to show this exceptional degree of intransigence thanks on the one hand to consistent repression, political controls and the double function of the Wall as a block and an escape valve and on the other to the comparatively high and well-secured standard of living that it offered its population. It had to be able to afford this animosity towards reforms, despite the fact that this severely tarnished its domestic and international reputation, because, in the probably accurate opinion of its representatives, if the regime had relaxed its hold or been more open at any point after 1961, it would have had the famous knock-on effect that happened in 1989.

It is the coincidence and intrinsic linkage of the features briefly summarized here which make the initial conditions and history leading up to the 1989 upheaval appear exceptional. The GDR was an economic state without being a nation state.[22] It endeavoured to offset this deficiency by invoking an 'anti-fascist' legitimation that negated its own national history. Despite its economic successes, its fragile statehood was threatened by the continual offers of a nation state made by the FRG, whose mere existence and frequently also its policies weakened the internal GDR opposition. The GDR was able to extricate itself from this confrontation with the neighbouring state in the West only by physically locking its own population in, to which end a building project was embarked on that on 9 November 1989 finally proved to be not a 'protective wall', but instead the Achilles' heel of the whole Eastern bloc system.

The course of the transformation process in the GDR

The most important difference between the GDR and its former 'brother countries' is certainly the fact that the transformation there took the shape of the state's contractual undertaking to dissolve itself and the merger ('accession') of the country with the other German state. The inhabitants and territory of the former GDR were subordinated to the legal, economic, currency and social system of the former FRG. By contrast, the legal system initially remained intact in the other former 'brother countries'.

This unique division of roles between internal and external agents can be explained by the fact that a dissident movement or internal opposition played a lesser role in preparing the upheaval in the GDR than elsewhere.[23] Only in the German case, given these internal and external factors, were people ready at hand to determine further developments and introduce economic, political and social reconstruction, namely the political leadership of the former FRG. In the other Central and East European countries the old legal framework and, above all else, the old administration and its staff continued to operate: a state of affairs that offered the 'old structures' of the elite corresponding opportunities to put a spanner in the works of reconstruction. Only the GDR, thanks to the reserves of people mobilized in the West, was able to 'afford', for example, to replace 50 per cent of the judiciary, as well as large sections of the academic intelligentsia in the social sciences and humanities. Owing to the dominant role played there by external forces, the GDR's case had less to do with a transformation 'from above' or 'from below' and more with a change 'from outside'.[24]

In addition to the rapid loss of non-competitive jobs, the GDR's labour force was also hit by functional disqualification as a consequence of the transfer of institutions from West to East Germany. The introduction of new institutions and technologies and the sudden assertion of 'Western standards' in all walks of life, something the labour force of the GDR was not prepared for, objectively devalued and subjectively discouraged the people there. Grimm (1992: 1063) writes: 'Knowledge and abilities which had been trained in the socialist society, the patterns of orientation and the modes of reaching understanding that functioned there, these are all largely unusable in Western society. Thus, the leading role fell to the West in almost all areas of society, whereas the East was condemned to learning.' This devaluation and discouragement of the labour potential was also a cause of the level of unemployment (in particular among women, of whom 90 per cent were incorporated into the world of work beforehand), which is probably unique in the history of industrial society. It is noteworthy that this unemployment exists despite uniquely high relative losses owing to migration westwards by members of the population of East Germany, which has dropped to below 16 million and continues to fall. Nowhere else is migration so attractive and (for legal, linguistic and cultural reasons) so 'cheap'. Moreover, not only do these losses through migration stand out quantitatively, but they must also be considered a signal of a catastrophic development policy and a demographic disaster. The high proportion of men points to further losses through migration, namely by the women and children who then 'follow'. The high number of younger people will cause the birth rate to fall further and will also diminish the ability of the 'overall labour force' in East Germany to upgrade its qualifications. After all, in Grundmann's words (1992: 58–9), it is 'the highly motivated, healthy, well-educated or intellectually capable achievers who disappear westwards'. Thus the decision to press ahead with unification as quickly and as radically as possible generated self-perpetuating time pressures (see Bialas and Ettl: 1992): the social and economic adjustment of living standards to those in the West has to be effected as quickly as possible in the interests of preventing further losses through migration.[25] The more rigorously this adjustment is accomplished, however, the more living conditions for the lion's share of the population of the 'acceding territory' change – in a manner which motivates them to migrate if at all possible, which in turn generates time pressures, and so on, and so on.[26]

A further unique feature of the transformation in the GDR was the role the political opposition played there. In the GDR the number of potential counter-elites was greatly reduced over the years by emigration or forced emigration to West Germany, to which this circle of people (for example, Wolf Biermann, Jurek Becker, Erich Loest, Sarah Kirsch, Monika Maron and Manfred Krug) always had access.[27] This explains why no equivalent of Vaclav Havel emerged there. And, equally, in the GDR there was no samizdat network of oppositional communications, but rather West German publishers.[28] As a consequence, after the Wall came down there was a dearth of charismatic individuals who symbolized the change and were able to lead it from an independent vantage point.

Leaving aside its size, the internal GDR opposition exhibited other characteristics that under the given conditions disqualified it from playing a decisive political role in the transformation process. On the one hand the (weak) domestic opposition, as Krüger (1992: 49) states, 'unlike that in Poland, Hungary or the Soviet Union . . . above all consisted of reformist socialists';[29] there was an almost total lack of conservative and national forces, or at any rate, as Kocka (1990: 486) avers, 'the decisive breakthroughs in the GDR occurred without being fuelled by national slogans'. Still fixated on the identity of their country as that shaped by a particular mode of production and form of political rule, for all their opposition the opposition in the GDR wanted a 'different' GDR, not the end of the GDR.

On the other hand national slogans, when they did arise in the shape of 'We are one people', did not refer negatively to liberation from foreign rule, but positively to the GDR economy being restored to good health from outside, by West Germany. Those who proclaimed it did not want a 'different' GDR, they wanted no GDR whatsoever. Thus elsewhere the notion of nationality conveyed the idea of a gain in sovereignty within a state that persisted in its traditional borders (or claimed new ones). In the case of the GDR it signalled a waiver of sovereignty.[30] After hundreds of thousands of GDR citizens had initially left their country behind them between the summer of 1989 and that of 1990 and following the Unity Treaty and the accession of the GDR to the territory covered by the West German Basic Law, the GDR dissolved itself in compliance with article 23. This switch in direction that the West German political elites pushed through had confined the GDR opposition, which in autumn 1989 had still spoken out on behalf of change, to the sidelines by the time of the elections to the People's Chamber[31] of 18 March 1990; in fact, unlike those in opposition in other countries in Central and East Europe,[32] they lost any chance of taking part in the process of rebuilding their country.

Everywhere else the talk was of 'reform' or 'transition' or of the 'path to Europe', that is, of a carefully focused process whereby the countries involved changed themselves. In the case of Germany's 'new federal states', by contrast, this became a matter of the 'process of unification' or the 'completion' of unification. This 'completion' was undoubtedly perceived by all concerned primarily as coming under the jurisdiction and being the task of the political elites and institutions in the old federal states. Terminologically speaking, this shifted the position of the 'former GDR', granting it the role of a more or less pliable object that was encumbered with a frightening range of burdens from its past. While the new political elites in the other East and Central European countries attempted to whip up support among their respective populations for the project (which was in places opposed) of taking the (political, economic and cultural) 'path to Europe' and giving things the necessary 'push' in this direction, in the GDR the 'path to Germany' was taken within a very few months by means of the quite unprecedented 'pull' exerted by a *tour de force* in Bonn.

The unique mode of transformation – and it was probably the only one that was politically practicable – to be observed in the GDR initially offered clear advantages over the mode of transformation adopted in the other countries. They had, as it were, to repair their sinking ships while still at sea, whereas the GDR was retrofitted in the FRG dry dock. The others had to pull themselves out of the quagmire by their own bootstraps, whereas the new German federal states were assisted by a high-power salvage crane. However, this external steering of the transformation process also brought with it specific disadvantages that did not occur in the other countries. Wiesenthal (1992: 172) is playing things down when he writes: 'the former GDR's special status is not something merely to be regarded as a privilege'.

What were the disadvantages? First, the oft-described signs of an unpleasant socio-psychological 'state of affairs'. These disadvantages include the brisk speed of institutional change in all walks of life, which, unlike in Hungary and Poland, also prompted panic-like disorientation, resignation and increasing protest from a population not used to reform debates and open political conflict. Moreover, the initiative taken by the FRG was experienced by the population of the former GDR as a personal deficit in democracy (and thus as an accentuated continuation of the status quo ante),[33] because, owing to its status as a minority, and a (relatively) economically weak one at that, it was predominantly prevented from effectively taking part in the redesign of the social order. The same applies to the role played by the native East German political institutions. The people of the GDR have been confronted with completely unfamiliar laws and institutions and, as it were, treated collectively as infantile owing to the consequent loss of practised and reliable 'interactive knowledge', to use

Wiesenthal's term (1992: 174). A third disadvantage specific to the former GDR was that the pain and shortcomings of the transformation have been experienced not as absolute, but rather as relative deprivation. The population of the GDR does not suffer from the otherwise ubiquitous poverty, but as a consequence suffers all the more from its backwardness with regard to the levels of income, employment, infrastructure and affluence in West Germany, with which it had been led to believe it would soon catch up. Whereas under the old regime the GDR had had a leading and pioneering position *vis-à-vis* the state socialist 'brother countries', and its pride stemmed from this fact, its population has suddenly found itself in the position of bringing up the rear in the process of German unification. Thus the objectively favourable conditions of the transition have made it subjectively more painful than in other transitional countries.

The speed of unification has created an extreme potential for disappointment. Pursuing the goal of 'catching up' has ensnared the East Germans in a mad dash for modernization that has inevitably had a socially disorganizing impact and goes hand in hand with the enduring frustration of those who have to regard themselves as being at least a generation behind things and, for all the absolute progress made, still relatively 'backward' and are regarded thus by others. In the GDR growth rates which in Poland would be considered a beneficial and encouraging success to be presented to the public serve only to stress the distance still to go in order to reach the defined goal of equal living standards in both halves of Germany.

By virtue of the fact that the GDR was transformed by positive legal fiat and 'from outside', its population was neither given the chance nor challenged to make its own, morally discerning contribution towards shaping its own future. It was treated politically as immature and not given sufficient moral encouragement,[34] whereas the West German population was rapidly morally overtaxed (in view of the signs of resistance to fiscal increases to fund unification), with sole jurisdiction for the future of the GDR falling to the elites there. Only in the case of Germany is the subject of transformation not identical with the object thereof.

More tangible than such symptoms of political and social alienation were the economic disadvantages of the GDR as an exceptional case (see Pickel 1992). The economic and currency union created a situation which not only, as in all the other countries, led more or less swiftly to the collapse of the Eastern and Western export markets, but also led to the sudden and at least temporary collapse of the domestic market. What Wiesenthal has called the 'unexpected volume elasticity' of Western suppliers and their sales strategy for conquering territory combined with GDR consumer behaviour, motivated by a sense of protest, to cause a decisive decimation of domestic production. Owing to its abrupt integration into the world economy with effect from 1 July 1990, industrial production in East Germany had fallen by the year-end of 1991 to a third of 1989 levels (Bialas and Ettl 1992: 6). The result was an enduring level of unemployment which was unprecedented in the entire history of industrial society and must, from a realistic point of view, be put at almost 40 per cent for the foreseeable future.

This level of unemployment takes on the quality of an extreme case – and not only for quantitative reasons, but also qualitatively – for it has evidently and expressly been caused by state agencies, in particular the activities of the Treuhandanstalt (German privatization agency), and has been desired or tolerated because of the primacy of privatization (via natural restitution) over employment ('return of property first, compensation second'). Responsibility must be assumed for it politically. At any rate, the political elites in the West who are unequivocally responsible for the state of affairs cannot appeal to some 'inherent characteristics of the world market' that politics is powerless to prevent, as can be politically advantageous for the elites in other cases of mass unemployment, because, unlike that in Poland, Hungary and the CSFR, post-Communist privatization in Germany, as David Stark has shown (1992a: 51), has been shaped to an extreme degree by statist and discretionary features.[35] What is involved here is the paradoxical case of state-led denationalization. The principle of 'return of property first, compensation second', which transparently obeys party political interests and corresponds to the business interests of sections of the West German population, marks a political decision on the course for the future that was to have a strong impact. Let us take the case of the available mass of state companies not up for 'return'. In the former GDR matters such as who is recognized as owning what production plant (however it may have been divided up or recombined) at what price and point in time and with what consequences for regional and employment policy are all decided not, as elsewhere, by the market or management or coupon clipping or a bank syndicate or a holding company or a ministerial committee, but by the Treuhandanstalt.[36] It is politically explosive to suspect that the interests of West German economic enterprises in preventing a structural surplus in supply (the term here is 'capacity adjustment'), for example in the electronics, power, steel and chemical sectors, may have played an important role here. Yet it is a suspicion that is often echoed in the sections of the population affected by de-industrialization.

Results

With regard to the level of economic integration of society in the former GDR into the overall German economy, champions of an encouraging scenario have become a scarcity. This is not just because the lag in income development, employment, available housing, ecological conditions and infrastructural development is larger than was prophesied during unification by all sections of the West German political elite (irrespective of whether this was an act of deliberate deception or just self-deception). Indeed this gap will remain wide for some time to come. Economic integration – understood here as the interpretation of the situation in a positive-sum game in which there are no absolute losers in the long term - has additionally been rendered difficult by the fact that the continuing shortfall in welfare can clearly be seen to have political causes, that is, to result from decisions. Thus voices can be raised calling for the opposite decisions to be taken. The Hungarians, Poles and Czechs are not able to attribute their economic difficulties, which in absolute terms are far larger, to anyone other than their past masters and thus, in the final analysis, to 'themselves'. Now that those masters have been forced from power such an ascription no longer triggers conflicts, simply because there is no conflicting party. Things are different in newly shaped Germany, where the redistribution from West Germany to East Germany is not subject to institutional regulation and has become the main issue in conflicts on distribution policy. Here, in the guise of investors, buyers and tax payers, not to mention those paying higher interest or social security contributions, there is an opponent in the struggle for distribution, as well as an addressee for claims (or as the focus for aggression). And this is true even though there is no widely shared moral standard[37] for this completely new case and – unlike in collective bargaining or the existing financial redistribution of tax income between the federal states in Germany – there are also no institutionalized rules of procedure from which one could derive which of the two sides 'has a right' to what.

The problem of economic integration is further complicated by the fact that both conflicts of distribution – that between East and West, and that between labour and capital – ineluctably dovetail. This happens at a point marked by, among other things, two obvious questions that are becoming ever more explosive for domestic policy. First, what compensation in terms of distribution policy (as opposed to the pleasant feeling that one has done one's bit for solidarity) are West German employees entitled to in return for having subsidized, by means of taxes and social insurance contributions, up to 50 per cent of private capital formation in East Germany? The second question is the mirror image of this: what taxes or duties over and above their voluntary commitment in East German investments can fairly be levied on those 'higher income groups' whose resources are needed to ameliorate unemployment and the housing shortage in East Germany? There is simply no equivalent for such unusual 'diagonal' distribution conflicts between Western tax payers and Eastern investors in the other post-Communist countries. This is also true of the way in which the conflicts over East–West distribution are caught up in conflicts between the Bonn central government and the federal states in West Germany, between the southern and the northern states[38] and between the public and private sectors.

Findings are no more favourable if we examine the degree of the former GDR's political and institutional integration into the overall German political system and the prospects for improvement here. On the basis of the Unity Treaty and by using article 23 of the Basic Law for accession the GDR is certainly incorporated into the territory governed by this Basic Law, which has been changed only marginally for this purpose. As a direct and indirect consequence of the events of 1989, however, and more than at any other time in its history, doubts have been raised as to whether the German constitution, with regard to more or less important articles in it, is able to cope with these events; there have been corresponding pressures for revision. We must conclude from this that in the mid-1990s the solid consensus on the constitution such as supported the development of West Germany as it was and which was preserved by adherence to article 146 (which stipulated that a new constitution should be drawn up for all Germany) is less robust than prior to unification of the two Germanies. Although in the run-up to the general election of December 1990 the West German party system was transposed on to the former GDR, when it comes to mobilizing and integrating the electorate or recruiting members for the elite it does not function there nearly as well as was usual in the former FRG. A further cornerstone of the West German political order is also most certainly being sorely dented, namely the system of 'cooperative federalism' and the 'intrinsic linkages of the polity' with its flexible division of powers and resources. This is because the enormous financial strain engendered by the unification process can be borne only by central government, which to this end has been prompted to strengthen its central powers. Moreover, the economic and budgetary problems in East Germany prevent the federal states there from playing the full-blooded role of *Länder* in keeping with the model of those in West Germany.

The political system in the old FRG was characterized by a great degree of cooperation and consensus between the agents of the central state, the parties, the judiciary, regional authorities and functional bodies representing specific interests, such as the employers' associations and the trade unions. This system relied on self-administration, consultation and continuing compromises, and can hardly be extended in the short term to apply to conditions in East Germany, owing to the tremendous time and cost pressures it has engendered. Besides, unification threatens to disturb quite decisively the fine-tuned mechanics of this horizontal and vertical mediation of interests. One example of this is the 'acceleration laws', another the executive's forced march to adjust the academic and health systems in East Germany to those in the West. Hitherto valid procedural rules and customs have clearly been dented in this process. In the face of this observers from East Germany have been prompted to diagnose an 'Easternisation' of the practices of the German state, in other words the approximation of German government to the largely opaque development of state powers and attempts at steering that were typical of the state socialist system.[39] The impact unification has thus had on the institutional system in West Germany has tended to be all the more disintegrative, the more unexpected the impact itself is. The expectation that had been nurtured everywhere was, after all, that unification was a process which largely took place 'over there' and not 'at our front door'.

Finally, an interim assessment of the mode of national cultural integration does not look rosy. The upheaval which occurred in Hungary and to an even greater extent in Poland unfolded in harmony with a national liberation movement that brought to mind that of 1848. The national motif emerged in East Germany at best only briefly and in an instrumentalized version, in keeping with the particularities of the GDR's history and the country's history before 1949, as it was not a national society, but a society defined by a territory and an economic order.

The tortured terminology with which the Germans refer to what will remain in the foreseeable future the central object of German politics is symptomatic of this – and no doubt forms fruitful terrain for the sociologists of language. We use the expression 'former' or 'ex-GDR' to refer to this object as if it were a nullity, something that no longer exists. The term 'the five new federal states' is unfortunate in two respects: it divides the structure, that is, turns one unit into five units, especially as these five units did not exist until after the end of the GDR; and it is incorrect, as the eastern part of Berlin, the former 'capital city of the GDR', the sixth section of the new territory, is simply forgotten. The term 'East Germany' is, by contrast, admittedly correct in terms of the international agreements, which preclude the emergence of parts of Germany even further east. But it hides behind geography, as if where the 'East' started depended on where the speaker was standing and not, which is clearly the case, on a western border of the 'East' which was clearly present in people's consciousness. And the 'acceding territory' or 'the territory mentioned in article 3 of the Unity Treaty' merely conjures up discontinuity via terminology[40] in the face of economic, cultural and political continuity that is manifest every day. The only term that at least has the advantage of being correct would be the (admittedly unusual) expression 'the GDR', by which I do not mean the 'German Democratic Republic' but instead the 'Grid covered by the Deutsche Reichsbahn', the former GDR railway. Perhaps such a term also bears using because it focuses unabashedly on an object with reference to a fiscal and administrative restoration and repair strategy to be initiated by West Germany.

Not only linguistically, but above all institutionally, the particular circumstances have condemned that structure to shapelessness (see Abromeit 1992) which had managed to gain acceptance at least for its name only in the second half of its existence (in West Germany in the fifties and sixties the GDR was, for completely different reasons, still referred to as the 'so-called GDR'). By 'institutional shapelessness' I mean that the GDR cannot be addressed; it has, as it were, relocated without leaving a forwarding address. To give such a social state of affairs a name is to grant it recognition and allow it self-recognition. West German linguistic usage prevents precisely this from happening for that part of GDR society which has quite definitely and factually survived the demise of the GDR state, for that language merely mirrors the 'commandeering' organizational practice of West German associations and West German party politics (see Wiesenthal 1992: 177). Abromeit (1992: 445) speaks fittingly of a 'gap in representation', which has been 'created by the widespread feeling in Eastern society that it has somehow got itself into a colonial situation . . . into the role of a conquered ethnic group; the colonial power (which is one that does not wish to be understood as such) has left it no institutions or organizations that could instil it with a degree of self-confidence'. One can, as is the paternalistic, disaggregating habit of West German politicians, 'talk' to the 'people' in East Germany, but not to a totality of these people, treated as a legal entity.[41]

The Federal Republic of Germany belongs to that minority of West European countries in which territorially based ethnic and linguistic conflicts play no role and which have succeeded in taking the bite out of religious and inter-regional conflicts by means of strongly federalist structures. This unobtrusive and federally structured form of political and cultural integration is in danger of being lost in the course of the unification process, which has engendered the main code of 'Ossi' (Easterner) versus 'Wessi' (Westerner). As a reaction to this ambivalent collective experience of being incorporated into the former FRG and at the same time excluded from it an unofficial special identity would appear to be gradually emerging among those who, with a slightly indignant undertone, term themselves 'upright GDR citizens'. Following the collapse of the old social order the population of the GDR is having to face the outside judgement of and condemnation by the public in the West German part of the country, whose political leadership largely recognized the GDR regime politically and granted it economic support. This multi-faceted relationship is unique among the post-Communist countries and results in resentment, myths and cognitive dissonance, which further shores up the special identity of the GDR population, perhaps even serves to ensure its subsequent 'ethnification'.[42]

This special inner German identity is no doubt not just a reaction to the conditions of unification, however, but also a cultural residue of political socialization in which, with the exception of practice in adjusting to the common routines and guarantees of a constitutional democracy, four political and cultural leaps in modernization have not occurred. And yet the four are precisely those that decisively shaped the younger and middle-aged cohorts in West Germany. What I have in mind is first the discussion of the history of Nazism, the Second World War and the annihilation of the Jews, something that played a minor and moreover one-sided role in the GDR, which had officially been declared 'anti-fascist'. Secondly, the GDR experienced neither a student movement nor the cultural and ethical forward momentum of the women's movement. The equal opportunities by and large granted women in the world of work were the result not of successful feminist demands, but of a 'state feminist' reaction to a lack of labour power. Thirdly, the GDR was a society which spared itself the trials of multi-cultural coexistence owing to the very low number of foreigners resident there – and those that did live there were often in military installations or confined to barrack-like hostels. Fourthly, the GDR was officially an anti-fascist and internationalist state which accorded high priority to the needs of the 'scientific intelligentsia'; but the nationalization of such values stripped them of any social validity.[43] These circumstances need not cause one to concur with Engler's biting diagnosis of a 'lack of civilization' (1991: 84), but they do mean that enduring breaches in overall German cultural integration are to be expected which can hardly be papered over with symbols of national unity with any hope of success.

IV

All the characteristics of the starting conditions, course and results of the upheaval in the GDR thus far suggest that this territory was a structure in which conditions were highly unlike those in all the other former 'brother countries'. But this too would be a questionable conclusion. Giving my argument a further twist, I therefore wish to present a few considerations in conclusion that are meant to elaborate the extent to which the GDR only superficially appears to be a deviant special case and in truth is the prototype and model for the paradigmatic problems facing a post-Communist politics of transformation, in that it will, with a greater or lesser time-lag, determine the path of developments in the countries referred to in the comparison here.

For a series of reasons, including central security and economic interests, the Western democracies cannot leave the post-Communist societies to their own devices. It is not just the vital interest in a beneficial control of migration that speaks in favour of this. Only if East European societies can be given the prospect of a consolidated liberal and democratic political edifice and of reliable economic reconstruction, that is, if the achievements underlying the shape of Western societies are transposed successfully eastwards, is there a chance that the populations in these countries will not transpose themselves westwards to the benefit of neither side. In addition to the problem of controlling migration, the upheaval in the 'new East' places issues of security, economic and trade policy and, not least, ecological interests back on the West European agenda (cf. Bomsdorf et al. 1993: 59–81).

The consequences for the West of the collapse of the bipolar view of the world and the understanding the West accordingly had of itself are more subtle. Western Europe is not only caught up in an elementary crisis of meaning and cohesion, to which both the EC and NATO have been exposed since the end of the Cold War. Its achievements are also unexpectedly being put to the test, a test to which transnational organizations and regimes, ranging from the UN via the World Bank to the EC and the West European Defence Union,[44] are having to face up. The order of the day, and there is by and large a consensus on this, must be a completely new type of strategy for transnational developmental cooperation and a defence partnership with the countries of East Europe. In order to have any prospect of success such a strategy would have to take great care to avoid any streaks of paternalism, discrimination and patronization, and it must certainly not allow the suspicion to arise that it is staking out territory for itself in the East. The enormous economic costs of these tasks, which Western countries and their transnational organizations will have to meet, are not justified simply in terms of investment (that is, only by covering these costs now can an even larger tide of costs be avoided in the future). They are justified also by fiscal criteria, for the end of the Cold War brought with it opportunities for savings in military costs, the dimensions of which should match the financial burdens that are on the agenda.

But even if the West were able to afford to sit back and watch developments from the viewpoint of its own medium-term interests, it would already be implicated morally in the post-Communist transformation process and thus appear jointly responsible for the results by virtue of the fact that almost everywhere Western societies are considered the political, institutional, economic and cultural example that societies in transformation hope to model their futures on, not to mention the fact that the West itself assumes this exemplary function and pioneering role[45] and propagates it. Klein (1993: 64) writes: 'In other words what is being tested in the East is what the universal evolutionary qualities of the West are capable of and whether they do indeed have a universal character.'

The German case is in fact not just one example or a deviating special case of these new East–West relations, but an exemplary model for them. The change of epoch marked by the end of state socialism brings to light not only the shortcomings of the social order that has collapsed, but also a deficit in the capitalist democracies of the West. Despite the universalistic principles proclaimed there (and presumably also institutionalized), principles that can be viewed by all human beings and implemented, the institutional system underlying this social order is possibly incapable of grounding and founding itself or even of assisting with any attempts to imitate it elsewhere. Evidently the attempt involves reconstructing a building for which the building plans have got lost and the genesis of which was attributable to unique, contingent, non-repeatable evolutionary circumstances that generated 'occidental rationalism' as a whole as a highly particular phenomenon in world history.[46] Whereas it is no problem to set up a production plant for cars at a foreign location or, for that matter, to 'clone' tried and tested laws or constitutions, the same does not apply for the institutions and cultural patterns which form their basis and 'spirit'. Should this fear prove founded, it would be possible, embarrassingly enough, to denounce the universalism of the market and of democracy as a luxury philosophy – as the particularism of rich countries, for whom their 'triumph' over state socialism would at the same time be the beginning of the definitive deflating of their claim to be superior in unifying all humankind. Be that as it may, much would seem to suggest that the capitalist democracies in the West must subject themselves to far-reaching institutional change before they can do justice to their claim, and it is a claim that has as yet not been put to the test, to represent what M. Brie has called 'a real generalizable social construct'.

It is clearly far too early to answer this question. However, it is worth bearing it in mind here in order to elucidate what is at stake for the First World in the beginning of a process of revolution which purportedly involves only 'catching up', but which will in fact lead to the merger of the Second and First Worlds. What is first at stake is whether Western democracies will be able to shield themselves from the external effects of the collapse of the Eastern system by setting the threshold even higher without losing their identity in the process,[47] and whether they will be able to avoid becoming infected, as it were, by the structural and moral shortcomings of the collapsed system. And what is secondly at stake is whether the state of society achieved in Western democracies today is adopted by the post-Communist societies as an attractive goal for their own further development or whether they reject it – be this owing to the mental relics of a nostalgic critique of capitalism, in other words sour grapes, or to anti-modernism becoming virulent. For what is finally at stake is whether this goal can be attained with Western assistance in a way that is both reasonable and rendered comprehensible to all involved, given that these societies do not have the means to achieve it themselves, or whether, should the answer be negative, the social model posed by the OECD world is clearly unique in world history, and able to retain its privileges only because it has pulled up the ladder behind it.

The transformation of the former GDR functions as an exemplary case in point for these three main questions, a test-run on a laboratory scale being made under what are still exceptionally favourable conditions. Let us consider what might happen if this perforce pioneering experiment, which all quarters hope will be forthcoming and the West German side with daring self-confidence has explicitly promised, were not to succeed in the long term. The failure of the German example of a process of transformation supported and fostered from outside would then necessarily and decisively discourage the other post-Communist societies, who would in turn be prompted once more to seek out paths of their 'own' that deviate from that of Western modernity.

8

Economic 'Hardware' and Institutional 'Software' in the Two German Transitions to Democracy: Comparing Post-1945 West Germany with Post-1989 East Germany

> *In the West, after 1945, they [had] only to clear away Hitler and his instruments of power, the heads of the party and the SS, and from behind all the destruction wrought by the war a society emerged that was essentially intact.*
>
> WOLF JOBST SIEDLER

Few will dispute the proposition that building a constitutional government on a workable democratic foundation in what remains of Germany in 1949 constitutes an unprecedented task ... If one adds to this governmental nightmare the social and economic problems resulting ... from forced immigration, the results coming from the levelling of all classes and the proletarianization of the middle class, from the psychic trauma ... and the all-consuming fear ..., then, and only then, does one approach a sense of the obstacles in the way of 'rebuilding the German constitution'. (Friedrich 1949: 461–2)

Exchange and delete a few words in this 46-year-old quotation from

Carl Joachim Friedrich and you get the essence of much of the contemporary writing on the transformation problems after state socialism. What emerges from this quotation is the same tone of drama and near-despair in facing the seemingly unsurmountable problems of the re-normalization process of an entire polity, economy and society after the demise of an authoritarian regime. This striking case of *déjà vu* suggests that post-totalitarian transitions are more or less all of the same kind. After all, many of the West German political elites' pronouncements made during the months preceding unification (October 1990) and all-German federal elections (December 1990) appeared to be carried away by the notion: 'Since we Germans coped and managed so impressively after 1945, the new post-1989 reconstruction should be little more than child's play.'

It is this apparent equation of 1945 with 1989 that I would like to take issue with in the following comparison of the two German transitions, namely the West German (WG) transition after 1945 and the East German (EG) transition after 1989. In chronometrical time 1949 (the year of the constitution of the West German post-war state) relates to 1945 (the year of the breakdown of the old regime) as 1993 does to 1989 in the case of East Germany. One way to account for differences between the two cases is to argue that a problem will always look easier in retrospect, after its viable solution has been found, than it does ex ante. Such reasoning, that things do not always turn out as badly as they looked, can surely provide a source of comfort. This, however, is not the line of argument I wish to pursue here.

Although I find it hard to prove, I wish to start from an intuition: the sense of accomplishment, the feeling of being on the right track and of moving with adequate speed in the right direction, was much more pronounced on the part of all parties involved, participants as well as observers, in 1949 than it is in the mid-nineties. Could it be the case that post-fascist German reconstruction in the period 1945–55 was a much smoother process which appears, not only in retrospect, as a clear and linear success story if compared with what we know so far, as well as what we can predict on the basis of current evidence, about the course of the post-Communist reconstruction after 1989? And, if this is so, how do we account for the apparent paradox that the reverse relationship would seem to be so much more likely, given that the situation the old regime left behind in 1945 was one of a total moral catastrophe, as well as vast physical destruction, whereas the regime that crumbled in 1989 committed neither genocide nor wars of aggression, and nor did its end result in hunger and the destruction of much of the physical basis of civilization? At any rate, to demonstrate this difference and to account for this apparent paradox is what I intend to do within the confines of this chapter. How is it that the more difficult case of transition was resolved more smoothly? What is wrong with the popular premise that the post-1945 case was in fact the more difficult one?

It goes without saying that the comparison deals with two parts and two historical periods of one country, divided for four decades, with its shared features of national, cultural and political history and institutional heritage. Moreover, the comparison is further invited by the fact that both of these transitions were aiming at the restoration of some form of liberal democracy and welfare state capitalism. Also, both regime transitions took place following the demise of a highly ideological 'totalitarian' regime, one fascist, the other state socialist. And, perhaps most importantly, political elites have conceptualized and presented to the public the task of transforming the economy and polity of the former GDR in terms of a replica of the prescriptions adopted after 1945. For instance, one of the lessons presumably drawn from the transition after the Second World War and implemented after 1989 was that currency reform must precede political reconstitution. Another lesson was that a constitution, in order to become widely accepted, need not be adopted through a plebiscitary procedure as people will 'get used to' the new order even if they have not been given the chance to decide on it in a formal constitutional referendum.

The analogy between 'then' and 'now' is clearly part of the cognitive frame that has been promulgated by the (West) German political elite since 1990. This is evidently a high-risk intellectual operation as it may well involve either or both of two mistaken assumptions. First, the smooth transition and rapid recovery experienced after 1945 may be due to factors other than the much celebrated introduction of the neo-liberal 'social market economy' through Ludwig Erhard (cf. Abelshauser 1993). Secondly, even if the neo-liberal reading of the post-1945 transition is tenable, the post-1989 situation may be different from the alleged precedent in so many of its background characteristics that analogous prescriptions cannot be relied upon to generate comparable outcomes.

Let us look first at the differences in the parameters governing the two post-totalitarian crises of 1945 and 1989. I will then explain the apparent paradox that the reconstruction of an institutionally well-rooted form of democratic capitalism proceeded much more smoothly in the first than in the second case despite the much more desperate situation that prevailed at the beginning of the former. I begin by looking at nine ways in which the two cases are clearly different.

Economic starting conditions

WG From a comparative perspective the economic breakdown of what was to become the West German economy was clearly extreme. The war had brought the physical destruction of many millions of lives, of industrial assets, buildings, the infrastructure (energy, transportation, public administration and services) and homes. Severe shortage of food was the overwhelming domestic policy problem in 1945–6. In the big cities more than half of the houses had been destroyed. Homelessness was a mass phenomenon: 10 million refugees from the eastern territories of the former Reich were counted in Germany in 1946. A concise account of the situation, given by a staff member of the American Department of State in 1949, reads:

> With the collapse of the Nazi regime, the economic life of Germany had come to an almost complete stop. Between four and six million Germans had been killed or permanently disabled; approximately as many again had become prisoners of war. Altogether about 25 million had lost their homes and property or were facing expulsion. All major cities had suffered severe damage from air raids. Most of the important highway and railroad bridges had been blown up by the retreating Germans in a futile last-minute attempt to stem the tide. In Western Germany, less than 10 per cent of the railway track mileage remained in operation. The Rhine and most canals were closed to traffic. Industry and coal mines were at a standstill. The roads were crowded with more than five million foreign workers and Allied prisoners of war and an approximately equal number of German air-raid evacuees, disbanded troops, and refugees from the East. National and regional administrations had ceased to function, and local police forces lacked the strength and authority necessary to maintain public order ... As a consequence of the war and defeat, Germany sustained what may be the sharpest percentage reduction in national wealth suffered by any nation in modern times. (Sanderson 1949: 111, 167)

EG The economic condition was much more favourable. In terms of per capita output the GDR economy was commonly ranked at the lower end of the best-performing dozen of industrial societies worldwide. To be sure, a slow and largely unrecognized economic decay set in in the mid-eighties, but the only economic crisis in the history of the GDR occurred in 1990 following the end of the regime. It was triggered by the sudden transformation and economic unification (*Wirtschafts- und Währungsunion*, effective on 1 July 1990), which involved the loss of much of the country's export as well as domestic markets.

Military force and territorial change

WG As a result of the Second World War the German Reich had suffered a total military defeat, followed by unconditional capitulation. The country was divided by the victorious Allies into four zones, all of which were occupied and tightly controlled by military forces.

EG The use of military force was conspicuously absent, during both the short process of the regime's breakdown (when local concentrations of repressive military forces, for example in Dresden, could be prevented from being deployed) and the reconstruction of the new regime. If anything, one could speak of a sharp diminution of the role of military force, as the East German Army (NVA) was rapidly abolished, substantial numbers of Soviet occupation troops were contractually scheduled for withdrawal and the remaining German military forces were cut by more than 20 per cent of their former (West German) personnel and budget. The pattern of territorial reorganization was also diametrically opposed to the one that unfolded after 1945. Whereas post-war Germany was divided in 1945 before reconstruction, it was unified in 1990 after the demise of the old regime, and reconstruction efforts were shaped by the politics of 'reunification'.

Migration and demographic change

WG Massive waves of refugees from the East flooded the country before and for several years after the regime's breakdown. The dominant pattern was an inward flow of people. In spite of millions of military and civilian deaths, the population in the territory that was to become the West German state was greater in 1945 than it had ever been before. Thus despite a decline in the labour market participation rate, the effective labour supply was probably unchanged before and after the war (Carlin 1993: 41).

EG There was a massive outward flow of people to West Germany, mostly (but by no means exclusively) before unification in the period from September 1989 to October 1990. In fact the mass exit that eventually turned out to be uncontrollable caused the regime's breakdown. As a consequence there was considerable loss of manpower and human resources, and a long-term demographic change was initiated in the former GDR as people of child-bearing age were most likely to leave the country, resulting in a sharp drop in the birth rate.

International constellation

WG The breakdown of the old regime and the subsequent reconstruction period coincided with the start of the Cold War and the break-up of the American-led anti-Nazi alliance with the Soviet Union. As a result the gradual incorporation of West Germany into economic and eventually military alliance (NATO) with the West became imperative from the point of view of American foreign policy, which soon came to abandon the Morgenthau Plan and in 1947 replaced it with the European Recovery Programme (ERP, or Marshall Plan) as a far-sighted component of the strategy for pushing back and containing Communism. The identity, legitimacy and historical mission of the new West German state was seen to reside in its anti-totalitarian essence: in its being simultaneously the virtuous antithesis to the evil past and to the equally bad East.[1] The obvious lesson to be drawn from the breakdown of the old regime was domestic accommodation on the basis of pluralist democracy and transnational (European and North Atlantic) economic, political and military integration, as it was initiated and completed by leaders such as de Gaspari, Schuman, Monnet, Spaak and Adenauer.

A common characteristic of all post-fascist democracies – Austria, Germany, Italy, Japan – has been the presence of a temporary 'constitutional dictatorship' (Friedrich 1953: 694ff) designed to impose a democratic regime upon the defeated nations. The transition to democracy takes place in two steps: first, the rights of sovereignty are transferred to the victorious power(s) and secondly, after some time interval in which institution building takes place, sovereignty is transferred back to the successor state of the defeated regime. Only after the constitutional and institutional premises of a liberal-democratic political order were put in place were a gradual devolution of political power from military to civilian authorities and eventually the restitution of sovereignty to the post-fascist nations accomplished. As power was gradually devolved to the putatively indispensable German experts and administrative agencies, the original emphasis upon the political purges of political and administrative elites began to recede as early as 1947.[2] Thus the post-fascist national states were by no means annihilated, but were revived as bearers of sovereignty and newly constituted in a carefully supervised process of transformation cum devolution. Even in this process of the 'dictatorial' foundation of democracy the Allies were careful to avoid creating the impression that the constitutional order was just imposed from a position of military strength and without the consent of the German people (Pfetsch 1986: 15). The Western Allies acted as – and desired to appear to be acting as – mere temporary catalysts assisting in the process of political and economic transition.

EG The breakdown of the old regime coincided with the end of the Cold War and the political integration of the European Community. It was followed by the dissolution of transnational organizations in East Central Europe (CMEA, Warsaw Pact). Neither East Germany nor any other post-Communist country within the former CMEA has been in a position to enjoy the benefits that derive from the fact that others (including, in the case of the embryonic West German state, former enemies) now take a vital strategic interest in the country's rapid economic recovery. There is no longer a source of antithetical self-identification available within the framework of military blocs and transnational alliances, other than, perhaps, nationalism. As transnational integration under the hegemony of the Soviet Union was one of the main characteristics of the old regime, the new leaders emphasize national independence and a competitive rush to join, as individuals, Western transnational organizations such as the Council of Europe, the European Community or NATO. At any rate, post-Communist countries in general and the ex-GDR in particular are by no means considered by the Western countries as valuable strategic partners in commerce and defence, but rather as a more or less unwelcome new burden. The post-Communist East is seen as a source of threatening uncertainties rather than a strategic asset.

Moreover, in the case of the former GDR, political decision-making capacity, control over fiscal resources and selection of political elites have remained so far, and are likely to remain for the foreseeable future, firmly in the hands of the West German centre of all-German political power. Unlike the pre-1945 regime, the pre-1989 regime has not resulted in the build-up of an emigrant elite (numerous though the emigrants were) that was willing to return and to assume responsibilities in the reconstruction effort. While the Western Allies quickly overcame their (partly justified) distrust of German elites after 1945 and soon handed over administrative and political responsibilities to them, West Germans seem to have been more reluctant to allow for, never mind actively encourage, an analogous process of devolution.[3] In the mid-1990s there is not a single institutional body provided for in the German political system that could serve as a specific representative of the whole of the former GDR and its citizens.[4] East Germany did not survive state socialism as a political unit in the same way as (West, and eventually all of) Germany survived the Nazi regime. It has almost literally disappeared from the political and institutional map – at the same time, however, surviving and increasingly asserting itself as a spooky mental phenomenon forming a bond of community among those sharing memories of their GDR past, as well as a stigmatizing device in the hands of those who do not share these memories. Needless to say, the new *Länder* enjoy the constitutional rights of policy-making and self-government that the Basic Law assigns to all of the old *Länder*. But, given their financial dependence upon the federal budget, these policy-making capacities often turn out to be nominal. Their share in the population of the new Germany (less than a fourth), together with a carefully crafted scheme that grants the West German *Länder* a two-thirds majority in the Upper House (*Bundesrat*), puts the new *Länder* in the position of a structural minority.

The newly integrated East Germany also underwent the process of 'regime imposition', though this imposition was backed not by foreign military force, but by a contractual agreement (Unity Treaty) between the sovereign governments of the GDR and the Federal Republic. The terms of this contract stipulated that at the point in time when the contract became effective (which was at midnight on 2 October 1990) one of the two parties that had concluded it would cease to exist as a subject of international law. This legal annihilation of the GDR did not, however, also annihilate the social and cultural identity and the collectively accumulated historical experience and economic conditions of the GDR; it simply deprived all these particular aspects of the former GDR of its institutional shell. As a consequence there was no two-tiered transition period, as in the West German case, during which processes of closely supervised elite formation, re-education, recovery and gradual self-transformation could have taken place, but a sudden, one-step process of institutional transplantation.

The moral qualification of the past

WG The old regime was seen as being the perpetrator of war and other crimes, most significantly the Holocaust. As a consequence military defeat and economic breakdown were widely seen as 'deserved' in retribution for these crimes. The leadership of the old regime was sanctioned for criminal acts and partly liquidated, its ideology thoroughly discredited and effectively banned. Functionaries of the old regime could survive in office (as they in fact did in large numbers) only by dissimulating their involvement in that regime or because they were held indispensable by the new occupying authorities. Initially rigorous measures of denazification were quickly abandoned as the issue was soon removed from the political agenda by both Allied and domestic elites.

The breakdown of the old regime took place in the form of military defeat, which could have been anticipated for at least two years

(Stalingrad) before it actually happened. This defeat came at the end of an extended period of invasion; it did not come as a surprise to anyone.

The mode of coming into being of the old regime was that of a quasi-constitutional acquisition of dictatorial powers by the Nazi Party in the period from November 1932 to March 1933. It was largely supported and approved of by the German electorate, and the regime continued to enjoy broad support until the early forties.

EG The old regime was seen as the natural, initially even promising and morally superior outcome of the breakdown of Nazi Germany. It gradually lost virtually all of its moral and political appeal, but it was still considered by most of its population as an 'error' growing out of good intentions, rather than a 'crime' growing out of bad ones. At any rate, the presence of the old regime was generally (and rightly) seen not as a matter of autochthonous choice made by the East German population, but as an imposed political and economic order that was established as a consequence of the war's outcome and the subsequent shift in the relations of international power. No equivalent to genocide and a war of aggression burdened the moral balance sheet of the old regime; even whether GDR military forces were present on CSR soil during the Warsaw Pact invasion of August 1968 remains to be ascertained. As the result of the breakdown of November 1989 the leadership of the old regime has been deactivated and sanctioned mostly through disqualification rather than criminal prosecution, though border guards and their commanders were put on trial. Limited continuity of ideological and associational patterns of the old regime (newspapers, the Party of Democratic Socialism) is permitted under the new regime of liberal democracy. An extended and highly politicized conflict over the scope and level of sanctions to be applied against functionaries of the old regime has emerged. This conflict is not mitigated by considerations of the 'indispensability' of certain skills and qualifications as a virtually unlimited supply of skilled manpower can be imported from the western part of the country.

The definitive breakdown of the old regime was triggered by a single and poorly prepared decision to open the Berlin Wall, which was taken by second-level SED leaders on 9 November 1989. In spite of the turbulent events of the two preceding months ('campsite' migration to Hungary, occupation of West German embassies in Prague and Warsaw), this decision and the events that followed it came as a breathtaking surprise.

Duration of the old regime

WG Duration was just twelve years, and old pre-1933 political and economic elites, partly even academic and intellectual elites, together with their associational contexts and networks, were still available for reactivation (Communists, Social Democrats, Christian Democrats; trade unions). The opposition to the old regime stood ready to assume an active role in the reconstruction process.

EG The old regime lasted much longer, namely forty-four years, and there was much more pervasive eradication of pre-1945 (that is Nazi) elites. In 1989 there was no one alive who would have been familiar with the institutions and rules of democratic capitalism from his or her own experience and who at the same time would have been available for elite positions, as these institutions and rules had been suspended for no less than fifty-six years. The long duration of the regime provided ample opportunity for a thorough exchange of elites, institutions and cultural (including linguistic) patterns. As a consequence of the pervasive change of the system's 'software' ('roles and rules') that had taken place in the period of one and a half generations even oppositional groups that had become active under the old regime were not ready, capable or permitted to assume leadership roles in the reconstruction process.

Proportions of the problem of economic reconstruction

WG In spite of the vast destruction of human lives and material assets, there prevailed a basic continuity of economic institutions and mechanisms before and after 1945, including core elements such as the institution (and much of the staff) of the civil service (*Berufsbeamtentum*), the tax system, social security corporations, local governments and academic institutions. To be sure, the Nazi economy was an authoritarian corporatist war economy, but still based upon private property and predominant market forces, technical innovation and efficiency. The economic condition was one of institutional continuity, a condition that was partly reinforced by the ERP and other American economic policies.

> We can observe that in the area of public, institutional and organizational regulation, norms and rules of law were retained that went back to well before 1945, to the Weimar and even imperial periods. Basic structures proved remarkably resistant to the reform zeal of the early

post-war era, especially that of the occupation powers – at least in the Western occupation zones. (Diestelkamp 1986: 88)

As a result 'capital' as an institutional 'relation of production' was firmly established, and hence no privatization effort was needed (apart from the abolition of wartime and post-war rationing and other forms of bureaucratic regulation, and the dismantling of some of the conglomerates imposed by Allied forces). Capital just happened to be partially destroyed as a physical entity, not capitalism as an institutional reality. Moreover, the severe damages inflicted upon the West German economy through the war had occurred mainly in the primary (food, fuel) and tertiary (transportation, administration) sectors, rather than the core industrial sector itself. As a consequence of these damages, by the end of 1947 national income had reached just half the level of 1936 (Carlin 1993). Generally speaking, the reconstruction problem of the post-1945 period is simply one of reviving and marginally reforming, in the spirit of the Freiburg school and Walter Eucken, an old economic order, the viability and continuity of which were soon almost universally recognized in spite of initial, but rapidly failing, demands for the large-scale nationalization of productive assets and banks.

Recovery was further facilitated by the availability of a highly skilled and motivated workforce, virtually unlimited domestic markets and the long-term advantage of the simultaneous modernization that took place in the process of reconstruction of cities and industrial plants. This modernization later, partly due to the Korean War, which provided an 'essential demand boost' (Carlin 1993: 39), allowed West Germany to become, from the late fifties on, one of the world's leading exporters of manufactured goods. Cooperative trade union politics of wage restraint allowed productivity to grow faster than real wages, thus contributing to rapid capital formation. All of these factors helped to set the stage for a hardly miraculous 'economic miracle'.

The institutional framework of the nascent West German political economy and political order can best be described as a hybrid in which three major elements were merged. First – and most explicitly on the constitutional and associational levels, including the party system – (revised versions of) Weimar traditions, as well as traditions dating back even further, were revived. Secondly, and in spite of the dramatic breakdown of the old regime, much of its legal order, personnel and authoritarian 'spirit' was maintained. Lastly, and certainly least importantly, some elements dictated by the American, British and, to a marginal extent, French occupation powers were added, such as a strong version of federalism, a weak presidency, the elimination of plebiscitary elements from constitutional life and the constructive vote of no confidence. In the urgent need for reconstruction of the economy and polity, traditions of the first and the second kind were even more stubbornly relied upon – after, that is, early and short-lived designs for a fundamentally renewed social and political order (such as the Christian socialism of the Christian Democratic Union's Ahlener Programm) were quickly abandoned. Knut Borchardt (1983: 45) writes:

> Even the most radical political, economic and military break can change only relatively little in the conditions that have accumulated in a society hitherto. That which has accumulated continues into the new period, pushes history forward and makes itself felt. In so far as past conditions make themselves felt, they facilitate overcoming the rupture of major systems. But, on the other hand, through their existence they limit the flexibility and potential of historical processes.

EG These continuities stand in sharp contrast to the deep rupture that occurred in the parallel process of post-war reconstruction in East Germany and later the GDR. The entire 'institutional software' of the old regime (as well as most of its predecessor regime, the Weimar Republic) was rather abruptly abolished and virtually all of the economic, administrative, political and academic elites (large parts of which had left the East anyway) were replaced. This much more pervasive institutional change in the Soviet occupation zone was certainly one of the major factors that delayed and distorted the process of economic recovery in the eastern part of the country, thus inviting the unpleasant speculation that still another round of radically 'new beginnings', as has taken place in the eastern *Länder* since 1989, is likely to repeat the experience of the diseconomies of institutional discontinuity.

The situation in East Germany after 1989 can be described as a basic discontinuity of economic and political institutions. Privatization, marketization/liberalization and the separation of state budget from private economy come as institutional novelties to which habits, expectations and economic attitudes must be adjusted. Capital is reasonably intact as physical assets, but not as the institutional pattern of property rights and the regulatory mechanisms attached to them. Severe shortages of food, fuel, transportation, housing and public services were unknown in the post-1989 transition. The problem was not the physical reconstruction of the productive apparatus, but the institutional reorganization of the entire economic and political system, which involves the enormous transaction costs of privatization and restructuring. The condition is one of sharp institutional discontinuities, which were exacerbated by the simultaneous occurrence of the deepest post-war recession in the national and international economy. In the GDR since 1989 the problem has been one of building an entirely new economic order that encompasses its legal and constitutional premises and cultural foundations.

The labour force is highly skilled, but unfamiliar with the technical, legal and institutional standards governing the new economic order. The economic breakdown that occurred in 1990 was not only of export markets (due to monetary reform), but also of domestic markets, which are being supplied by West German manufacturers with whom most of the GDR plants, given their outdated technical standards and managerial strategies, cannot successfully compete. Wage increases are far in excess of productivity increases thanks to the efforts of West German-led unions to prevent the transformation of East Germany into an internal 'low-wage country' (in which case investors would see strong incentives to move east) or, which amounts to the same, a low-income country (in which case East German workers would come under pressure to move west), with both further fuelling the West German labour market crisis.

As a consequence of all of these factors no realistic prospect of an 'economic miracle' is to be found in East Germany, in spite of the massive funds[5] supplied by the West German *Länder*, as mandated by the constitutional terms of unification. The long-term sustainability of such funding, moreover, appears precarious for fiscal, economic and ultimately political reasons.

Level of politicization of civil society

WG This was very low due to three factors. First, political activity and political conflict were repressed partly through internal mechanisms, such as the desire to 'forget' and ignore what happened before the 'zero hour'. The dominant political climate is perhaps best characterized as the attitude of self-inflicted amnesia that prevailed until the mid-sixties and thrived on an economic condition in which there were 'more important things to worry about than the past', namely food, fuel, housing and the well-being of family members. Given the nature of the recent history that had just resulted in a total military, economic and moral catastrophe, the only cognitive frame that fitted the situation was the self-attribution of the causes of this situation to all or parts of the German people, not to any outside agency. Moreover, this self-attribution had to assume, to a limited extent, the quality of self-blame, as the benign notion of having been ignorant, deceived or just erroneous was clearly not enough to account for the scope of what had happened. Self-attribution and self-blame did not, however, burst into an open and possibly cathartic political conflict, but, on the contrary, resulted in a telling kind of silence.

The fact of this silence and calm is uncontested in the literature, while its historical evaluation most certainly is not. Lübbe (1983: 585, 587, 594) approves of it in functionalist terms:

> This holding back was the social-psychologically and politically necessary means for the transformation of our post-war populace into the citizens of the Federal Republic ... [The] restraint in the public thematization of individual and institutional Nazi pasts characteristic of the early history of the Federal Republic [was] a function of the effort ... to integrate the putative parties into the new democratic state. This holding back of the discussion [of the past] was premised on the proposition that it was politically less important to ask about one's past than about one's future intentions.

At any rate, the overwhelming problems of coping with daily necessities had a strong depoliticizing impact. The main concerns, next to the provision of food and fuel, were missing people and prisoners of war (Klessmann 1984: 56). Mass political activism was also checked through external mechanisms of control of the occupation regime and its licensing and re-education activities. The dominance of consensus politics was further strengthened by the emerging Cold War, which resulted in anti-Communism becoming the major premise of all spheres of public life. The prevailing political culture in Germany during the fifties is well captured in Almond and Verba's famous study (1963: 312):

> The contemporary political culture ... reflects Germany's political history. Awareness of politics and political activity, though substantial, tends to be passive and formal ... Informal means of political involvement, particularly political discussion and the forming of political groups, are more limited. Germans are often members of voluntary associations, but rarely active in them. And norms favoring active political participation are not well developed.

In this climate of an acquiescent political culture a rapid convergence of political extremes towards the middle ground could evolve, as was eventually defined by the constitutional consensus of 1949. Even before the formal reconstitution of German sovereignty the quest for convergence and unity and the attempt to overcome entrenched ideological and programmatic divisions (particularly the Christian/ Socialist division) dominated the politics of all major parties. After the first *Länder* elections of 1946–7 great coalitions of Social and Christian Democrats were formed in nine out of ten *Länder*. This convergence was motivated by a reaction to the failure of the Weimar Republic, the causes of which were widely seen to lie in the dynamics of excessively polarized political forces.[6] It was further motivated by anti-fascist and anti-Communist premises shared by virtually all the new political parties, as well as by the overwhelming priority of presumably non-ideological political problems, such as the need to rebuild the economy of a country devastated by the war (Thränhardt 1986: 24ff).

The constitutional order of the Basic Law in turn further institutionalized the depoliticization of West German society, as it was inspired by a sense of distrust in the people. It is a constitutional document that has aptly been characterized by its moderation and sobriety, the absence of programmatic proclamations and a strong protection of civil rights and liberties, as well as of the rights of the *Länder*. As a consequence political parties were instituted as the guardians of the people, and on top was the Constitutional Court as the guardian of parliament and the party system; the stability of the new political order thus resided not in the empirical consent of the people, but in the multiple institutional safeguards protecting the essence of the newly established constitutional order.

Secondly, there was no political opposition to the occupying forces (with the exception of limited resistance to the dismantling and removal from Germany of industrial plants as reparations in kind or *Demontage*), who were largely welcomed as 'liberators'. Blaming 'them' or others was out of the question. Since 1945 West Germany has greatly benefited from the fact that the incipient state was initially deprived of any sovereignty and was thus not permitted to be an agent, but was initially seen and treated, both from within and from the outside, as an object at the disposition of others (Niclauss 1974: 46). The constitution-making process itself was guided by a remarkably broad and inclusive consensus prevailing among the political parties involved, as they were licensed and revived by the occupying powers and led by reactivated leaders, concerning the lessons to be drawn from both the failure of the Weimar Republic and the experience of the Nazi dictatorship (cf. Golay 1958; Fromme 1962; Sörgel 1969). International as well as national political forces were united on the basis of a common political project, the implementation of which was greatly facilitated by the fact that it was only after a period of ten years after the defeat, namely in May 1955, that full sovereignty was restored to the new state.

In the meantime a two-tiered process of the 'foundation of democracy' (Niclauss) was allowed and encouraged to take place. On the upper tier the occupation regimes imposed the basic principles of the new political order and retained their dictatorial power, if certainly with a view to its gradual abolition. And on the lower tier the *demos* of the new West German state was gradually – first on the local level that was conceived of as *Kindergarten der Demokratie* – and increasingly allowed to play its role within the democratic process through elections, legislation and the selection of administrative elites. This two-tiered process allowed for a highly successful and beneficial coexistence of an imposed order and self-imposed rules, or of the consequences of military defeat and the accomplishments of gradual reconstruction of the West German polity and economy.[7]

This strategy of a gradual and guarded devolution of power to indigenous agencies was most consistently pursued in the American occupation zone. The *Länder* that belonged to that zone (Württemberg-Baden, Bayern, Hessen and Bremen) were the first to adopt state constitutions, which they did as early as by the end of 1946. At the same time partial federal powers and elements of sovereignty were restored to them. The applied bottom-up and anti-centralist philosophy of 'letting the German public and German agencies learn democracy by practising it' (cf. Benz 1984: 59) had its somewhat delayed impact also in the British-occupied *Länder* of the Bi-zone and eventually also in the French zone. The success and failure of these re-educational efforts were monitored in the American zone by vast projects of public opinion survey research. In contrast, the occupying power of the Soviet zone pursued a very different strategy of tight control which amounted to a rapid elimination of all forms and forces of political agency that did not conform to the political priorities of the Soviet Union, most spectacularly the Social Democratic Party through its forced fusion with the Communist-dominated Socialist Unity Party (SED) in 1946. In what was becoming the West German state a dense network of mildly antagonistic cooperation among representative groups evolved between 1946 and 1949 under Allied guidance. It encompassed the military governments of the Western zones, the *Länder*, the reconstituted political parties, unions, employers' associations, co-determination in the steel industry, inter-zonal councils and conferences (most importantly the *Wirtschaftsrat* established in 1947 and later the constitutional assembly of the *Parlamentarische Rat*), embryonic legislative and judicial bodies and various administrative and self-governing agencies. It also encompassed a rich variety of cultural institutions, journals, newspapers and other media. The majority of these agencies were staffed by people who had their political, professional and intellectual roots in the political system of the Weimar Republic.

The formation and operation of this configuration of political forces was distinctively a matter of elite politics, with elements of mass mobilization, movement politics or populist appeals being conspicuously absent. No parallel to this wealth of elite-dominated indigenous pluralist forces has emerged in the former GDR since 1989 (any more than it did in the nascent GDR after 1945). Nor can it conceivably be permitted to emerge now as an autochthonous network since every potential domain of public affairs and collective action has effectively been placed under the control of branch organizations of the West German institutional system of intermediary bodies.

Thirdly, the experience of economic recovery, or the prospects thereof, led, after the currency reform of June 1948, to the concentration of all energies on efforts to restore prosperity within the framework of the newly revived 'social market economy'. As 'all of us' were suffering from the military and economic defeat, the scope for redistributive conflict, in stark contrast to the post-1989 situation in the new *Länder*, was limited. But rather generous social policy and co-determination arrangements were still introduced and further helped to reduce sources of potential conflict. They were partly initiated according to a logic of preventive response to a perceived challenge of 'social progress' accomplished by the 'other side' in the incipient Cold War. One of the driving forces of both Social Democratic and Christian Democratic social reforms was a shared 'theory of magnetism' that was based on the premises of anti-Communism and national unity. In the words of the Social Democratic leader Kurt Schumacher:

> From any realistic German perspective, there is no other way to achieve German unification than to make the West a magnetic force whose pull on the East must then be so powerfully exercised that, in the long run, the mere possession of an apparatus of power will provide no reliable means against it. (Quoted in Benz 1986: 145)

As a consequence of all three of these favourable factors – a low level of political conflict, a slow and gradual transfer of sovereignty and a steady and rapid economic recovery within the framework of a social market economy – the West German consolidation process took a uniquely rapid, centripetal and consistent course in the period from 1949 to 1959, resulting in an unusual condition of lasting political calm that was eventually brought to an end by the movements that emerged in the second half of the sixties. This powerful trend of centripetal accommodation is illustrated by the fate of the broad alliance, ranging in the late forties from the Communist Party to well into the leadership of the Christian Democratic Union (CDU), that advocated various and rather vague programmes for reconstruction comprising democracy, socialism and non-alignment. All these alternative ideas and proposals had disappeared from the political scene in West Germany by 1956, the year when the Constitutional Court declared the Communist Party (KPD) unconstitutional and thereby banned it. Throughout the post-war history of West Germany the CDU performed the vital function of absorbing into its ranks what remained of the nationalist political Right and of thus reducing it to political invisibility. As a further indication of the streamlining of the political field and the dynamics of centripetal accommodation, the number of political parties represented in the Bundestag declined from ten to four from the 1949 to the 1957 elections, and it was the first and so far only time in German parliamentary history that a party in power, the Christian Democratic Union, has been capable of increasing its share of the vote over two successive elections (Dietze 1960: 118). Finally, the consolidation was epitomized by the basic reversal of the programmatic outlook that was adopted at their Godesberg convention in 1959 by the oppositional Social Democrats, who from then on accepted and recognized the consolidated post-war political economy of West Germany, including its international role and military integration, as a valid and lasting arrangement.

The net effect of all three of these factors was, at least throughout the first fifteen years of the Federal Republic's (pre)history, an extreme condition of political calm that is surely unparalleled in any of the democratic periods of German history, either before or after the period under consideration. This tranquillity was due to the institutional encapsulation of political conflict, the unfolding of a massive economic positive-sum game and ideological convergence and containment. The repertoire from which political ideas could be derived, as well as the motivation to derive, adopt and advocate them, had been narrowed down by the lessons drawn from both the war and the Cold War. The ideologies of the old regime were most obviously discredited, but so were also successively various conceptions of anti-fascism, socialism and large-scale nationalization, economic democracy, neutralism, nationalism and various strands of anti-modernism. What remained was the peculiar mix of restoration and new beginning, aspirations inherited from Weimar and models adopted from America, economic liberalism and societal corporatism that soon came to dominate the political economy of West Germany as both a theory of legitimation and soon, with the unfolding of the 'economic miracle', its increasingly uncontested and firmly established practice.

EG Politicization of civil society is very high, which is due to three reciprocal factors. First, there was no silencing power of collectively repressed guilt, but, on the contrary, a gradual but consistent increase in popularity of the view (and its electoral manifestation) that the 'old regime was not that bad after all'. Opposition to what is widely seen as an equivalent of the occupation regime, namely West German 'new masters' and functional elites dominating all sectors, is common and intense, as is the discourse of blaming the 'Wessis'. On the other hand an equally widespread and legitimate desire to settle accounts with the oppressors of the old regime surfaced. The collective sources of failures of the old regime are seen, where they are seen at all, as errors for which 'we' cannot rightfully be blamed, not as crimes for which the entire nation must accept some measure of blame. To the limited extent to which the old regime can be seen to have committed criminal acts, these can be – and in fact are – attributed to the lasting control of Soviet leaders over much of the GDR's foreign and domestic policies. Also, what was (and still is) seen to go wrong under the new regime is largely and most definitely not accepted as a self-inflicted burden, but attributed to the actions of others, namely West Germans, including previous West German policies that provided a measure of political and economic credit to the old regime in the name of *Ostpolitik* and *détente*.

The high intensity of political expression and activism (which manifests itself, for instance, in the unheard-of use of hunger strikes for settling industrial relations disputes and the protection of jobs) was further legitimated, in the case of post-GDR politics, by the tradition of the oppositional 'citizens' movements' that had sprung up under the old regime in 1989. Thus the newly acquired political resources of democratic citizenship are used, in often vehement and passionate ways, in the service of the promotion of economic interests and the expression of political splits along both the West–East and the past–present axes, as well as, increasingly, the nationalist German–non-German axis. The economic interests, in turn, are typically framed (and thereby intensified) not in terms of absolute improvements over the previous situation, but in terms of lasting deprivations relative to the West German population with which the East Germans are now politically and legally, but not yet economically, unified.

The prevailing economic experience of the new *Länder* is not one of recovery gaining momentum, but rather one of a protracted crisis with uncertain distributional outcomes within the framework of a decisively less 'social' market economy, at least if compared with the conditions of social, job and housing security that were provided by the old regime. At any rate, the pains of the economic transition are responded to by very vocal complaints targeted at highly visible West German individuals and bodies, such as the privatization agency (Treuhandanstalt), not self-blame. Conversely, and as there is no longer an inter-systemic challenge in terms of a rivalry over 'social progress', there is no effectively perceived need on the part of West German elites to respond by measures designed to redistribute income, wealth or power. All of this adds to the climate of highly politicized discontent and protest, which also concerns the issue of xenophobia and the priority German nationals should take over the entitlements of foreigners.

In the fifties rather generous and progressive social security, co-determination and housing policies were advocated and implemented in West Germany with an eye to the goal of 'preserving national unity' against the GDR claim to represent the forces of social progress. Ironically, the goal of preserving this unity by means of social policies has dropped to a much lower rank in the current political agenda of German politics at the very point in time at which such unity must be built. The pace of economic recovery in East Germany is not being accelerated by the two kinds of tail winds that worked in the first decade of the Federal Republic: first, the American and West European strategic interest in the rapid economic recovery of West Germany[8] and its integration into a Western Alliance and, secondly, the 'preventive' logic of extensive social reform and social progress provided by the Cold War.

Elite and institutional continuities

WG The overall strategy of the occupying powers was to initiate and encourage a tightly supervised process of institutional reconstruction of the German polity and economy that would follow the logic of selective restoration of those patterns of the country's institutional tradition that appeared acceptable and innocent. Among the patterns to be resurrected were, on the political and constitutional levels, federalism and local self-government, a somewhat revised party and electoral system, the organization of social security, the system of industrial relations (including the 'dual' logic of workers' interest representation on the company and industry levels), the civil service, the professional and commercial chambers and the independent, yet protected and privileged, status of the two major churches, the media, academic institutions and the professions. On the economic plane it included the restoration (or rather preservation) of the arrangements of a capitalist market economy with a strong element of associative representation of classes and sectors. By 1948 'the business sector was largely rehabilitated, and the labour movement firmly in the hands of moderates' (Carlin 1993: 53). This strategy of selective and supervised restoration stood in sharp contrast to the revolutionizing attempt of the Soviet occupying power in its zone, which amounted to a complete reorganization of German society, economy and polity and involved the abolition of its entire previous institutional set-up.

The strategy of selective and supervised restoration was all the more easily implemented as, due to the comparatively short duration of the Nazi regime, the memories of these institutions were largely present among the adult population and, most importantly, the people were also available with whom both economic and political institutions could be staffed and thus relatively quickly put into operation.

The combined outcome of the restoration strategy and the re-installation of pre-Nazi political (as well as former Nazi administrative and economic) elites and managerial personnel was a pattern of transition in post-war West Germany that was largely and to an increasing extent determined by the results of institutionalized group conflict among indigenous elements such as political parties, territorial units, organized interests and pluralistic political and cultural forces. At least after the formal inauguration of the Federal Republic of Germany in 1949, but in important policy areas long before that date, the transformation and reconstruction became a matter of conflicting domestic bodies and activities, group negotiations and electoral politics, and was no longer a matter of the unilateral decree of the occupying forces. The roles and rules which were to govern the second German republic were smoothly and easily restored, and its 'bearers' put to work. It is this latent continuity and quick reactivation of the 'institutional software' of social and political life that accounts for both the success of the transition after 1945 and the major differences we see if we compare it with the post-1989 transition in East Germany.

EG All the institutional legacies of the old regime have been rendered obsolete and illegitimate, even the demonstrably more successful ones, such as the GDR health system (Offe 1992). They are being replaced by a new order that is not agreed and negotiated by indigenous representatives, but imposed from the outside. As a consequence former elites and managerial strata, where they have not been removed from their positions because of having been excessively involved in the old regime, suffer 'functional' disqualification, as the rules and routines, standards and legal norms according to which they are now supposed to operate are entirely new and unknown to them. The judicial, managerial, administrative, political and academic personnel required to operate the new institutions must therefore also to a large extent be transplanted from West Germany.

To a much lesser extent than was the case with the West Germans after 1945, the East Germans of the 1990s can be said to be, through their representatives and mechanisms of interest intermediation, the authors and masters of their collective destiny and of the route the transformation will take. Being deprived of an initiative mediated through associative action and structurally incapacitated to recapture it, because no such things as indigenous forms of East German collective action have been allowed to survive or to come into being, the role they can play is restricted to three rather impotent responses to the new conditions.

First, individual adaptation is resorted to as opposed to collective action, and the 'exit' rather than the 'voice' option is chosen. Individual adaptations of people facing the prospect of unemployment are basically of a defensive sort, such as migration, long-distance commuting, abstaining from having children (cf. Wagner 1992) and undergoing retraining.

A second prevailing response to the pains of transformation is that since 'they' (meaning the West Germans) have taken the initiative, they should also see to it that the pains do not become excessive. This response amounts to an appeal for more and more funds and social protection, which, however, is becoming increasingly weak as it is not backed up by any significant bargaining power other than the warning and/or threat of the rise of anomic forms of social conflict or, more recently, in the 1994 and 1995 federal and state elections, the protest vote in favour of the revived former state party, now called the Party of Democratic Socialism.

Thirdly, some people in some positions seem to be able to rely upon forms of collective action of a non-institutional sort (popularly referred to as *rote Socken, alte Seilschaften*), for example cliques, clans and personal connections developed under and preserved from the old regime. Non-institutional and often highly expressive (if equally highly ineffective) forms of collective action are also employed for the defence of economic interests of (often small) groups, such as, as mentioned before, when hunger strikes are staged in order to defend jobs in the mining industry. In all these types of responses (individual coping, 'Wessi' blaming, protest voting, informal pursuit of interest) it is evident that the power and transformative impact they are likely to generate are very limited. These responses indicate rather than help to overcome a prevailing condition of fatalism and passivity. While traces of the first and third type of response, individual coping and reliance on informal groups, can certainly be found in the West German early post-war history as well, the decisive new element is the presence not of a nation in trouble, but of a politically and economically weaker minority within a recently revived nation state in trouble. It is this unprecedented scenario – as well as the resultant and bilaterally assumed responsibility of the old *Länder* to assist the new *Länder* in overcoming their economic and fiscal hardship and the lack in the new *Länder* of a representative political 'voice' and bargaining power – that, taken together, make the reconstruction of the East German economy so uniquely difficult.

Conclusion

The paradox that emerges from this comparative review of some of the major characteristics of the two transitions is that the East German case, which is much less dramatic and catastrophic in its initial (moral, economic, military) conditions, does not turn out, as one might expect, to be the case in which the problems of transformation and reconstruction are more easily overcome in 'objective' terms and at the same time experienced as being more easily manageable. The depth of the abyss would seem to allow for a much steeper and more sustained way out, with a clearer and much less contested direction. This appears also to be the logic behind a strangely sad remark that I heard being made in Moscow. 'You Germans', a Russian intellectual said, 'were in a much more fortunate position after 1945 than we Russians are now after 1991. For you had at least an occupation regime capable of prescribing and imposing a new political, economic and territorial order.' The assumption that was so popular with the West German political elites before and immediately after unification may have been based upon a *non sequitur* – the assumption, that is, that since 'we' succeeded after 1945, we are all the more certain to succeed, and by applying the same methods and institutional prescriptions, in the 'easier' case of the post-1989 transformation.

To be sure, in order to describe the situation as paradoxical something like the following spatial metaphor would have to be shown to apply. There are two cases of transition, one (1945) over a long distance and the other (1989) over a comparatively short distance in terms of the effort needed to bring about full economic recovery and political normalization. What needs to be substantiated and explained is that the long distance was bridged much more smoothly, more successfully and faster than has so far been the case with the short distance. Both of these empirical claims – the length of the distance and the success of the transition – may be controversial. Let me briefly spell out why I believe that – and in what sense – both of them are valid.

As our comparative review of some of the major parameters of the situation has demonstrated, the distance that had to be covered in the 1945 case was enormous, both in absolute and in relative terms. The country to be rebuilt had endured devastation, military defeat, unconditional surrender, huge waves of refugees, moral ignominy, international isolation and the ultimate delegitimation of all existing political institutions and elites. None of these grim features of the 1945 situation – or certainly not all of them or on the same scale – was present in 1989. After all, the per capita output of the GDR in 1989 was probably correctly estimated to be equivalent to the one achieved in West Germany by some point in the sixties, well after the reconstruction period was successfully concluded.

On the other hand the more intangible preconditions of economic reconstruction, such as human resources, the spirit of mobility, efficiency and technical modernization, as well as the basic institutional set-up of a private, capitalist economy, were all in place at the beginning of the West German reconstruction, as were political elites from the previous regime, the Weimar Republic. What was also in place was an externally stimulated and encouraged 'sense of direction', a widely shared notion of the values and goals that the new regime must pursue with high priority, namely a 'social' market economy and a liberal democracy within the institutional framework of strong federalism. This convergent orientation of all major political forces was as much inspired by Anglo-Saxon models of liberal democracy as it was inherited from the welfare state project of Weimar, which together amounted to a widely shared ideological mix of 'restoration' and 'new beginning' (cf. Kocka 1979). All of these cultural, personal, institutional and ideological 'software' resources stood ready for immediate use. Given these circumstances and conditions, the post-1945 transition was in fact easier to accomplish than the one after 1989.

In East Germany after 1989 the reciprocal situation applies. The 'hardware' – the stock of machinery, buildings and infrastructure – may be outdated and rotten, but it has not suffered from anything like the large-scale destruction that had taken place in the 1945 case. Up to its end the GDR was an economic system that was able to feed, house and employ its citizens at a level of prosperity unequalled by any of the other state socialist countries. But here the bottleneck variables appear to be elite, institutional and cultural factors. The intangible, or 'software', resources – mentalities, routines, habits, modes of coping,

cognitive frames and expectations, familiarity with institutional patterns – that turn out to be of a surprising strategic significance as
determinants of a sustained and successful process of reconstruction
seem to be missing.

To put my argument in a nutshell: the 1945 breakdown taught people both what not to do and what to do as a consequence, whereas
1989, in the words of Soviet reformer Yuriy Afanas'yev, has just
shown the world 'what not to do' – without any positive lesson. To
continue for a moment with the teaching metaphor: even if there is a
curriculum, there is no one who is uncontestedly entitled and capable
to teach it. In contrast to 1945, 1989 did not offer an unambiguous
'opportunity for positive reconstruction'. The situation in 1945 was 'a
calamity, but a calamity with a positive side', a calamity, in the words
of Friedrich (1953: 626) paraphrasing Burke, that brought the 'prescriptive force of tradition' to bear upon the situation. In contrast, 1989
lacked the energizing and directive power of the 'zero hour' (Stokes
1991: 19). Instead of an unequivocal conclusion, what remained from
the old regime was a multiplicity of institutional designs, ideologies
and concepts of social order that remain largely incompatible.

Social and political forces that emerge in the aftermath of state
socialism are split among three centres of gravity, namely the
('golden') pre-Communist past, the ('better' aspects of the) Communist
past, with the security, equality and authoritarian-paternalistic protection offered by it, and the 'better future' of prosperity to be achieved
through an emulation of Western-style democratic capitalism.

There is hardly anything that proponents of the three orientations
making up this triangle of forces could easily agree upon, and there is
no domestic or external power capable of effectively imposing the
ground rules of a political space in which all three of these political
forces could possibly coexist.

First, in contrast to the German situation after 1945, the ('golden')
past that is being referred to as a guideline for reconstruction is not a
relatively recent past of the better traditions of the failed Weimar constitution and its project of a democratic welfare state. Instead it is a
distant pre-democratic past made up of all kinds of myths of ethnic
nationalism and other communal bonds.

Secondly, given that the caesura has been much milder and the continuity of elite as well as mass habits and 'mental residues' of the old
regime much greater in 1989 than 1945, the rejection of the old regime
is more ambiguous and its prospects for some kind of ideological survival much greater.[9]

Thirdly, given the need for a fundamental institutional reconstruction of the polities and economies of post-Communism, the prospects

for success are far too bleak to inculcate much of the trust and confidence that would rapidly improve the situation. It is this absence of the unequivocally promising and relatively painless path of modernization that explains, in the case of the new *Länder*, why the hope for the blessings of a 'social market economy' remains much more qualified and much less hegemonic than was the case in the early post-war years in West Germany.

In short, the field of political forces is not unified and constrained by a shared and militarily enforced rejection of 'totalitarianism' (in either of its two versions), which was the condition of post-fascist democracies in the context of the incipient Cold War. Instead history has left the post-Communist societies behind without a clear instruction as to what to do. History's vote of no confidence in state socialism was not a 'constructive' one. The field is rather torn between the three poles of the post-Communist triangle that constitute the much wider political space in which the post-1989 reconstruction efforts occur. In that sense 1989 was not a 'revolution', if that term implies the construction of a new order built upon new ideas, but just the crumbling of an old regime with highly indeterminate consequences for the building of a new order. The most striking thing about 1989 was the absence of new ideas.

The attempt to develop such ideas was often marked by the tacit recognition of its futility. 'Anti-politics' (G. Konrad) or the desire for 'living in truth' (V. Havel) are as respectable as authentic statements of a personal existential condition as they are vacuous if taken as formulas guiding the conduct of public policy. To be sure, all kinds of synthetic hybrids can be developed in between the three poles of the post-Communist political space that is made up of the longing for the 'golden' past, the residues of the state socialist past and the hopes for a prosperous future within the institutional framework of welfare capitalism. The strongest of these hybrids is an ideological alliance of the two pasts, which amounts to an appeal to statist-authoritarian protection cum national pride and ethnic patriotism. Second comes the nationalist–liberal hybrid, an alliance of the economic modernizers with the patriotic or regionalist conservatives. Least strongly developed and least auspicious is the liberal–social democratic alliance, which would retain some transformed welfare state guarantees of the old regime while combining it with the economic institutions of democratic capitalism.

My thesis is that, contrary to appearances, the post-1989 case poses the more difficult problems of transition, and the idea that 'if we have done it once, we can easily repeat the success' is deeply misleading. The factors that made the post-1945 case so comparatively easy were the following:

most of the economic institutions of capitalism were intact, and the internal as well as external economic conditions of the reconstruction period were generally favourable;

the collective 'social capital' (Putnam 1993) of mental dispositions, habits, routines and attitudes that favoured economic reconstruction and democratic accommodation were intact, and they were supported by widely shared memories and traditions taken from the pre-fascist period;

indigenous elites experienced in the operation of a democratic social market economy were available and helped to contain the level of politicization, as did the fact that the nascent West German state was for some time deprived of full sovereignty;

the international constellation of forces predetermined an external interest in the rapid recovery of West Germany.

The clear absence of these four factors makes the East German transition much more uncertain in its course and eventual outcome, for which the West German experience cannot serve as a reliable model.

9

The Left after the West's Victory

To an unforeseen extent the collapse of the state socialist systems in Central and East Europe drew all the teeth of the Communist parties in the West, which had constituted a marginalized political force since the mid-seventies at the latest. Moreover, it shattered the respectability and the credit of 'left-wing' political, cultural and economic ideas as a whole. In the 1990s these ideas are considered to have been disproven by history, and the purported refutation is no doubt the key parameter of domestic and international policy. Only in Central and East Europe (excluding the Czech Republic) have leftist 'post-Communist' parties with opaque party manifestos scored successes either in linking the transition to a market economy to goals of social justice or in merely delaying the transition. In the European Union, socialist and social democratic political programmes, by contrast, which credibly promised social security, economic modernization and full employment, have since disappeared from the agenda, just as most left-wing parties have disappeared from government. In conclusion, it is therefore worth casting a glance at the fate which the events of 1989 to 1991 held in store for left-wing ideas and projects.

Throughout the post-war period complaints about the obstacles and slander they faced under Cold War conditions were part of the standard repertoire of democratic socialists. The success the German Christian Democrats (CDU) had in the 1953 general election with their slogan 'All the paths of socialism lead to Moscow' made things difficult for social democrats and socialists, as did the fairly idiotic slogan the CDU came up with in 1976, 'Freedom or socialism?'. Or rather this was always the somewhat self-pitying assessment of the Left. Events since 1989 have made it necessary to correct this analysis. Could it not be that the chances of success of 'left-wing' political projects and interests were more favourable during the Cold War (and precisely because of it) than they have been since the end of that war?

(1) The historical burden that rests on the Left's political projects in the mid-1990s is not something that has arisen recently as a consequence of the distortions of the ideas of socialism perpetrated by their Soviet Communist practitioners. For this reason alone the historical genesis of this distortion and the final collapse of the Soviet system are a central topic in the Left's attempts to find its political bearings. I wish, as a contribution to these efforts, to untangle one thread in the complex fabric of causal links.

The successful military struggle against the Third Reich gave the Stalinist regime and the hegemony of the Soviet Union such permanent credit on the domestic front, within the Eastern bloc and in the international community that the Soviet empire managed to stay alive well beyond its historically justified lease of life. Indeed we know today that the empire was factually doomed to failure in socio-economic and political terms. And the actual course that the failure took was of such a merciless nature that no one would have foreseen it. Just as interesting as the question of 'why' it happened is the question of why 'it' did not happen at a much earlier date. Why was it possible for the knowledge that the economic and political constitution of state socialism was not sustainable to be repressed and suppressed for so long by, among other things, the deployment of military means?

An explanation that goes part of the way towards answering this reads as follows: the military and economic resources which the Soviet system controlled as a consequence of its victory over Hitler's Germany, as well as the political and moral hegemony to which it could for so long lay successful claim, relieved this system of the necessity of 'learning', that is, of releasing its own structural premises for reform to be used for such. The successful outcome of the Second World War and the consequent expansion of the territory of the Eastern bloc both served to prevent those responsible for the success from being able to learn.

Under this hegemonial regime and given the dynamics of the Cold War, a fixed idea was nurtured and persisted until the eighties in the bloc dominated by the Soviets: namely an unchanging image of an enemy. According to this image, the situation during the Cold War was to be interpreted in line with that of 1941, that is, with a view to the potential vanishing point of a conceivable Western surprise attack. The internal and international structures of the Warsaw Pact, including this 'cognitive frame' of a latent Western willingness to attack, are clearly a hangover from the experiences the Soviets had in the Second World War. It was this canonical interpretation of the situation which prompted the allied members of the Warsaw Pact to believe it rational to subordinate themselves to the military and political leadership of the Soviet Union and increasingly to subsidize the Soviet Union economically by supplying it with capital goods. The heroic picture painted retrospectively of the liberating deeds of the Red Army and also the future-oriented estimation of possible instances in which they would again have to rely on the Soviets for military protection against Western attacks both to a certain degree provided reasons for recognizing Soviet predominance and knuckling under. The fear of the Comecon elites that was fuelled by challenges to their rule sparked by the domestic potential for conflict also fits smoothly into this legitimatory frame. Or rather it did at least as long as it was possible to classify such potential for conflict as merely deriving from the Cold War and thus as ideological phenomena that were either caused and encouraged by the West (be it solely by virtue of the latter's factual existence and the function it played as a political and economic model) or would objectively help the West in the imagined scenario of military confrontation between the blocs. It was impossible to view internal opposition as anything other than the work of 'fifth columns' which were 'objectively' the puppets of the West – this was the constant justification given for the military repression from 1953 (in Berlin) to 1981 (in Warsaw).

Under the sway of this cognitive frame the Comecon countries embarked on a socio-political learning programme that was 'mistaken', that is, it was foreseeable that it would prove unsustainable in the final instance. And even the coercive means of Soviet power would not have been sufficient to impose this programme on them against their will. Without the horror of the Second World War and the role the Soviet Union played in it, namely that of victim of attack and of victor, there would have been no adequate basis for the other Comecon members agreeing to the Soviets' role as ideological, economic, political and military leader, irrespective of how they were squeezed into agreeing to this. The flip side of this agreement and the official agreement to everything for which the Soviet Union stood was, however, that attention was directed away from questions of what the 'Soviet path' was able to offer and in general away from questions of the need for reform or reform options. These blind spots when viewing themselves led to a loss of the endogenous potential for transformation, which simply cannot be axiomatically rejected as inconceivable and impossible to implement. 'Learning from the Soviet Union means learning to win' was the premise of a learning programme that was wrong, and yet speaking out and attacking its absurdity was punished as a crime against the sanctified foundations of the 'community of socialist peoples'.

The rigid definition of this misleading learning programme was a remote effect of the Nazi regime and its politics of conquering East Europe. By its annexation of and military attacks on the countries in the region, it established the traumatic linchpin of political thought and all political fears in Central and East Europe. And the Soviet leadership was able to conserve these fears strategically and exploit them to preserve its power. The negative reference point, that one might fall victim to an attack from the West, programmed the positive reference point, 'the loyalty to the alliance with the Soviet Union' as the sole power that had not only not been defeated, but had transformed the war of aggression launched against it into a defeat for the aggressor. By subordinating themselves to the interests of the Soviet Union as a consequence of this motivation, the political elites in the other Comecon countries rigidly adopted a course that was equally hopeless in moral, political, economic and military terms. In this regard the destructive consequences of the adherence to this programme amounted to the 'delayed' victory of the German aggressors, to the extent that quite unintentionally they tricked the Soviet Union and its allies in the Warsaw Pact into the trap of a Pyrrhic victory. Seen thus, the Nazis, by attacking the Soviet Union, were the first link in a causal chain that did not come to an end until 1991 – an end which left the Soviet Union the paralysed economic and political victim of its own military successes.

It would clearly be necessary to prove two arguments to elaborate this hypothesis. First, the causal argument that it was the victory over Nazi Germany that initially caused the Soviet regime to start down the road it never veered off between 1945 and 1989, namely to be rigid and anti-reformist, and that the said victory furnished it with those crazed forms of legitimation which enabled it continually to pre-empt any nascent domestic questioning of its justifications. Secondly, the counterfactual argument that culminates in the following proposition: if the preparations, battles and outcome of the Second World War had not had this potential for shaping the further structural development of the Comecon countries, then potential for reform and opportunities for development would have been able to emerge that would perhaps have averted the sorry end of the Soviet Union and with it the subsequent problems that have arisen and are so topical in the mid-1990s.

Conversely, should one of the following two findings be shown to have substance, then this would weaken the hypothesis. First, it might be possible to demonstrate that the fact that the Soviet regime, by dint of the Bolsheviks having seized power, was forced to adopt structures and to develop in specific ways that precluded its independent and promising political and economic modernization was a course fixed from the very outset (that is, from 1917–24 onwards) or one which dated back to older legacies of Russian culture and history, and was not the product of the Second World War and its outcome, namely that the Soviet Union developed into an imperial power. If this were the case, the structural errors which were confirmed in 1991 would have to be seen solely as resulting from the foundation of the regime and its institutional premises and not from their deformation through war and subsequent codification. Secondly, and conversely, it might be possible to show that the Second World War and its consequences by no means served to shape structures and the further course of events as strongly as my hypothesis assumes. Rather, we might claim that opportunities for self-correction did indeed exist or emerged anew, but were not seized or were blocked for reasons other than those which have to do with war and the consequences of war.

Any investigation and conclusive evaluation of this hypothesis would clearly require a medium-scale research project in modern history, something that cannot be offered here. However, the origins, course and outcome of the Second World War should be paid greater attention in a historical explanation of the events of 1989–91 than is usually the case in Western discourse on the economic and moral shortcomings of the Soviet system. What we need to understand is not just what was 'wrong' with the Soviet system. The question as to 'second-order errors' is of key interest here: why was it not possible to correct first-order errors? At any rate, only an explanation of the circumstances in which East European state socialism arose and collapsed can form the point of departure for answering the question of whether the events of 1989 are 'a historical refutation' of socialism or not.

(2) For a long time the failed social experiment of state socialism of the Soviet type enjoyed an ambiguous form of credit in the West too. There, certainly in the first two decades after the war, many believed that that system might forge a stable political order which would abide by international agreements, and the believers were to be found not just in the Communist parties that were loyal to Moscow, but well beyond them, even among the ranks of conservative proponents of *realpolitik*. In fact the belief was that in the domains of relations between employers and employees and of social policy on the one hand, and in the development of the productive forces by means of the 'scientific-technological revolution' on the other, that form of state socialism might develop a certain appeal or at least respectability *vis-*

à-vis the capitalist democracies in the West. The Soviet Union and the Warsaw Pact countries were taken seriously in the West not only as a potential military threat, but also as the foundations of an economic and socio-political project that fought tooth and nail against the West's ideas and structures and was by implication considered a potentially stable social order capable of further expansion – and certainly not as a clear absurdity. The presence of a completely different model for organizing industrial society, and one that took up the international, unifying banner of justice and peace at that, was a challenge that had to be met from the viewpoint of the Western political elites not only by building new missiles but also, given the conditions of the Cold War and the existence of the two Germanies, by suitable socio-political endeavour. Wiesenthal (1992: 163) remarks: 'Be it as a latent threat, as normative justifications or as an institutional heuristic method, the influence of socialist ideas is evident in the processes that led to the forming of the modern welfare states.'

This leads to a further counterfactual argument. In particular, German social policy in the fifties would not have taken the dynamic and 'progressive' form it did had it not been for the challenge of the opposing system behind the Iron Curtain. The impact on domestic policy of the confrontation with that system can be seen with exceptional clarity in the case of the history of social policy in West Germany. They could equally be outlined with reference to endeavours in the domains of science and education policy triggered by the 'Sputnik shock'. Adenauer believed that external security and internal stability were closely related owing to the exposed position of West Germany in the East–West conflict. His social reforms were intended, Hockerts (1980: 285) claims, 'to make the West German state ... socially resilient, ... in the sense of taking the offensive, of making West Germany attractive for the East German population' and to wrest any arguments such as 'First pensions, then rearmament!' from the hands of the opposition of Social Democrats and trade unions in West Germany (p. 416). Such strategic and tactical considerations meant that the thrust of the Cold War fuelled the fires of socio-political progress.

In West Germany, as Klessmann (1984: 301) states, 'important socio-political initiatives also served to immunize the population against socially radical claims ... At the same time, the reference to the "occupied zone" sufficed to block any calls for reform.' Conversely, some of the success of the (social democratic) Left certainly stems from the well-considered accommodating approach, in fact what was even at times an attempt to outdo the other in the domain of social policy, which its liberal and conservative opponents adopted in order to prevent the Left from serving as a bridgehead for the 'other side'. And even it was solely in order to immunize social democratic and socialist parties and trade unions against the advances of those situated on the other side of the Iron Curtain, the non-socialist political forces in the West believed it was advisable to accommodate the Left politically to a greater extent than it would otherwise have had cause to do. As a consequence we can safely say that the fact that life under Cold War conditions was apparently the norm afforded West European societies as a whole and the active leftist socio-political forces unearned gains which unobtrusively assisted in socio-politically progressive programmes being adopted – in a manner quite unlike that which many theorists in the Western Left always assumed or at least claimed to assume took place.

In the competition between the systems, social policy exercised not only the above defensive functions, but also an aggressive function. To quote Hockerts again (1985: 254), it was 'aggressive in the sense of ensuring that West Germany remained appealing for the population of East Germany in order to avoid the division of Germany solidifying any further. Thus the reforms on welfare provisions had the (additional) function of supporting the "magnet theory" of German reunification supported by all the major political camps of the day.' If it had not been for the prohibition of the German Communist Party (the KPD, which was controlled by East Berlin) by the German Constitutional Court in 1956, the German Social Democrats (the SPD) would not have enjoyed that factual monopoly on the left of the party spectrum which enabled it to embark unchallenged on the new course of domestic and foreign policy inaugurated by its Godesberg Programme of 1959. Thus, at least in the period from 1949 to 1961 and possibly in the seventies too, during the phase of 'full employment' in West Germany East Germany served permanently to remind West Germany of social policy and to stimulate innovation. In this manner – and perhaps we can see this fully only with the benefit of hindsight offered by the nineties – it unintentionally assisted the consolidation of West Germany and the institutionalized social peace there which was of such importance for the West German success story.

Another counterfactual question is whether the 'German model', with its corporatist and concerted 'social market economy', would ever have arisen or had a chance of survival without the continual reminder and challenge of state socialism (a reminder then exploited under the conditions of the Cold War) and the 'competition between the systems'? Schneider (1988: 162) avers that 'the intellectual and specific individual, practical challenges of socialism decisively shaped West Germany's social conscience and its liberal market economy. In fact even within the West, with its basis in competition, they created a more favourable climate for solidarity, stimulating an ability to reach a consensus on fundamental issues and helping advance the economic unification of Europe.'[1] To this extent there is a clear basis for the hypothesis that in many areas state socialism formed the 'exoskeleton' of Western democracies: its presence enabled them to process challenges of social and technological policy productively and in so doing to demonstrate that they were economically, militarily and, moreover, morally 'better' than the only operative counter-model for an industrial society, namely the state socialist variant.

If this is the case, then in the mid-1990s we must ask which constellations of social policy will emerge and what chance of success they can have now that this challenge, or rather the covert impact of external assistance in innovation and consolidation, has ceased to exist.

The East Berlin economist Dieter Klein (1993: 67) has suggested that 'the preservation or even the expansion of the social components of capitalist modernity is in the balance', and much has confirmed his assumption – and not only because the cake available to feed social policy and redistribution now has to be cut up differently in order to be shared by the federal states in East and in West Germany. The fact that there is a dwindling of the political-strategic motivational basis for the willingness to bake a cake of the usual large proportions for social policy and redistribution, specifically in the context of the new problems of industrial locations and competition, may also play a role here. The GDR offered the FRG a mirror image, opposite which the latter was able to find economic and moral confirmation domestically and internationally; it was thereby able to legitimize its own claim to being clearly the morally and economically 'better' Germany in all respects, in order to defend itself, as it were, against the GDR's claim to legitimacy through an anti-fascist heritage. Kocka (1990: 492) states that 'soon the Federal Republic of Germany will no longer have a GDR with which to compare itself and confirm its own validity. *This* source of legitimation for the FRG is gradually drying up.'[2]

This finding would suggest that the fact that such pressure is drying up may perhaps have instigated the regression in social policy, or at least the stagnation of a policy of social security and redistribution. There are two sound causes for such an assumption following German unification, which, taken together, have led to a marked shift to the right in the domestic political spectrum in Germany.

First, the unexpected burden placed on West Germany's economy and tax payers by the tasks of economic reconstruction in the new federal states and the new competitive conditions of the Single European

Market has caused decidedly 'materialist' (as opposed to 'post-materialist') political themes to be pushed to the top of the domestic political agenda. The themes are those of growth, exports, competitiveness, the industrial hub, monetary stability and relieving manufacturing of the burden of taxation and levies, as well as genuinely 'materialist' themes of 'civil' order, to be guaranteed by the police. At the beginning of the eighties, shortly after the foundation of the German Green Party and on the occasion of the marriage of the new social movements, the general prediction was for a trend towards a post-industrial society in which the significance of 'materialist' realms of politics geared towards guiding values such as growth and social and military security would recede. And, so went the forecast, in their place 'post-materialist' political aims based on autonomy, participation, ecology and securing peace would blossom and perhaps lend a strong impetus to a 'post-industrial Left'. In the mid-1990s this speculative position, which was quite daring at the time, has proved to be completely erroneous.

Secondly, German unification caused a relative weakening of the Left and its election potential, above all in East Germany. Bürklin (1992: 16) writes in this context: 'From the viewpoint of an electoral sociology, the losses the political Left incurred were unexpectedly high. And I say unexpectedly so, because on the basis of the socio-structural composition of East Germany and the traditional political culture there, the leftist parties could have counted on a higher degree of electoral support.' In those instances in which leftist parties scored electoral successes in East Germany, as in most of the other post-Communist countries, it was the successor parties of the former Communist state parties that benefited and not, with few exceptions, Social Democrats or Green parties.

(3) Until the very end the Soviet Union derived its legitimation from the fact that it was a world power shoring up peace. This claim was, as we can now see, well justified – though in a manner quite unlike that in which it was put forward. The Soviet Union did not prevent a war between the First and Second Worlds, because such a war was not on the cards, or certainly not in the sense of a 'hot' war. Rather, the most acute danger of military confrontation in the post-war era occurred during the Cuba Crisis of 1962. It did, however, clearly prevent wars within the Third World (though it did not, as Vietnam shows, stop those between the First and Third Worlds) or ensured they did not escalate to a world scale, for, given a situation defined by the two opposing political blocs, such wars would have involved incalculable risks. The Gulf War was not possible before 1991

and would certainly have been prevented during the regime of the two superpowers. Above all, the Soviet Union's policies prevented wars within the Second World, because it effectively repressed the potential for ethnic conflict in Eastern Europe and in the Asian parts of the Soviet Union.

Moreover, the Soviet Union erected that 'Iron Curtain' along the western border of the two blocs from which Western societies objectively profited as it functioned as a barrier to migration. The existence of this barrier spared them (or at least the Germans, who had not been tried by the problems of post-colonial domestic 'minorities' of a demographic or other nature) from having to face the test of the strain of multi-ethnicity, a test which they are failing so abjectly in the mid-1990s. The new migration conditions which have emerged with the disappearance of the Iron Curtain (in which context it is, incidentally, no longer a matter of the 'demand-pull' migration of the sixties as was regulated by labour market policy but instead of 'supply-push' migration) are sorely trying for the traditional 'internationalist' and 'republican' professions of the European Left and their rejection of a form of politics restricted to nationalist considerations. The fact that there is now no Soviet Union fulfilling the two latent functions of securing peace and blocking migration is confronting the West European countries with problems and challenges which for the duration of its existence the imperial Soviet regime benevolently spared them. The Left is badly prepared for the hardly surprising insight that upbeat welfare state policies had their socio-moral roots in widely shared intuitions on justice that stemmed in part from national communities. As a consequence the 'moral effort' required proves to be all the greater if the needy recipients of the fruits of redistribution are no longer 'our sort of person'; the community is still far more prepared to grant such benefits to the latter rather than to 'aliens'. Indeed the more 'aliens' there are, the more the moral effort necessary for social policy fails to be made, as is shown by the symptoms of populist and in part violent xenophobia and 'the chauvinism of affluence' witnessed in a unified Germany. The Cold War – and equally the framework of nation states whose sovereign rights were by and large unimpaired – more or less saved the Left from having to concern itself with the thorny problem of the exhaustion, even within its own ranks, of the indispensable moral resources that had to be exploited in order to grant non-nationals positive rights.

A further contribution which the existence of the Soviet Union certainly made to the development of the Western countries and which is now sorely lacking was to secure, albeit indirectly, the political, military and ideological cohesion of the NATO members. In retrospect the

Cold War, anti-Communism and the need for transnational cooperation appear to have formed the cement which held the Western states
together under the hegemony of the United States and which is now
crumbling by the day.

For the duration of their existence the Communist regimes resembled
a deep freeze. The function of deep freezes is to freeze processes (of a
chemical and biological nature that depend on higher temperatures)
and thus ensure that foodstuffs remain edible. The metaphor refers to
both aspects: something is prevented from happening and something is
preserved. What was blocked was the political process of cultural modernization which took place in the West and can be studied there as the
'normal' side-effect of industrial development. The important upshot of
this modernization is that differences (between lifestyles, types of education, religious confessions, political parties, economic interests, cultural patterns and so on, and also between income and wealth) are not
only permitted; in the framework of a liberal-democratic state, as well
as the institution and procedures of a democracy of competition and of
the welfare state, they are also rendered undamaging to the extent that
there is no threat to the fundamental premises on which the integration
of society and the society rest. This social and political-cultural process
of modernization is blocked by regimes of the Soviet type or at least
braked decisively, while at the same time they press ahead with technological and scientific modernization at as fast a pace as possible.

This explains why the societies 'thawing' in terms of culture in the
mid-1990s are typified by a lack of experience in dealing with difference – and that includes equally the institutional routines for dealing
with difference. To put it somewhat boldly, East European societies
have suddenly been confronted with more economic and cultural difference than their inhabitants are either used to or able to tolerate, and
more than the existing institutions there are able to regulate and render compatible with the respective societies.

This shortcoming can prompt two diametrically opposed forms of
pathological reactions, namely the rejection of difference and the
strategic exploitation of difference. By 'rejection of difference' I mean,
above all, a clinging to 'communal', informal and 'primordial' forms
of social organization, perception, thought and action. The recourse to
primordial social categories, such as is repeatedly virulent in the
ethno-nationalism of the East European countries, can be explained
psychologically as a despairing attempt to ward off the alien, the different. It is an attempt via the forging of a community to bring factors
to bear which tame the differences that persist, allowing them to be
treated as something of a secondary priority and as essentially unimportant. In short, difference is not permitted – or at least only within

the framework of community bonds, whereby it is not permissible to differentiate between the validity of the respective bonds.

On the other hand we are seeing a strategic, unrestrained and institutionally unregulated exploitation of difference between these communities and also between individuals who do not participate in the cohesive force of such communities, which as often as not are mere mirages. This is true for ethno-nationalist civil wars at the macro-level, for party, factional and inter-organizational struggles at the meso-levels[3] and for such forms as lurk behind all the corners of a predatory, aggressive and parasitic type of mercenary, kiosk or 'smash-and-grab' capitalism at the micro-level. Taken together, they call into question both the system and the social integration of the post-Communist social formations in a way that has dire consequences. In Eastern Europe it is precisely this vicious type of capitalism that is emerging, a type subject to little institutional control, and this is surprisingly and suddenly putting the socialist critique of this post-Communist regime back on the agenda. What is involved is clearly a variant of that form of capitalism which in the last third of the nineteenth century triggered socialist criticism of it, gave birth to the major socialist movements and parties and demonstrated the moral and scientific justifications of that socialist critique. What I have in mind is an unregulated form of capitalism which is accompanied by mass poverty and insufficient social security and which probably unleashes the 'productive forces' only intermittently. The historical function, albeit by no means the dominant strategic intention, of the socialist and social democratic parties after the First World War was to reduce the inhibitions of the mass of the proletarian electorate *vis-à-vis* the workings of the state by integrating them into the political system – and today's post-Communist societies clearly challenge such parties once more not only to fulfil their critical function, but also to tackle precisely this 'constructive' function. Essentially the historical achievement of the socialist and social democratic parties and the trade unions associated with them was to accord wage earners – in their capacity as workers and as voters – a place for active involvement in the competition-based democratic welfare states. What we are witnessing in Central and Eastern Europe in the mid-1990s, by contrast, is mass apathy and political disintegration. For this reason alone there is a 'functional need' in the East for socialist parties and for themes that mobilize the population, for there, without the introduction of social rights of protection and civil rights, the achievements of the market economy and democratic liberties on their own will persist only with the greatest difficulty given the costs and turbulences of the transformation process.

If the state of affairs sketched so cursorily here, including the dynamics of an unregulated market economy not subject to institutional structures *in statu nascendi*, is the result of differentiation having been blocked under the Communist regime, then in retrospect the regime must not only be charged historically with having (co-)constructed a social and economic structure, not to mention a political culture, incapable of dealing with difference, but also credited with having controlled the dangerous effects on the domestic and international fronts of the lag in modernity it had itself preserved and intensified over a lengthy period of time. In fact the said regime must perhaps even be given a certain historical legitimation for having done so. Outwardly the regime gave the international system a bipolar structure defined by the arms race and deterrence strategies of the Cold War. Within the Eastern bloc this led to the effective prevention, indeed to the factual impossibility, of military conflicts between ethnic groups or nation states (see Anderson 1983: 12; Hobsbawm 1990: 207). Internally the compulsory economic system of labour, production and distribution did not result in greater and increasing efficiency. However, and this should not be underestimated given the state of the countries' economies today, it did ensure output that provided the authoritarianly guaranteed and socio-economically secured social satisfaction of the population. Moreover, phenomena such as mass unemployment or revolts based on hunger were beyond the ken of the societies in question, something that has again changed today. It is therefore safe to say that the Comecon and Warsaw Pact regime the Soviet Union established on the one hand led to pathogenic backwardness in modernization in respect of the political, cultural and institutional differentiation of the societies affected by this regime, yet on the other helped prevent the dangerous consequences of this deformed development from exploding either at home or abroad.

This assertion is not meant as moral window-dressing for a thoroughly discredited and irreversibly defunct regime after the event. Instead it is intended merely to pinpoint more exactly the problem facing the creation of a policy of order and peace in the post-Communist world in the mid-1990s. Such a policy must tackle the subsequent damage arising from and the heritage of the old regime's social structure, politics and culture. It must avoid relying on the compensatory and disciplining achievements of that regime (and in retrospect they were clearly considerable), yet at the same time it does not have institutional alternatives at hand that are suitable for transplantation. The state socialist regimes were themselves able to solve the lion's share of the problems which they created or the causes of which they had preserved. Moreover, they were the source of challenges that were taken up productively and inventively by the capitalist democracies in the West and rebuffed. Both are no longer the case. This is the dominant factor in the formation of political agents and agendas in the post-Communist countries and the West alike. The problems we were spared by the automatic side-effects of state socialism, that is, the problems of shoring up peace in Central and Eastern Europe, the problems of economic underdevelopment and of migration due to poverty, are problems we are now having to solve with our own means, namely those of the capitalist market economy and of liberal democracies. The West profited from the achievements of state socialism and is affected and challenged by its collapse. We benefited far more from the functioning of the Second World than from exploiting the Third World, and we must now substitute those advantages with means drawn from our own system.

In the attempt to put this agenda into practice the West's prioritization of the Third World over the Second changes. What is initially clear is that the end of the Cold War is by no means good news for those sections of the Third World dependent on aid from the First World. Many countries in the Third World were formerly able to gain a relative advantage from the contrast between First and Second Worlds in that they could switch allegiances strategically from the one protecting power to the other, threaten such a switch and manage their geo-strategic resources accordingly (such as naval bases, other military installations, sources of raw materials and so on). Such threats and such resources are now useless. Furthermore, above all in Western Europe, the strategic interest in the enduring reconstruction of the countries of the Second World has been increased. Quite apart from the cultural and religious affinities with the societies in Central and Eastern Europe and the solidarity this prompts, akin to that spawned by the Spanish and Catholic background of Latin American countries, this is because, were the reconstruction not to be a success, this would have a far more direct impact on Western Europe than the continuing immiseration of African and South Asian society. Cultural and geographical proximity, and the fact that Western Europe is not separated from the Second World, as it is from the Third, by seas and oceans that act as barriers to migration, together lead to a shift in the focus of European development policy away from the fixation on the South and more to the East. Or at least this is a widespread and quite plausible fear in Third World countries. This narrowing of the focus to conditions in the North also poses a challenge for the West European Left, which has traditionally always seen its internationalist task first and foremost as an equitable regulation of the relations between North and South.

Notes

Chapter 1 The Structure of Industrial Societies: the Joint Characteristics and Shortcomings of State Socialist Societies and Democratic Capitalism

1 'Power is the ability to afford not to learn' (Deutsch 1966: 111).
2 What I claim was the inability of the state socialist regimes to monitor themselves contradicts the presence of a highly developed system of informers only superficially and at first glance. For such a system institutionalizes the arbitrariness and idiosyncrasy of a form of gathering, receiving, interpreting and using information. This informer system is, as it were, comparable to a person with strongly impaired vision who refuses to wear glasses, but now and again picks up a magnifying glass when it seems appropriate. In general we can say that such information has a value only as information which 'everyone else' knows about, and not just the recipients of it. Only such second-order knowledge (what Weber called information that had 'gone down in the administration's files', where the opportunities to consult such files were public knowledge and were given an organizational structure) guarantees that the contents of first-order information are not selectively ignored, paranoidly misinterpreted or strategically 'forgotten' - in other words that the use to which such information is put remains open to examination and its value as information remains concealed. 'Private information' is just as little information as private money is money or a private language language.
3 This does not explain why in the individual state socialist societies the social sciences had developed to such differing degrees and exhibited such different levels of intellectual maturity. Of the Comecon countries outside the USSR, Hungary and Poland were clearly the most advanced in this regard, with the German Democratic Republic (GDR) and Czechoslovakia (CSR) bringing up the rear. See chapter 7 for possible explanations.

4   The following sentence is supposed to exist in all East European lan-
    guages, fittingly describing the maxim that was so often adhered to in
    state socialist societies: 'As long as "they" only pretend to be paying us a
    decent wage, we too will only pretend to be working.'

Chapter 3 Capitalism by Democratic Design? Democratic Theory Facing the Triple Transition in East Central Europe

1   I owe this parallel to unpublished work of J. Elster.
2   In their expectation of a proletarian world revolution the founders of the
    Soviet Union dispensed with indicating the geographical position of the state
    in its official name, Union of Soviet Socialist Republics. This is probably the
    only modern example of a state's forgoing the name of its place in the world.
    Even the United States of America operates with such a self-localization,
    though it is a misleading one since it concerns the entire continent. In the
    case of the Soviet Union what was perhaps meant as an invitation to other
    'Soviet Republics' that might be emerging elsewhere in the world to join the
    Union turned into an invitation to all the bearers of hitherto oppressed and
    denied ethnic and national identities to secede, for they no longer had any
    reason to include themselves in the empty category of 'Soviet citizen'.
3   Cf. J. Habermas's defence (1985) of 'civil disobedience' as conducted in the
    name of widely shared norms and values of civility itself.

Chapter 4 Ethnic Politics in East European Transitions

1   Nairn (1990: 30) goes as far as to claim, with a view to the rise of ethnic
    politics in Eastern Europe, that 'nationalism is not now (and never was in
    the past) . . . a counter-current . . . interfering with the majestic mainstream
    of Progress: nationalism *is* the mainstream'.
2   To give a descriptive account of the state, volume and intensity of ethnic
    conflict in post-Communist Eastern Europe and the former Soviet Union
    in the mid-1990s is not part of my agenda in this chapter. A rough idea of
    the magnitude of the problem is given by the fact that in the early nineties
    twenty out of twenty-three borders between the republics of the former
    Soviet Union alone were contested for ethnic reasons by irredentist or
    secessionist movements (Lendvai 1992). On the other hand the borders
    that are least likely to be disputed are those that are marked by the former
    Iron Curtain.
3   As stipulated by articles 2 and 3 of the Bulgarian constitution, which deny
    the right to form autonomous territorial units and declare Bulgarian the
    only official language. Article 11, section 4, prohibits parties based upon
    ethnic or religious identities, and article 12, section 4, bans all political
    activities based upon religious affiliation. Article 36 declares the use of the
    Bulgarian language a 'duty' for all citizens. Article 44, section 2, declares
    illegal all organized activities inciting ethnic or religious hostility. Given
    the actual ethnic division of Bulgarian society and the presence of a strong
    Turkish minority, all these seemingly 'unitary', ethnically neutral stipula-
    tions imply the non-recognition of the Turks and their ethnic identity.

Ethnic politics can thus take the form of denying the social fact of ethnic divisions and of failing to recognize the rights of ethnic groups. In view of the actual existence of a Turkish party, the Movement for Rights and Freedoms (MRF), and its potential for engaging in ethnic conflict (which might even have been supported from abroad) had it been banned from participating in the October 1991 elections, the Supreme Court allowed the MRF to take part.

4 The standard response of Jörg Haider, leader of the Austrian nationalist-liberal Freiheitliche Partei, to charges of racism and chauvinism has been that his party is in no way *ausländerfeindlich*, but just *inländerfreundlich*. It is thus not the perceived ethnic incompatibility of people coming from abroad that led to their discrimination and exclusion, but the calculated economic incompatibility of their being poor and dependent upon 'our' resources. Ethnicity often serves as little more than a proxy in this economic calculus.

5 On 29 March 1990 Slovak deputies of the Czechoslovak federal parliament proposed a motion that the name of the state should from then on be written as 'Czecho-Slovakia' (as it was in the interwar period) rather than Czechoslovakia. The Czech majority voted in favour of the compromise that the spelling proposed by the Slovaks should be used in Slovakia, but the unhyphenated version should be used in the Czech Lands and abroad. This decision was perceived by the Slovak public as deeply insulting, and the elimination of the hyphen was protested against the next day by a crowd of 80,000 people at a mass rally in Bratislava. In this case a compromise could be found. On 12 April the parliament changed the official state name to Czech and Slovak Federal Republic (CSFR).

6 This escalating interplay of violations of two different sets of norms, and the dynamic and intensity of conflict resulting from it, is conceivably quite 'natural' in post-Communist societies, where inherited ethnically hostile attitudes were never overcome, but rather their manifestation was repressed and constrained by a superordinate regime of coerced ethnic peace and 'internationalism'. As the demise of Communist rule has upset this hierarchy of norms, the intense clash of particularistic tribalism and universalistic standards of citizenship is hardly surprising. A telling example is the Estonian intellectual who defends the legal discrimination in this reborn nation against resident Russians by saying that the Russians are (now) rightly considered as inferior because they (previously) considered the Estonian language as inferior and failed to learn it.

7 A practice that is now being totally reversed and with passionate care by the Statistical Offices of post-Communist governments. Cf. Statistics Committee of Latvia 1992, which contains highly detailed statistical breakdowns of distributional variables, ranging from occupational positions to divorces, by ethnicity.

8 Both the Estonian Citizenship Law passed by the Supreme Council of the Republic on 26 February 1992 and the Latvian Citizenship Law of 15 October 1991 are clear cases in point. As the acquisition of property to be privatized is contingent upon full citizenship status, and as this status is made extremely cumbersome to acquire by these laws, foreign ethnic groups (which include, in the case of Latvia, half a million non-Latvians born in Latvia) are effectively barred from becoming owners of land (as well as from the right to vote).

9 More precisely, a distinction can be made between two levels of inauthenticity. First, ethnic politics always pretends to be based upon some self-evidently valid foundations of the community, while in fact these foundations are 'invented', imagined, construed and designed by invoking linguistic, religious, cultural, historical or dynastic group characteristics which are thus a matter of strategic choice rather than collective 'essence' (cf. Anderson 1983; Elwert 1991). Secondly, this construct can be invoked and adhered to in authentic or strategic ways.

10 Needless to say, there is no easy way to tell 'sincere' and 'responsible' ways of using the law, democratic politics, the welfare system and state-organized cultural institutions from 'unauthentic' and 'unreasonable' ones; but this difficulty does not invalidate the analytical distinction.

11 Most importantly, these parameters include their own military, economic and cultural resources; the anticipated strategic action of other ethnic groups, as well as that of relevant 'third parties'; and the political support they enjoy in their own societies and ethnic groups.

12 In view of such strong claims we may usefully remind ourselves of the paradox that the claim to self-government of ethnically homogeneous groups is historically quite new. Most historians would probably agree that the apotheosis of this moral claim did not occur earlier than the rise of the modern nation state. Most nationalists, in contrast, tend to base the claim to self-government on an (often 'invented') history that dates back many centuries, if not millennia. As a consequence the right supposedly acquired in the course of this history seems to have remained mostly unclaimed in the course of this history (Anderson 1983; Elwert 1989: 441). Nor has the right to constitute a political unit on the basis of primordial ties of a community been universally claimed. More often than not the sequence was reversed, following the principle of 'We have made Italy, now we have to make Italians.'

13 The aggressive energies of ethnic mobilization 'may be released in three main directions: against identifiable minorities living in the midst of a majority . . . , against a neighboring ethno-territorial formation . . . with the aim of redrawing borders, and against the imperial center and the hegemonistic nationality' (Zaslavsky 1992: 107). In the case of the Russians in the Baltic states as well as in Moldavia, and in the case of the Serbs in Croatia, all three of these characteristics coincide.

14 For example, the direct and opportunity costs of multilingualism. Direct costs occur when forms must be printed in two or more languages, instead of one. Opportunity costs occur when children have to study a minority language at school, and thus lose the time and opportunity to study subjects of greater value in terms of their employability, and also if they fail to learn a second language the command of which would later provide them with access to a larger labour market.

15 More specifically, the presence of ethnic conflict together with the amplifying effect of the liberalization of the rules of democratic participation (voting rights, communication rights, rights to form associations, movements and parties) will undermine both the legitimacy and the governance capacity of post-Communist states and thus destabilize them. Cf. Kolarova 1992.

16 As, for example, Hobsbawm (1972: 399) argues: 'Nationalist movements tended to take root first in areas (and perhaps strata) for whom modernization was sufficiently present to present problems but not sufficiently advanced to offer solutions.'

17 All East European Communist regimes are post-war creations. But while most of them were created through military force as a consequence of the Second World War, there are the two cases of the Soviet Union (after the First World War) and Yugoslavia (after the Second World War) where the Communist takeover of power was an endogenous phenomenon. In both the revolution was accomplished through the effective and self-imposed repression of ethnic divisions and conflicts in the name of a Communist-ruled federal republic (replacing, in the case of Russia, a pre-existing multi-ethnic empire). It is worth noting that it is precisely these two countries which have become the scene of the most vehement and violent ethnic conflicts following the demise of Communism. This can be interpreted as being based on the notion that the former multi-ethnic unity in these states alone was unequivocally due to Communist rule, and hence must be abolished with its end. In all other post-Communist states the multi-ethnic composition of their populations was inherited from pre-Communist times, and the impulse to undo it with the demise of Communism is therefore weaker.

18 'Historians are to nationalism what poppy-growers in Pakistan are to heroin-addicts: we supply the essential raw material for the market' (Hobsbawm 1992: 23). A comparable role is performed by linguists and philologists and literary intellectuals who both explore and codify the 'national heritage' and standardize the national language (cf. Anderson 1983: 46ff, 72ff).

19 According to a report in *Der Spiegel*, no. 7 (1992), 161, a team of historians at the Ukraine Academy of Sciences is busy discovering and reinterpreting the 'Ukraine philosophy of the sixth to ninth centuries' in order to establish the roots and to document the traces of a new Ukraine identity in the distant past.

20 In Bulgaria 'there is a lot of evidence that the communist party organizational structures and resources were used to mobilize nationalistic rallies' in order to 'prevent the consolidation of the emerging oppositional organization in a grand anti-communist coalition' (Kolarova 1992: 7; cf. Troebst 1992).

21 And probably rightly so in the 'national Communist' cases of Albania, Romania and Yugoslavia.

22 Leslie Green (1982) has developed an interesting model of rational nationalist voting behaviour. Voting is an act of investment (aiming at uncertain future material returns which tend to be unequally distributed), as well as an act of consumption (aiming at certain present immaterial, equally distributed express benefits of symbolic self-identification of the voters). Using this model, we may hypothesize that under conditions of economic turbulence and a 'new' party system, both of which do not allow for rational political investment decisions, and given the voters' lack of practice and experience with political investment decisions and their fear of inequality, voters rationally tend to attach greater weight to the consumption than to the investment aspect of voting. Furthermore, responding to this disposition of the voters, parties would equally rationally rely on supplying the strongest conceivable express benefit to voters by 'offering ethnic nationalism to the voters as a consumption good' (Green 1982: 239).

23 Prazauskas (1991: 587) claims that within the former Soviet Union ethnic groups that enjoy union republic status more often dissociate themselves

from nascent ethno-national movements than those who do not have some equivalent of a 'state'. Thus ethnicity appears to be negatively correlated with constituted nationhood.

24 Linden (1991: 33) argues that 'the appeal of nationalism is partly residual; that is, the result of the failure of other ideas or ideals to galvanize popular support, energize strong feelings of loyalty, or create effective and attractive institutions'.

25 Following the logic that Bulgarians apply to their Turkish minority: 'After what we have done to them, we'll be devastatingly punished unless we continue doing it to them.' This is the logic of political nihilism, the classic example of which is a statement Hitler made five days before the German attack on the Soviet Union on 16 June 1941: 'Whether just or unjust, we must be victorious. That is the only way. And it is right, moral and necessary. And once we have been victorious, who will ask us about our methods? As it is, we have so much on our record that we must be victorious; for otherwise our entire people, we as its leaders first ... will simply be erased. So let's get on with it!' (Fröhlich 1987: 696).

26 'Perverse' at least as measured by the ordinary notion of market exchange, where some positive service is exchanged for positive payment.

27 The preference of politicians to be 'a big fish in a small pond' can be helped through ethnification. This is sometimes even what voters suspect to be the case. As was demonstrated in a 1992 survey, 61 per cent of the Czechs and even 65 per cent of the Slovaks 'suspect the motives of their politicians and agree that they are only using the question of nationalism for their own purposes' (Deis 1992: 12).

28 These ethnicity-based 'group profits' must be distinguished from the costs of granting rights to ethnic minorities, such as the costs of having forms and signs printed in two languages or installing interpreting equipment in courts. From the point of view of the majority 'our' costs and 'their' profits add up to a strong objection.

29 'The landscape of civil society is very flat ... In all post-totalitarian polities the relative flatness of the landscape of civil society has created problems for politicians, because it is hard to represent amorphous groups ... In the context of post-totalitarianism's flattened landscape the easiest hopes and grievances for politicians to mobilize relate to ethnicity' (Linz and Stepan 1992: 136).

30 'In a social situation where the old regime was collapsing ... the members of the non-dominant ethnic group would see the community of language and culture as the ultimate certainty, the unambiguously demonstrable value. Today, as the system of planned economy and social security breaks down ... language acts as a substitute for factors of integration in a disintegrating society. When society fails, the nation appears as the ultimate guarantee' (Miroslav Hroch, as quoted in Hobsbawm 1992: 25).

31 If the three modes in which political interests are pursued can be described as 'having', 'wishing' and 'being', it is probably easiest to compromise on material issues and most difficult in the case of identity issues ('being'). In the latter case the smallest concession, if it affects aspects of the 'identity' of individuals, is tantamount to total loss, while the very divisibility of material possessions makes it easy and rational for people to sacrifice some of their property in order to keep the rest. 'Wishing', or the pursuit of normative goals, principles and values, appears to occupy an intermediate position in this respect.

32 Schöpflin (1991b: 61) gives the following illustration: 'If minority language schools are set up, what should the language of instruction be and for which subjects? Should the history of the minority be the only history taught or should the history of the majority be taught as well? And in what language? How much teaching time should be allocated to the majority language and what should be done with technical subjects? Should these be summarized in the majority language? (If not, members of the minority will have their mobility and hence their life opportunities severely curtailed.)' It is in the nature of all of these questions that they do not allow for a quantitative compromise, and that any concession encourages further demands. Cf. also Brzezinski 1989: 10.

33 Even if the right were granted and a referendum held, the decision emerging from it would not necessarily be recognized as binding, particularly if the margin of the majority were narrow. For people feeling very strongly about either side of the issue are likely to resort to the counterfactual argument that the empirical outcome of the referendum must not be taken as binding as voters have been deceived, manipulated, bribed or discouraged from participating in the referendum, or simply corrupted by the experience of the status quo. Kirschbaum (1992: 13) argues that the experience of federal 'Czechoslovakism' imposed by the Communist regime may have corrupted the national consciousness of the younger generation. At the same time he claims: 'It is clear that the Slovaks do not accept the Czechoslovak proposition. The Czechs must come to understand that they too have to give it up.'

34 The *locus classicus* of this logical loop is Fraenkel ([1932] 1968: 102): 'If the current Reichstag were capable of undertaking a reform of the constitution, then such a reform would not be needed. The very impossibility of bringing about a constitutional reform via parliamentary means demonstrates its necessity.'

35 In view of this dual cooperation problem the analogy of 'therapeutic intervention', as proposed by Senghaas (1992: 116–38), is clearly misleading: the situation cannot be equated to the relationship between patient and therapist as there is more than one 'therapist' involved.

36 Compared with the interwar period, it is doubtless right to highlight as an important difference 'the relative absence of territorial claims in the region' (Linden 1991: 34), or to state that 'there are no external predators now, such as Fascist Italy, Nazi Germany, and eventually Soviet Russia' (Brown 1991: 37). But these differences do not necessarily prevent paranoic fantasies and scenarios of international war or national economic dependency, which concern both the bellicose desires of neighbouring East European countries and predatory ambitions of Germany and other West European states, from spreading in the region. At least the official discourse of the Serbian leadership seemed to rely quite heavily on such interpretations of current realities.

37 The sequence of demands typically runs as follows: from the right to use the language in public to the right of primary and secondary school students to be taught the language outside the state school system, to the right to have language instruction included in the regular curriculum, to the right to be taught in the minority language, to the right of having minority language teachers trained at the tertiary level and books and programmes published by publishing houses and (state-operated) electronic media, to the right to bilingualism in courts (as opposed to the right to be

represented in court through an interpreter), the local administration and regional parliaments (cf. Engelbrekt 1991: 3; Troebst 1992). As there is no obvious stopping point within this sequence, rational majority politicians may be determined from the beginning to stay away from this slippery slope and to resist even the smallest of concessions (as the Bulgarian legislature, which is dominated by the Bulgarian Socialist Party, did in a reversal of policy on 1 October 1991, shortly before the elections) – with which decision they are only all the more likely to incite ethnic conflict rather than putting it to rest.

Chapter 5 Disqualification, Retribution, Restitution: Dilemmas of Justice in Post-Communist Transitions

1 Elster offers the following radical plea: 'Because nobody is innocent, nobody should be put on trial. Because everybody suffered, nobody should be compensated ... One might imagine a public autodafé of the pre-communist property records as well as of the archives of the security police and those of the communist party. Something like this would be my own ideal preference' (1992b: 17, 3). The question is whether such a sweeping disregard for matters of degree will be acceptable to masses and elites of post-Communist societies, and to sufferers and dissidents of the old regime.
2 The Nuremberg Trials come to mind as a potential model, though misleading in the case of East European transitions. A more fitting example are the events in Romania of Christmas 1989, ending with the televised execution of Ceauşescu.
3 A moving and compelling example is Kukutz and Havemann 1990.
4 That is to say, there is not the remote probability that someone is going to rebuild the Berlin Wall or order people to be shot who wish to escape across it. And everyone agrees on this and welcomes it. Hence there is no need for either deterrence or reminders.
5 This type of argument, applied to the war and genocidal crimes of the German Nazi regime, has been made by Lübbe (1983) in an essay that became one of the catalysts of the German *Historikerstreit*.
6 In the Polish debate on how to deal juridically with the past, the proponents of a 'thick line' approach seem to keep the upper hand. The 'thick line' means that 'we should not too intensively investigate our recent history in order to avoid blind vengeance, which may lead to another tragedy' (Falandysz 1991: 30). This attitude also governed Spanish post-1975 policies, in which a return of the horrors of the Civil War was feared more than anything else (Rovan 1992). Where horrors of civil war or martial law are both vividly remembered and their return cannot be categorically excluded as a possibility, the general approach adopted towards past wrongdoing seems to be more lenient than in countries, such as Germany, where neither of these conditions prevails.
7 This is at least as hard as is the other, prospective case of justice, namely the more often debated case of the rights of future generations.
8 Such an analysis would have to include, in addition to post-Communist regimes, at least the following groups of cases: post-fascist democracies (West Germany, Japan, Italy), Quislings and Vichy-type collaborationist

regimes and post-authoritarian democracies in Latin America and Southern Europe. I shall limit myself to occasional references to these other cases.

9 There is a clear interaction between the two factors just discussed, namely practice (or governing capacity) and theory (or historically conditioned awareness of the problem). This interaction is illustrated in many East European countries. As one can hear Russian intellectuals in Moscow argue: 'As we do not have a hope of doing anything about the personnel of the old regime except for eliminating the very top strata, it is not worth thinking about what we *would* do if we *could*.'

10 I mean this in the same way as it was meant by Robert Michels, who, in his book *Political Parties*, set out to prove his 'iron law of oligarchy' and selected working-class organization as the case to examine because, or so he thought, if the hypothesis was confirmed there, it was valid everywhere.

11 Below I will come back to the problem associated with crediting the former GDR with the quality of a *Rechtsstaat* and its implication of executing the norms of criminal law as general norms.

12 I owe this tripartite distinction of approaches to an oral communication with Jon Elster.

13 An example of how the means of criminal justice can help to compensate victims directly (other than through the psychological benefit of seeing one's oppressor being punished) would consist in the perpetrators being fined and the revenue from the fine, in cash or kind, being destined for the victim. Another example is the formal repetition of a trial in which the defendant had been sentenced by the old regime. If she or he is found not guilty by the new trial, the defendant will enjoy the 'positive sanction' of being rehabilitated, as well as perhaps compensated in cash in proportion to the length of the term to which he or she had been illegally sentenced.

14 The reader should be warned that, throughout this chapter, I shall remain at the level of a qualitative empirical analysis of normative argumentation. Formal legal rules and normative arguments are being considered, not the quantitative frequency with which they are being applied or employed. Thus the legal norms that have been adopted, the range of alternatives from which they have been chosen, the juridical practices of their application and the normative reasoning behind them, as well as objections raised against them, will be reviewed. As a consequence a further warning is required. Given the recentness of the discourse under review, most of the (German) materials are on the one hand journalistic accounts, opinions published by intellectuals or statements by politicians and legislators, or on the other legal norms; a philosophical, historical or social science scholarly literature (apart from some technical-legal contributions and classical treatises such as Kirchheimer [1961: ch. 8]) on the matters I am concerned with is still largely missing.

15 European Convention for the Protection of Human Rights and Fundamental Freedom of 4 November 1950, article 7, section 2. Extensive reliance on such bases for criminal prosecution would soon begin to discredit the new regime by making it vulnerable to the charge of 'Stalinist methods of de-Stalinization' and of violating Havel's dictum 'We are not like them!' It is noteworthy in this context that the Federal Republic of Germany, when ratifying this convention on 5 December 1952, did so under the stated proviso that article 103, section 2, of the Basic Law (which

requires punishability to be stated in positive law valid at the time of commission) limits the extent to which the above stipulation can apply.

16 For example, tenured professors and other state employees who were also party activists and/or are working in 'ideologically sensitive' subject areas must undergo, in spite of their being tenured, a renewed examination of their professional competence.

17 'Stasi' is the popular short term for 'Staatssicherheitsdienst' (State Security Service), which was a large-scale political police apparatus for domestic surveillance run by the GDR Ministry of State Security. For an analysis of its structure and operation, cf. Ulrich and Schröter 1991. Equivalent organizations existed in all other Comecon countries.

18 In the case of restitution its costs may be borne not by 'society as a whole', but by specific groups and individuals who may feel victimized, such as tenants of residential houses or employees who lose their jobs. In the cases of retribution and disqualification the revelation of acts that have been committed by agents of the old regime against ordinary citizens may give rise to outbursts of hatred and despair, leading to either unlawful acts of private revenge or numerous and lasting psychological disturbances on the part of victims. They may also lead to the (alleged or actual) perpetrators being overwhelmed by feelings of guilt, shame, fear or alienation so intense that some of them have committed suicide, most conspicuously Gerhard Riege, a member of the German Bundestag, after having been exposed as a Stasi informer (February 1992). Both of these types of secondary consequences affecting victims (revenge and despair) are being anticipated in the German debates of the 1990s, in which it has also been proposed that psychotherapeutic services be made available to victims to help them to come to terms with their emotional shock. Such services are, of course, quite useless with regard to another category of disturbances likely to emerge as secondary consequences of retribution. These consist of the opportunities for blackmail, denunciation and strategic accusation which are created as a by-product of retribution procedures and which certainly have the potential of poisoning civic and political life for many years.

19 To call for extreme and bluntly illiberal sanctions against leaders of the old regime for the sake of thereby exposing liberals and leftists within the new regime for their allegedly insufficient determination to condemn the old regime is a game, widely being played in East Central Europe, that is motivated by an undeclared 'third-order effect'.

20 'The purge has been most forcefully denounced by those who were the boldest dissidents under Communism' (*New York Times*, 12 April 1992). An exception to this rule is the German case, where former GDR dissidents are consistently to be found among the most vehement advocates of harsh measures against supporters of the old regime. This may have to do with the fact that, only in the German case, it was not the strength of the voice of the opposition, but the suddenly available exit option of the mass of the population that caused the breakdown of the old regime, and further with the fact that the task of building a new regime fell not to the opposition, but to the West German government. Deprived of a past and a future role, many opposition activists seem to indulge in sterile resentment against their former oppressors.

21 This act is basically a set of legal rules regulating the lawful flow of information on Stasi activities and files. It also established a federal agency that

serves as a special archive in that it is granted the monopoly of legal possession and use of the files, and the act specifies to whom the information contained in the files can or must be made available – without, however, specifying the consequences that may result from the information that is being made available, thus leaving the actual disqualification effect contingent upon someone else's discretion.

22 The *Einigungsvertrag*, together with the supplementary documents that are part of it, is an extremely complex legal document 526 printed pages long, covering the entire substantive range of the legal order that was to become effective on the territory of the former GDR. In order to avoid lengthy references to its chapters, sections, subsections and so on, I quote from the most easily available publication of the *Einigungsvertrag* in book format by page number.

23 The substance of the Lustration Act can best be understood as a complex exclusion rule which follows the logic 'x only if not y'. On its x-axis, specified in article 1, it represents offices in the state sector that are to be filled in accordance with 'additional prerequisites' (meaning additional to a person's being elected, appointed or assigned); these offices range from the presidency to the position of head of a local branch of the State Bank. On its y-axis, specified in articles 2 and 3 of the law, it lists positions and functions which, if held or performed by an applicant, candidate or nominee for any of the x-positions in the period between 1948 and 1989, will automatically disqualify him or her from occupying that position. A certificate documenting that the person in question has not previously occupied any y-position is issued upon request by the Ministry of the Interior (article 4).

24 A rather trivial example is the withdrawal of privileges attached to medals   and   awards   distributed   by   the   GDR   government (*Einigungsvertrag*: 85).

25 The popular German neologism is *Warteschleife*, which evokes the idea of an aeroplane circling before being permitted to land.

26 Again the German case exhibits some exceptional features. Chapter XIX, section III of supplement I of the Unity Treaty provides an ingenious mix of 'political' and 'technical' justifications for disqualification. While the Czech Lustration Act declares a clear preference for openly political criteria for disqualification (with indispensability for reasons of national security being the only criterion for non-disqualification), the German counterpart relies primarily on technical incompetence (471) and assigns a supplementary role to the unacceptability of a public sector worker because of his or her previous political acts. At the same time the net effect of technical disqualification in the German case may well be as great as or even greater than that of the predominant use of political criteria in other countries, given that the skills of whole categories of occupations and professions (law, public administration, humanities) are largely rendered obsolete in the course of the fundamental institutional reconstruction that the polity and society of the former GDR have been undergoing. As German authorities can therefore rely to a large extent on the 'technical' section (4) of the above law and operate through 'ordentliche Kündigung', the use of the more controversial 'political' disqualification rules of section (5) ('ausserordentliche Kündigung') is often dispensable.

27 Or *abgewickelt*, another neologism as far as labour relations are concerned.

28 The argument has been put forward that it is unfair to apply the competence test to East German professors alone, and that either the West
German professors should have been tested as well or no test should have
been conducted.

29 This effect applies, among many other things, to academic life. Disciplines
such as law, economics, philosophy, sociology, history and political science
were kept under strict ideological and partly also quantitative constraints
by the old regime, and recruitment for teaching and research positions in
these disciplines followed those constraints. The upshot is that, in the discipline of sociology for example, the percentage of East German scholars
who have applied for newly created professorial positions (or re-applied
for their own former ones) is less than 5 per cent, with the prospect of success being even smaller. For younger West German scholars this means a
gold-rush for social science careers in the new East German *Länder*. The
same applies to judges, lawyers, managers, administrators and politicians,
many of whom are called upon for their services in a post-retirement
career. In other Central and East European countries such extra manpower
pools are largely unavailable. Even the Czechoslovak Lustration Act, generally considered a very harsh scheme for categorical dismissals, therefore
makes allowance for keeping irreplaceable military and security staff
employed in case their dismissal 'should interfere with an important security interest of the State' (article 3, section 2).

30 It is this eventuality that the authors of the Lustration Act seem to have
had in mind when making the further allowance that disqualification
should be suspended 'if the purpose of the Law should be counteracted
thereby' (ibid.).

31 This holds true with one interesting exception. The *Einigungsvertrag* (p. 9)
stipulates that those pieces of information obtained by the Communist
security apparatus through monitoring the mail and telephone conversa-
tions of citizens that would also have been legally available under the law
constraining the freedom of speech guaranteed by the West German Basic
Law may in fact be further used for purposes of criminal prosecution of
those who have been victims of such observation.

32 Note that the procedural problems discussed in the following come in
addition to the substantive doubt concerning the objectionable nature of
the activities of informers in general. To be sure, the passing of information
to the authorities that may harm the people about whom this information
has been gathered must often be considered morally and politically objectionable. But that does not make them punishable through disqualification.
As one of the more liberal-minded civil rights activists in the former GDR
has remarked: 'The secret passing on of information pertaining to the private sphere of others is not, by itself, punishable; if it were, all private
detectives and much private gossip would have to be prosecuted' (Richard
Schröder, *Frankfurter Allgemeine Zeitung*, 6 December 1991, 33).

33 Perhaps informal ways of carrying out 'justice' are even to be preferred to
formal criminal ones. Paraphrasing Talleyrand, Joseph Rovan (1992) has
suggested that after a dictatorship has come to its end 'purges should be
short and bloody'.

34 In the mid-1990s Romania, in spite or because of its use of this extreme
form of sanctioning, is clearly the case among all Central East European
countries that has done least to overcome the Communist regime and its
power structures.

35 Instead of being punished the defendant 'would only suffer the ignominy of the compulsory publicity given to the delinquencies through television and the press' (Bence 1991: 7). Similar ideas and proposals have been forwarded in Germany under the title of 'Forum' or 'Tribunal' (cf. Schönherr 1992), and the Bundestag has created an investigative commission which is charged with the task of writing a comprehensive report on the nature and operations of the East German regime and its forty-year history. If the state does not claim its right to punish, this could also be due to the fear of revenge and retaliation on the part of those to be punished or their supporters. This was the situation with military leaders in Argentina under the presidency of Alfonsin in the mid-eighties. A way out of this dilemma may be formal 'acknowledgement' of guilt combined with guaranteed impunity. Another one, adopted in Chile, is to expose the crimes without prosecuting or even naming the perpetrators.

36 The problem with the two preceding types of justification is that it is by no means self-evident that the Communist states had the intention – or in fact the option – of letting their social, political and economic life be strictly governed by standards of 'civilization' or 'rule of law', even if they had nominally accepted those standards as binding. They simply lacked an independent court system that would have been able to enforce those standards where they had been violated by 'higher' political purposes. These were societies not only with 'soft budget constraints', but also with 'soft legal constraints'. They were not rule-of-law states, but, according to their own understanding and aspiration, 'justice states' governed by substantive principles rather than legal formalisms. Any perpetrator of acts declared desirable or permitted by the political authorities could thus believe that the law nominally applying to and prohibiting those acts would be selectively invalidated and not enforced against him or her. It was therefore not an effectively 'valid' norm, and consequently it cannot be retroactively interpreted and enforced as such today – if the rule-of-law doctrine is to remain consistent. After all, the GDR has been rightly denounced as failing to live up to rule-of-law standards. 'Socialist legality' exempted many acts from prosecution as it denied the right to claim constitutionally guaranteed freedoms in court; had it not, the socialist state would have been forced to give itself up, for example by permitting free travel across borders. The 'law' was that the law would not apply (cf. Falandysz 1991: 27). It is plainly contrary to the rule-of-law doctrine to ignore this fact *post mortem* (cf. Jakobs 1992 for a compelling legal-technical statement to this effect).

37 An impression of this kind was created when Harry Tisch, the chief of the East German Trade Union Federation and long-term member of the nomenklatura, was sentenced for using union funds to rebuild his weekend house.

38 For instance, questions of such importance as who exactly ordered the results of the local elections held in the GDR in the spring of 1989 to be falsified on a massive scale, whether East German tanks entered the territory of the CSR on the occasion of the Warsaw Pact invasion of that country in August 1968, or who authorized the shoot-to-kill command to border guards, have still not been resolved for certain.

39 This defence was used by the former Czechoslovakian minister of the interior, Frantisek Kincl, in his January 1992 trial (*Frankfurter Allgemeine Zeitung*, 18 January 1992).

40 In a decision of October 1991 the Hungarian Constitutional Court denied the constitutional possibility of 'reviving' a limitation that has already passed, even if prosecution was not initiated while it was still valid. Given this ruling, a parliamentary vote, passed on 4 November 1991, in which the legislature lifted the statute of limitation was unconstitutional.

41 In the German case a group of states, led by Thuringia, introduced a draft legislation opening this option into the *Bundesrat* in January 1992 (*Frankfurter Allgemeine Zeitung*, 2 January 1992), the unsettled legal question being whether or not such procedural retroactivity is permissible under the Basic Law. An important difference between the decision of the German Bundestag to suspend the statute of limitation for murder and the suspension proposed to the Hungarian parliament was that in the former case (b) was slightly to the left of (d), whereas in the Hungarian case it was to the right as the statute of limitation had already been exhausted at the point the proposal was made.

42 Advisers to President Wałesa claimed that his main concern was with 'victim-oriented' rather than 'perpetrator-oriented' justice, and with relegating judgements about the past to the moral rather than the juridical domain (cf. Elster 1992b: 5).

Chapter 6 The Morality of Restitution: Reflections on Some Normative Questions Raised by the Transition to a Private Economy

1 For a review and critique of 'third forms', see Kornai 1990.

2 To illustrate: if it is held to be the duty of the international community to come to the military assistance of countries that are victims of foreign aggression, such a duty cannot apply only to countries that happen to be in control of strategic resources such as oil.

3 It is this danger which has led Luhmann to call for an *Ethikfolgenethik*.

4 Such reflexive or meta-rules may come in a procedural or a substantive version. 'Deliberation', 'arguing' and 'public debate' are examples of the former, while a rule such as 'abortion is prohibited unless the life of the mother is in danger' is an example of the latter.

5 The logic of such fallacious moral arguments can be compared to that of Freud's famous 'kettle' story. He relates 'the story of the borrowed kettle, which was returned with a hole in it. Upon inquiry, the borrower explained that, first of all, he hadn't borrowed any kettle, secondly, it already had holes in when he borrowed it, and thirdly, he had returned it free of holes and undamaged' (*Der Witz*, Frankfurt: Fischer, 1958, 167).

6 To illustrate: in a decision on abortion regulation in 1993 the German Constitutional Court declared it unconstitutional for abortion, even if permissible under the law, to be paid for through the public health insurance system. This decision was welcomed with a characteristic mixture of justifications by a conservative–liberal coalition of supporters of a stricter regulation of abortion. First, it is argued that it is the duty of the state to refrain from forcing participants in a mandatory insurance (such as the German Public Health Insurance GKV) to contribute to the financing of abortion services even though they may object to abortions on moral

grounds. It is also argued that making abortion more expensive will have the desirable consequence of operating as an incentive for more careful birth control practices. This is a clear case where two arguments are less effective than one in moral terms, as each argument can easily be shown to be deficient. If the first were to be taken seriously, pacifists should also not be forced to pay for the military apparatus. If the second were to make sense, a highly implausible empirical relation between the financial costs of abortion and the practice of birth control would have to be established.

7 Additional complications arise if the regime change goes hand in hand with the dissolution of the state, as in the former Soviet Union. This tends to further weaken the bonds between the 'old' and the 'new' regime since the former is no longer necessarily to be considered the legal predecessor of the latter.

8 This problem is, however, reduced by the fact that the bulk of the property to be restored was state-owned and no clear-cut owner exists (cf. Preuss 1993a), so no suffering from expropriation was experienced by anyone. On the other hand property relations under state socialism may now undergo a retrospective reinterpretation as workers may now begin to feel deprived of their status of former collective proprietors of the jobs that are now put into jeopardy by privatization and liberalization.

9 The restitution legislation in most East European countries seems to have been inspired by some moral intuition such as 'the more recent the injustice, the more urgent the need for redress'. In Czechoslovakia, to take an example, the first law, no. 403/1990, provided for the return of or compensation for property nationalized during the latest wave of nationalization (beginning in 1955), and only a year later law 87/1991 extended the scope backwards until 1948.

10 For some supplementary arguments as to why rectification entitlements tend to weaken over time, see Morris 1984; Sher 1981.

11 This is not to deny the existence of political organizations, such as the German associations of people expelled from the Czech Lands and other territories occupied by German troops during the Second World War (*Vertriebenenverbände*), which are specialized in nourishing feelings of deprivation as well as hopes of a future restitution. Yet it appears uncertain to what extent such organizations can manage to halt the operation of individual adjustment mechanisms in the longer run, at least in the absence of some official endorsement by governments and governing parties.

12 At first sight a striking similarity exists between the restitution of confiscated property and the acknowledgement of the foreign debt accumulated under the old regime. In both cases the post-Communist government tries to build up a certain reputation by assuming responsibility for the actions of its predecessor. Yet there is a decisive difference. Whereas the 'old' creditors are more or less identical with the possible 'new' ones and are hence needed for future lending, the progress of privatization does not critically depend on the previous owners or their heirs. Moreover, the smaller number of creditors makes it easier to overcome collective action problems. It thus comes as no surprise that the leverage of foreign creditors is considerably greater than the leverage of the dispossessed previous owners.

13 In addition, restitution may aim at a domestic 're-education' effect intended to teach the population at large the sacredness of property titles.

14 Note that there is a certain built-in potential for escalation if strategies are adopted for dramatic effect. If I suspect that you do what you do primarily in order to impress me, I fail to be impressed. In order to continue to impress me you will have to engage in ever more extreme – and costly – efforts. This game will become even more dynamic as several bodies (such as the governments of post-Communist countries) compete for the favourable attention of agencies (such as West European governments or banks) on which both sides know they depend. The logic of this game will soon lead bodies to resort to plainly irrational overdoses, following a rule such as 'the more I hurt myself, the more you will be impressed, the more I serve my interests'.

15 Neuber (1992: 21f) argues that large parts of the 'first generation' of reformers have been interested less in future political careers than in securing a critical mass of reforms in order to bind their anticipated populist successors.

16 Mechanisms such as the ones just discussed may also help to account for the often shrill, fundamentalist and 'Thatcherite' tone of 'ideological overshooting' that seems to prevail in much of the East European economic policy debates.

17 At this point the issues of economic reform and ethnic nation building intersect. A hidden agenda in defining entitlements to restitution may be to keep 'foreigners' (Jews, Germans, ex-patriates) out. Such an agenda would emphasize the semantic continuity of 'my' and 'our' property, of land as 'property' and as 'country', or of 'fences' and 'borders'.

18 An interesting experiment would be to imagine the course of the post-Communist Czechoslovak government if the expropriations and expulsion of the Sudeten Germans had happened under the Communist government.

19 Later amendments of the Civil Code have brought inheritance provisions into line.

20 It must be admitted that the question of what individuals belonging to the political elite can reasonably be expected to know (or do know but choose to ignore) is virtually unresearchable. Likewise, it may appear pointless to moralize about the requisite analytical effort a policy-maker would have to engage in in order to be accepted as serious and respectable. For the sake of the present argument, it is simply assumed that under any given condition there is a critical threshold of ignorance (or, still worse, ignorance about the depth of one's own ignorance) beyond which action becomes morally blameworthy.

21 In this respect Germany is an exception as compensation payments are to be largely financed by a levy on the restored property itself (*Vermögensabgabe*). Yet this system works only because the beneficiaries of restitution are, as a rule, West German residents.

22 In a more general context Munzer (1990: 428) speaks of the 'moral hazard costs' of compensation.

23 It must be admitted that this is a general problem of privatization under post-Communism, as argued in chapter 3. Yet the political nature of privatization is particularly visible in the case of restitution.

Chapter 7 A 'Special Path' of Transformation? The German 'Accession Territory' Compared with its East European Neighbours

1 The same analytical frame of course underlies basic conceptual tripartite distinctions such as that of market/state/community or interest/institution/identity. To adopt the terminology of pragmatism, one could speak here of the difference between the 'advantageous', the 'just' and the 'good'.

2 Approaches that compare the former GDR and the other Comecon countries are rare. The social scientists in East European countries would seem, for all their decidedly comparative studies, to regard the former GDR after 1989 as such a remote and favoured special case that it purportedly does not offer much in the way of instruction for the theory and politics of transformation in their own countries. And, conversely, scholarship (and also the politics of science) in the Federal Republic of Germany (and above all in East Germany) is dedicating itself in quite exclusive and somewhat provincial manner to studying the social and political change in the former GDR and thus neglecting a broader comparison at the level of Eastern Europe as a whole, such as has long since been the practice above all in the United States. Thus the uniqueness of the GDR is recognized predominantly by not including it in comparative studies and thereby at the same time veiling it in silence. Exceptions are the studies by Batt (1991a), Bruszt (1992), Stark (1992b) and Wiesenthal (1992). Where the GDR is included in comparative investigations, one of two perspectives predominates: a comparison of the systems in the FRG and the GDR or a comparison of the respective profiles of Nazi and late Stalinist 'totalitarianism'. Moreover, it would seem that even while it still existed the GDR was very poorly linked to the transnational networks of research in the social sciences in the Comecon countries, and little has changed in this regard since the Wall came down. At least in Hungary and Poland, and probably in Bulgaria too, the methodological level in the social sciences and the variety of topics addressed – never mind the state of publications, the volume of training, the opportunities to travel and make contacts and simply the linguistic access to the predominantly English-language international discourse in the social sciences – were better developed than in the GDR. For example, the Central European University, an ambitious project set up by George Soros, a Hungarian in exile in the United States, has institutes and contact offices in no fewer than fourteen post-Communist countries, but not in the former GDR.

3 This high degree of 'contingent' circumstances that led to the collapse of the state socialist regimes can be linked to the contingency of the circumstances under which this regime was established and kept alive by an external imperial power as a result of the war of aggression and the defeat of Hitler's Germany after 1945, unlike the situation in the Soviet Union itself after 1917 and in Yugoslavia after 1945.

4 This is probably why the Hungarians held the questionable notion of 'Central Europe' in such high regard: 'Geography is politics with other means ... To be Central European means not being East European Balkanites. It means better than the Russians, Rumanians, Bulgarians, or

Montenegrans. Central Europe became a program of distinguishing one-self from the ''barbarians'' ' (Miszlivetz 1991: 12).

5 This constitutes a new problem that the OECD countries, both individu-ally and collectively, must reflect on for the sake of their supranational totality: the ensemble of institutional inventions such as basic rights and mass participation, private property and market price formation need no longer be legitimated or fine-tuned as the result of evolution, the basic traits of which are ineluctable, just in the geographical area where it arose. Instead this ensemble must be re-erected at new sites character-ized by massive symptoms of post-Communist disorganization and overcome as a design problem facing national and international politics. The logical relation between 'the result of evolution' and the 'design problem' is the same as that between the tasks of caring for the forest and reforestation of an area on which there had previously never been forest. The project of 'cloning' capitalist democracy and planting sustain-able and 'related species' in the form of cuttings in foreign soil has already more or less failed once, namely in Latin America, under condi-tions that were culturally and politically less demanding. While the OECD countries have shown themselves able to globalize their mode of economic integration, namely trade, to date they have evidently not suc-ceeded in doing the same for their cultural and political-institutional form of integration.

6 This criterion excludes Albania, the Baltic states and the former Yugoslavian republics from consideration.

7 This criterion excludes the CIS states.

8 The break was already predestined to happen, given the repressive nature of both regimes, their condemnation of the Polish and Hungarian attempts at reform and of Gorbachev's policies, not to mention, in the case of the GDR, the open affirmation of the Tiananmen Square massacre on 4 June 1989. There was no willingness on the part of the party and state leader-ship to negotiate with the opposition, and nor would any member of the opposition have dared to propose such negotiations for fear of discredit-ing him- or herself.

9 In none of the other countries have laws been passed that are as far-reach-ing as the German law on documents held by the GDR State Security Service or the Czechoslovak Lustration Law.

10 The GDR and the CSR were, Batt (1991c: 377) avers, 'able to avoid open economic crisis, loss of control over basic macro-economic proportions, and exposure to the shocks transmitted from the world economy'.

11 Bruszt (1992: 65) writes: 'In Czechoslovakia and the former GDR, it was the lack of previous reforms that invited tabula rasa strategies, a fast departure from the old regimes.'

12 In this context the GDR differed from the CSR in that there was no equiva-lent there of the Charter 77 civil rights movement, let alone an equivalent of Poland's Solidarność or Hungary's reformist Communism.

13 We could equally well say that the GDR enjoyed comparatively favourable conditions (such as preferential loan and trade relations with the West) and was therefore in a position to buy its citizens' loyalty by providing affluence and security without reforms, whereas the Hungarian reformist Communists endeavoured to generate this 'political purchasing power' in the first place by means of economic reform. In Poland and Hungary the failure of these attempts at reform in the eighties led to polit-

ical disintegration and oppositional activities on a scale that hardly troubled the dreams of the GDR leadership right up to the very end (see Batt 1991c: 374–5).

14 As is well known, this difference had a decisive consequence: in September 1989 it was the Hungarian and Polish governments which expressly or factually reneged on their contractual obligations towards the GDR on the issue of 'camp-site' or 'embassy' refugees. By contrast, until the end of November the CSR upheld its duties in the Warsaw alliance (Pradetto 1991: 76). The CSR and the GDR were both characterized by the fact that the final phase of the collapse of the respective regimes was externally induced, namely by events in its socialist 'brother countries' Hungary and Poland, whose governments, unlike that in Prague, refused to declare the problem of the refugees in the embassies or camp-sites an 'inner-German' affair.

15 In quantitative terms domestic minorities formed no relevant potential for conflict in the two 'most homogeneous' countries in Eastern Europe, among other things because of the established and recognized minority rights they enjoyed. Of the 40 million inhabitants of Poland 95 per cent are both Polish and Roman Catholic, and 90 per cent of the 11 million Hungarians are Magyars, though the Catholic majority admittedly faces a strong Protestant minority.

16 In Bulgaria, and to an even greater extent in Romania, the change in regime was, historically speaking, much more a question of changes by the minute, with all the accompanying phenomena such as the spectacular case of arson in the Communist Party headquarters in Sofia and with the quasi-judicial, public execution of the president in Romania. It would be exciting, if too early as yet, to relate the stability and robustness of the results of the transformation process to the time involved; at least the Romanian example would appear to confirm the hypothesis of a positive correlation of the two variables. The seemingly paradoxical course taken by both countries stems from the fact that the extreme abruptness and at times violence of the change in regime did not lead to particularly far-reaching changes, but rather to meagre political and economic adjustment. To this extent we can speak here neither of a *transición pactada*, as most probably applies to the cases of Poland and Hungary, nor of a *tabula rasa*, as in the GDR and the CSR; instead, as the results of the first free elections in Bulgaria and Romania emphasized, there was a change of elite, but predominantly continuity as regards the system.

17 In Romania this was even true of the second free election, held on 26 September 1992, which at least led to President Iliescu being re-elected as president; the results of the second election in Bulgaria in October 1991 differed only slightly.

18 We cannot go into the elective affinities and correspondences as well as the possible causal relations between the above-mentioned features here; however, this would evidently offer social scientists a promising subject on which to form further hypotheses.

19 I wish to warn readers in advance that the argumentation here is admittedly focused on a goal, but is nevertheless motivated by three objections I have to my own approach: it progresses through hairpin bends and we are just entering the second bend.

20 In this context an attempt was made to replace the depleted 'anti-fascist' substitute legitimation with the strongly promoted image and reality of a

nation of top athletes and sportspersons. The GDR's sports elite functioned, as it were, as anabolic steroids for the nation; together with Cuba,
the GDR headed the world ranking for 'Olympic medals per head of population'.

21 In this respect the GDR can almost be compared with Bulgaria, the only
Eastern bloc country in which neither the elite nor the masses ever made
striking anti-Soviet statements.

22 It shared this feature with the FRG, which secured social integration predominantly via successes in economic and social policy.

23 Kocka (1990: 486) writes: 'On the whole, the internal opposition in the
GDR remained remarkably weak, much weaker than in the other countries, and that had to do with the in part enforced and in part voluntary
flow of real and potential dissidents into the Federal Republic, where they
were gladly received.'

24 The fact that the change in regime in the GDR was rendered irreversible
not by political action from above or below but by means of private emigration towards the outside (initially via Hungary and Prague, then
through the breached Wall) concurs with this (see Hirschman 1992).
Oppositional forces did not bring about the end of the GDR, they were
merely a short-lived accompanying factor.

25 As is well known, the migration of people from East to West Germany
triggered at least one of two problems, and caused both to a hitherto
unspecified extent: an overly great strain was placed on the West German
labour and housing market and there was a loss of human resources in the
East German economy.

26 In 1990 the immediate goal of West German policy, including that of the
trade unions, was to stop the flow of citizens out of East Germany into
West Germany. This was rational in the long term, because the migration
would make it seem as if East Germany had been 'restored to economic
health', whereas in the future the costs of reorganizing the economy there
would be all the higher. From the point of view of the trade unions, the
way to achieve this goal was to adjust wage levels swiftly; these are currently racing ahead of developments in productivity. This approach is
understandable, because the trade unions must be interested in ensuring
that East Germany does not become a long-term low-wage region that
repulses labour and attracts investors, or at least certain categories of
investor. The attempt to achieve this by adjusting wage levels is self-con-
tradictory, however, because any adjustment of wages over and above
productivity creates additional unemployment in East Germany, which
then sharply increases the propensity to migrate – and unemployment is
certainly a stronger reason for migrating than lower wages. These are
strategic paradoxes which do not arise in the other post-Communist countries, or at least only in a milder form, simply because the latter have legal
and cultural foreign borders.

27 The GDR and the FRG had, as it were, entered a symbiotic relationship of
mutual disposal of pollutants. The FRG stored its chemical waste in GDR
dumps and the GDR dumped its political 'waste' in the FRG.

28 The novelist Christoph Hein confirms this: 'Essentially the helpful proximity of the FRG was not helpful for the [GDR's] own development ... There
was no samizdat, there were simply West German publishers.'

29 As Friedbert Rüb pointed out to me, the most important criticism a GDR
citizen ever made of the GDR was notably a 'radical Communist'

appraisal of it which, quite unlike the approach of the Hungarian and Czech 'anti-politicians', took the regime at its word. I am thinking of Rudolf Bahro's *Die Alternative*.

30 Although this may run the risk of creating false associations, we could perhaps talk of the FRG having played the role for the GDR of a functional equivalent to the occupying forces which directed the post-war transformation in the FRG after the 1945 capitulation.

31 The election campaign in question was already managed from West Germany, with West German parties and promises made by West German politicians. This external conditioning of (procedurally flawless) democratic elections by means of attractive rewards offered and/or credible threats made by one state to influence the electoral behaviour of another pinpoints a problem for theories of democracy. The significance of the problem was highlighted a short time before then by the elections of 25 February 1990 in Nicaragua. *Mutatis mutandis*, what Batt (1991c: 386) writes of the GDR could equally apply to the 'election campaign' conducted from outside Nicaragua by the US government: 'The Federal Republic's governing party's ability to offer the East Germans the quickest, most sure route out of the existing morass of uncertainty determined the outcome of the election.'

32 After all, the presidents of Hungary, the CSFR, Poland and Bulgaria were all once prominent activists in the opposition and dissident movements – there is a spectacular dearth of parallels to this in the former GDR. There the few protagonists of the opposition were initially condescendingly accepted as 'lay persons' and soon forced out by Western 'personnel on loan'.

33 An excerpt from an interview with a mining deputy is revealing: 'In the past nobody in the plant could tell us what to do or throw us out. But today if you so much as mention the red socks worn by the management [their Communist past], then you are already accused of disturbing the peace.'

34 Wiesenthal (1992: 177) writes: 'Nowhere else was the political debate on the future of a post-socialist community so underdeveloped as in what was still the GDR.'

35 Here too many have spotted the continuity of the status quo ante, that is, of the autocratic paternalism of the old Communist Party regime.

36 The Treuhandanstalt is not duty-bound in its decisions on the tendered privatization of companies (or of operational sections it has spun off) to consider 'the best offer or some offer or other', as its tender advertisements would suggest. The statist and discretionary side to German privatization policy is also emphasized by the fact that the initial focus on managing the GDR's assets with a view to property rights, that is, the priority of re-privatization, has gradually shifted in favour of an orientation towards the function of property, or towards accelerating sluggish investment activity.

37 The questions are whether, to what extent, for what length of time and, above all, for what morally compelling reasons the West German providers of finance for East Germany should accept the burden placed on them on behalf of the 'acceding territory'. The burden takes the shape of prices, taxes, levies, contributions and interest payments; it will possibly soon also involve contracting wages and will thus impact on all citizens of West Germany. In respect of the moral reasons for tolerating this burden

the following negative arguments arise. It is hard to make the motive of 'national solidarity' plausible when others (countries, groups suffering hardship) need help even more urgently. Owing to article 23 of the German Basic Law, West German citizens had no opportunity to take these burdens upon themselves voluntarily by a collective declaration of intent, particularly as the political elites played down the scale involved by means of rhetoric. It is in the interests of East Germany itself that this burden be lessened, as any further increase would ruin the output of the West German economy to such an extent that its ability to shoulder a future burden left by unification would be sorely tried.

38 In East Germany, in particular in the states of Mecklenburg-Vorpommern and Saxony, the North–South divide in economic capability has already made itself felt, just as it is to be seen in West Germany, for example between Bremen and Baden-Württemberg.

39 The following appeared in the *Frankfurter Allgemeine Zeitung*: 'The state bureaucracy has currently all sorts of problems with stimulating the upturn in the East and would therefore like to get the planning and administrative procedures moving faster, by means of abrogating rules for a fixed period and for specifically delimited regions ... Essentially this involves curbing opportunities for objections and expanding the planners' muscle' (23 October 1992, 33).

40 In a similar vein, the rhetorical trope that the West Germans used after 1945 to describe the results of the Nazi period and the war was the 'zero hour'.

41 An interesting indication of this is the fact that for administrative reasons it is not possible to establish the number of migrants from the territory of the former GDR and the manner in which this number increased, even if such figures would not be unimportant in terms of population statistics.

42 This at least is the hypothesis of Grinberg and Levy, two Israeli sociologists, who orient themselves at least implicitly towards the example of the Palestinians 'becoming a nation' under Israeli occupation. They understand 'ethnification' to mean 'the conflictual relationship that develops between two unequal groups that prompts each side to 'discover' its cultural uniqueness *vis-à-vis* the other, even when the two share a common language, history, and national identity' (Grinberg and Levy 1992: 20).

43 On 8 March, 'International Women's Day', the official party line involved giving a high profile to the slogan 'Greetings and Thanks to Our Women'; such a use of the possessive pronoun, one that unmasks the actual self-understanding of those using it, would hardly have been conceivable even in the most provincial backwater in West Germany.

44 The following statement by Pradetto (1991: 92) can be considered the basic consensus among West European political elites, even if its practical consequences are far from clear: 'The acute economic and political state of emergency in these countries makes assistance and cooperation a necessity for any European policy, if the continent is not to disintegrate into economic and political opposites, into social animosity and nationalist feuds as in the past.'

45 As early as 1989 the EC initiated a cooperation programme for three East European countries, though its strange name, 'Poland, Hungary, Assistance for the Reconstruction of the Economy', was chosen in order to dampen the impact of this claim to hegemony: PHARE is the French for lighthouse.

46 Stark (1992a: 17–23) puts it this sharply, warning against a repetition of precisely that 'rationalist fallacy' which brought the Leninist regime to its knees. However, Stark overlooks the fact that what we have to date been able to regard as a strength of capitalist societies, namely that their development has been 'blind' and has involved decision-making that has been quite independent of other factors, has now become a weakness: its inability to break its own genetic code and to make it available to help the process of transformation in East Europe will expose it to the 'external effects' of the failure of this process. This weakness is at least an interpretation which one could characterize with an adage coined by the playwright Heiner Müller: 'There is no longer an alternative to capitalism; in fact, it no longer has an enemy, except for itself' (see also Pickel 1992).

47 In the mid-1990s our political elites are primarily interested in whether the outbreaks of violence prompted by a chauvinism of affluence in Rostock and elsewhere will damage 'Germany's reputation abroad'. They do not ask to what extent the bases for self-recognition of the second German republic and its moral-political aspirations within Germany have themselves possibly been just as dented. The vanishing point of this question is the fear that in the course of 'coping' defensively with the subsequent problems of the upheaval in Central and Eastern Europe, Germany's 'free democratic basic order' could be deformed in such a way that it would simply no longer be suitable as an object of 'constitutional patriotism'.

Chapter 8 Economic 'Hardware' and Institutional 'Software' in the Two German Transitions to Democracy: Comparing Post-1945 West Germany with Post-1989 East Germany

1 Note that the only two political holidays that were officially observed in the old Federal Republic were 17 June and 20 July, which celebrated the resistance to Communism and the resistance to the Nazi regime respectively.

2 'Since the [Allied] army authorities were concerned, first of all, with the need of getting the technical administrative machinery running again smoothly and as quickly as possible in order to ease the burdens of occupation and to prevent popular unrest and disease, political motives were generally subordinated to considerations of administrative efficiency in making new appointments' (Meyerhoff 1949: 199).

3 Compared with the short-lived and half-hearted denazification experience after 1945, the post-1989 purges of political, judicial, administrative, intellectual, managerial and professional elites were much more protracted and comprehensive, and political efforts to lift the statute of limitation even on minor wrongdoings of former officials are likely to extend this situation further into the future. The kind of benign neglect from which even ranking functionaries and economic leaders of the Nazi regime were to benefit after 1949 is not, as a rule, being offered to the staff of the Stasi and other agencies of the GDR, in spite of the vast differences in the quality of the criminal records of the two regimes (cf. chapter 5).

4 The striking absence of an association, political party or constitutional

agency that could claim to represent the whole of the former GDR and its interests in the post-1989 transformation is not hard to explain. First, the West German authors of the Unity Treaty, as well as the leadership of political parties and societal associations, did everything to annihilate representations of 'ex-GDR' identity and interests. But even in the absence of these 'unifying' pressures which have strongly discouraged the institutional preservation of GDR identities, it is hard to imagine how a reasonable representative agency of these identities and transformation-related interests could have been created, since GDR society was deeply divided as it emerged from state socialism. This is not just a division between winners and losers of unification, but also an obvious and deep division across the three major categories of losers, namely members and functionaries of the state apparatus and the ruling party, obsolete industrial workers and intellectuals and members of educated professional middle classes who formed the social and cultural base of oppositional movements and initiatives.

5   By any reasonable standard these funds exceeded the volume of the entire ERP aid (1,500 million dollars) by two orders of magnitude during the first three years after unification alone.

6   This 'anti-polarizing' emphasis is illustrated by the name that the Christian Democrats adopted ('union' instead of 'party') as well as by the principle of 'unitary' organization (*Einheitsgewerkschaft*) adopted by the trade unions. Cf. also the name of a new post-war intellectual periodical, *Die Sammlung*, invoking the notion of both reflection and convergence.

7   A psychological factor may have further assisted the transition, as well as the role played in it by the Allies in general and the Americans in particular. The fact that the victorious powers made an active and helpful commitment to rebuilding the country they had defeated came as something of a pleasant surprise to much of the German population and helped to build a great deal of moral credit for the Western powers and the values and ideals they represented. Much of the German population's prevailing perception of the occupation regime of the Western Allies (in sharp contrast to the perception of the Russians' activities in East Germany) may be captured by the formula: 'Although they certainly don't "owe" it to us, they are still willing to give it to us.' As a consequence of this perceived benevolence and generosity it appeared just prudent to submit to the decrees of the Allies. The reverse condition seems now to prevail in the post-1989 relations between East and West Germany. Here the formula would be 'Although they do owe it to us because they are compatriots and because we are their formerly much celebrated "brothers and sisters", they are still reluctant to share as much of their resources as we think we are rightfully entitled to.'

8   In a letter to President Truman, dated 12 August 1947, W. Averell Harriman suggested that 'the best reparations our Western Allies can obtain is the prompt recovery of Germany' (quoted in Maier and Hoffmann 1984: 31).

9   'Feeling that their predicament is not their fault but rather something imposed on them from outside, being socialized to the ethic of the paternalistic state, and retaining a sense that some of the bad old ideas are not really all that bad, they will find it more difficult to take advantage of their particular caesura' (Stokes 1991: 19).

Chapter 9 The Left after the West's Victory

1 The Cold War and the challenges created by the competition between the systems had a similarly innovative impact on other OECD countries. And the examples are not just limited to the first subsidizing of interstate highway construction in the USA, motivated by, among other things, military strategy, and the accelerated pace of expansion in education and science following the 'Sputnik shock'.

2 The 'comparative' legitimacy of the OECD world as a whole and of West Germany in particular was derived from both its higher economic efficiency and the moral and political qualities of a developed welfare and democratic constitutional state. Essentially, two diametrically opposed tacks can be taken when attempting to solve the legitimation problems of the West, an issue suddenly back on the agenda with the loss of a rival manifestly 'inferior' in both dimensions. On the one hand a solution can be sought via the challenging attempt to establish and redeem intrinsic and self-sufficient criteria for a political and economic order that are no longer based on an external reference point: in other words the claim would no longer be to be 'better' but to be 'good'. On the other the monopoly the Western model has in terms of the regulation of a social order could lead to the cynical practice of completely renouncing criteria of the 'good': as there is no enemy any longer, any factual state in the world is considered the best possible world.

3 In a conversation with me Elemér Hankiss, director of Hungarian TV, described the conflicts that prevail in that company as a 'daily civil war' – and, given the details he recounted, he was by no means exaggerating.

References

Abelshauser, Werner, 1993: 'Erhards Illusion', *Die Zeit*, no. 12, 19 March.

Abromeit, Heidrun, 1992: 'Zum Für und Wider einer Ost-Partei', *Gegenwartskunde*, 41 (4), 437–48.

Ackerman, Bruce A., 1977: *Private Property and the Constitution*, New Haven/London: Yale University Press.

Ackerman, Bruce A., 1992: *The Future of Liberal Revolution*, New Haven/London: Yale University Press.

Almond, Gabriel, and Sidney Verba, 1963: *The Civic Culture: Political Attitudes and Democracy in Five Nations*, Princeton: Princeton University Press.

Anderson, Benedict, 1983: *Imagined Communities: Reflections on the Origin and Spread of Nationalism*, London: Verso.

Badura, Peter, 1990: *Der Verfassungsauftrag der Eigentumsgarantie im wiederver-einigten Deutschland'*, *Deutsches Verwaltungsblatt*, 105 (23), 1256–63.

Bartlett, David, 1992: 'The Political Economy of Privatization: Property Reform and Democracy in Hungary', *East European Politics and Societies*, 6 (1), 73–118.

Bates, Robert H., 1988: 'Contra Contractarianism: Some Reflections on the New Institutionalism', *Politics and Society*, 16, 387–401.

Batt, Judy, 1991a: *East Central Europe from Reform to Transformation*, London: Pinter.

Batt, Judy, 1991b: 'Economic Transformation and Political Pluralism in Eastern Europe: Some General Reflections', London, unpub. MS.

Batt, Judy, 1991c: 'The End of Communist Rule in East-Central Europe: A Four-country Comparison', *Government and Opposition*, 26 (3), 368–90.

Bence, György, 1991: 'Political Justice in Post-Communist Societies', Occasional Paper, no. 27, Washington, D.C.: Wilson Center.

Bence, György, 1992: 'Retroactive Justice after Burke and Lassalle', Budapest, unpub. MS.

Benz, Wolfgang, 1984: *Die Gründung der Bundesrepublik: von der Bizone zum sou-veränen Staat*, Munich: dtv.

Benz, Wolfgang, 1986: 'Erzwungenes Ideal oder zweitbeste Lösung? Intentionen und Wirkungen der Gründung des deutschen Weststaats', in Ludolf Herbst (ed.), *Westdeutschland 1945–1955*, Munich: Oldenbourg, 135–50.

Bialas, Christiane, and Wilfried Ettl, 1992: 'Wirtschaftliche Lage und soziale Differenzierung im Transformationsprozess', Arbeitsgruppe Transformationsprozesse, Arbeitspapier 92/1, Berlin: Humboldt University.

Blanchard, Olivier, and Richard Layard, 1992: 'How to Privatize', in Horst Siebert (ed.), *The Transformation of Socialist Economies*, Tübingen: Mohr, 27–43.

Bohata, Petr, 1991: 'Vergangenheitsbewältigung in der Tschechoslowakei', *Jahrbuch für Ostrecht*, 32 (2), 325–44.

Bohata, Petr, 1992: 'Rückgabe oder Entschädigung in den osteuropäischen Staaten: CSFR', *Recht in Ost und West*, 36 (11), 321–4.

Bohrer, Karl Heinz, 1992: 'Deutsche Revolution und protestantische Mentalität', *Merkur*, 46 (9–10), 958–64.

Bolton, Patrick, and Gérard Roland, 1992: 'Privatization in Central and Eastern Europe', *Economic Policy*, 15, 275–309.

Bomsdorf, Falk, et al., 1993: *Die Risiken des Umbruchs in Osteuropa und die Herausforderungen für die Europäische Gemeinschaft*, Forschungsinstitut der Deutschen Gesellschaft für Auswärtige Politik e.V., Arbeitspapiere zur internationalen Politik, no. 74, Bonn: Europa Union Verlag.

Borchardt, Knut, 1983: 'Die Bundesrepublik in den säkularen Trends der wirtschaftlichen Entwicklung', in Werner Conze and Rainer M. Lepsius (eds), *Sozialgeschichte der Bundesrepublik Deutschland: Beiträge zum Kontinuitätsproblem*, Stuttgart: Klett-Cotta, 20ff.

Brown, J. F., 1991: 'The Resurgence of Nationalism', *Report on Eastern Europe*, 2 (24), 35–7.

Brünneck, Alexander von, 1984: *Die Eigentumsgarantie des Grundgesetzes*, Baden-Baden: Nomos.

Bruszt, László, 1992: 'Transformative Politics: Social Costs and Social Peace in East Central Europe', *East European Politics and Societies*, 6 (1), 55–72.

Bruszt, László, and David Stark, 1991: 'Remaking the Political Field in Hungary: from the Politics of Confrontation to the Politics of Competition', *Journal of International Affairs*, 44, 201–45.

Brzezinski, Zbigniew, 1989: 'Post-Communist Nationalism', *Foreign Affairs*, 68 (5), 1–25.

Burger, Josef, 1992/93: 'Politics of Restitution in Czechoslovakia', *East European Quarterly*, 26 (4), 485–98.

Bürklin, Wilhelm, 1992: 'Die Struktur politischer Konfliktlinien im vereinten Deutschland: eine Nation – zwei getrennte politische Kulturen?', *Forschungsbericht der Universität Kiel*, 34, 15–32.

Campbell, John L., 1992: 'The Fiscal Crisis of Post-Communist States', *Telos*, 93, 89–110.

Carlin, Wendy, 1993: 'Economic Reconstruction in West Germany, 1945–55: the Displacement of "Vegetative Control"', in Ian D. Turner (ed.), *Reconstruction in Post-war Germany*, London: Berg.

Cepl, Vojtech, 1992: 'Retribution and Restitution in Czechoslovakia', *Archives Européennes de Sociologie*, 33 (1), 202–14.

Chapman, David, 1991: *Can Civil Wars Be Avoided?*, London: Institute for Social Inventions.

Deacon, Bob, and Julia Szalai (eds), 1990: *Social Policy in the New Eastern Europe*, Aldershot: Avebury.

Deis, Michael J., 1992: 'A Study of Nationalism in Czechoslovakia', *RFE/RL Research Report*, 1 (5), 8–13.

Deppe, Rainer, Helmut Dubiel and Ulrich Rödel (eds), 1991: *Demokratischer Umbruch in Osteuropa*, Frankfurt: Suhrkamp.

Deutsch, Karl, 1966: *The Nerves of Government: Models of Political Communication and Control*, New York: Free Press.

Diestelkamp, Bernhard, 1986: 'Kontinuität und Wandel in der Rechtsordnung, 1945–1955', in Ludolf Herbst (ed.), *Westdeutschland 1945–1955*, Munich: Oldenbourg, 85–105.

Dietze, Gottfried, 1960: 'The Federal Republic of Germany: an Evaluation after Ten Years', *Journal of Politics*, 22 (1), 112–47.

Doyle, Jonathan J., 1992: 'A Bitter Inheritance: East German Real Property and the Supreme Constitutional Court's "Land Reform" Decision of April 23, 1991', *Michigan Journal of International Law*, 13 (4), 832–64.

Easton, David, 1965: *A Systems Analysis of Political Life*, New York: Wiley.

Einigungsvertrag, 1990: in *Die Verträge zur Einheit Deutschlands*, Munich: Beck, 43–569.

Elster, Jon, 1990: 'When Communism Dissolves', *London Review of Books*, 12, 3–6.

Elster, Jon, 1992a: 'On Doing What One Can', *East European Constitutional Review* 1 (2), 15–17.

Elster, Jon, 1992b: 'Retribution and Restitution: Backward-looking Justice in Eastern Europe', Chicago, unpub. MS.

Elwert, Georg, 1989: 'Nationalismus und Ethnizität', *Kölner Zeitschrift für Soziologie und Sozialpsychologie*, 41 (3), 440–64.

Elwert, Georg, 1991: 'Fassaden, Gerüchte, Gewalt', *Merkur*, 45 (4), 318–32.

Engelbrekt, Kjell, 1991: 'Nationalism Reviving', *Report on Eastern Europe*, 2 (48), 1–6.

Engler, Wolfgang, 1991: 'Die träge Masse des Habitus', in Michael Brie and Dieter Klein (eds), *Umbruch zur Moderne?*, Hamburg: VSA, 83–91.

Engler, Wolfgang, 1992: 'Die ungewollte Moderne: Individualisierung im Ost-West-Vergleich', Berlin, unpub. MS.

Epstein, Richard A., 1985: *Takings: Private Property and the Power of Eminent Domain*, Cambridge, Mass./London: Harvard University Press.

Falandysz, Lech, 1991: 'From Communist Legality to the Rule of Law', *Helsinki Monitor*, 2 (4), 27–32.

Fischer, Brigitta, 1992: 'Das Entschädigungsgesetz von 1991 und die marktwirtschaftliche Umgestaltung des Agrarsektors in Ungarn', *Südosteuropa Mitteilungen*, 32 (1), 35–44.

Fischer, Stanley, and Alan Gelb, 1991: 'The Process of Socialist Economic Transformation', *Journal of Economic Perspectives*, 5 (4), 91–105.

Fraenkel, Ernst, [1932] 1968: 'Verfassungsreform und Sozialdemokratie', reprinted in Ernst Fraenkel, *Zur Soziologie der Klassenjustiz*, Darmstadt: Wissenschaftliche Buchgesellschaft, 89–103.

Franklin, David, 1991: 'The Pull of the Past: Restitution and Rehabilitation in Post-revolutionary Czechoslovakia', unpub. MS.

Friedrich, Carl J., 1949: 'Rebuilding the German Constitution', pt I, *American Political Science Review*, 43 (3), 461–82.

Friedrich, Carl J., 1953: *Der Verfassungsstaat der Neuzeit*, Berlin: Springer.

Fröhlich, Elke (ed.), 1987: *Die Tagebücher von Joseph Goebbels*, vol. 4, Munich: Saur.

Fromme, F. K., 1962: *Von der Weimarer Verfassung zum Bonner Grundgesetz: die verfassungspolitischen Folgerungen des Parlamentarischen Rates aus Weimarer Republik und nationalsozialistischer Diktatur*, Tübingen: Mohr/Siebeck.

Frydman, Roman, Andrzej Rapaczynski, John S. Earle et al., 1993: *The Privatization Process in Central Europe*, London: Central European University Press.

Gagnon, V. P., Jr, 1994: 'Serbia's Road to War', *Journal of Democracy*, 5 (2), 117–31.

Golay, J. F., 1958: *The Founding of the Federal Republic of Germany*, Chicago: University of Chicago Press.

Gralla, Erhardt, 1992: 'Rückgabe oder Entschädigung in den osteuropäischen Staaten: Polen', *Recht in Ost und West*, 36 (11), 327–31.

Green, Leslie, 1982: 'Rational Nationalists', *Political Studies*, 30 (2), 236–46.

Grimm, Dieter, 1992: 'Verfassungsreform in falscher Hand?', *Merkur*, 46 (12), 1059–72.

Grinberg, Lev, and Daniel Levy, 1992: 'Reconstructing the Wall: a Theoretical Framework for the Analysis of German Unification', unpub. MS.

Grundmann, Siegfried, 1992: 'Regionale Disparitäten', *Utopie Kreativ*, 17–18, 52–63.

Habermas, Jürgen, 1985: 'Ziviler Ungehorsam – Testfall für den demokratischen Rechtsstaat', in Jürgen Habermas, *Die neue Unübersichtlichkeit*, Frankfurt: Suhrkamp, 79–99.

Habermas, Jürgen, 1990: *Die nachholende Revolution*, Frankfurt: Suhrkamp.

Habermas, Jürgen, 1992: 'Was bedeutet "Aufarbeitung der Vergangenheit" heute? Bemerkungen zur "doppelten Vergangenheit"', in Jürgen Habermas, *Die Moderne: ein unvollendetes Projekt*, 2nd edn, Leipzig: Reclam, 242–67.

Hirschman, Albert O., 1981: 'The Changing Tolerance for Income Inequality in the Course of Economic Development', in Albert O. Hirschman, *Essays in Trespassing: Economics to Politics and Beyond*, Cambridge: Cambridge University Press, 39–58.

Hirschman, Albert O., 1992: 'Abwanderung, Widerspruch und das Schicksal der Deutschen Demokratischen Republik', *Leviathan*, 20 (3), 330–58.

Hobsbawm, Eric J., 1972: 'Some Reflections on Nationalism', in T. J. Nossiter and A. H. Hanson (eds), *Imagination and Precision in the Social Sciences: Essays in Memory of Peter Nettl*, London: Faber, 385–406.

Hobsbawm, Eric J., 1990: *Nations and Nationalism since 1780*, Cambridge: Cambridge University Press.

Hobsbawm, Eric J., 1992: 'Whose Fault-line is it Anyway?', *New Statesman and Society*, 5 (199), 23–6.

Hockerts, Hans Günter, 1980: *Sozialpolitische Entscheidungen im Nachkriegsdeutschland: alliierte und deutsche Sozialversicherungspolitik 1945 bis 1957*, Stuttgart: Klett-Cotta.

Hockerts, Hans Günter, 1985: 'Ausblick: bürgerliche Sozialreform nach 1945', in R. von Bruch (ed.), *Weder Kommunismus noch Kapitalismus: bürgerliche Sozialreform in Deutschland vom Vormärz bis zur Ära Adenauer*, Munich: Beck, 245–73.

Holmes, Stephen, 1988: 'Precommitment and the Paradox of Democracy', in J. Elster and R. Slagstaad (eds), *Constitutionalism and Democracy*, Cambridge: Cambridge University Press, 195–240.

Ionescu, Dan, 1992: 'Romania's First Postcommunist Census', *RFE/RL Research Report*, 1 (11), 57–63.

Jakobs, Günther, 1992: 'Vergangenheitsbewältigung durch Strafrecht?', in J. Isensee (ed.), *Vergangenheitsbewältigung durch Recht*, Berlin: Duncker and Humblot, 37–64.

Jedlicki, Jerzy, 1991: 'Die unerträgliche Last der Geschichte', *Transit*, 2, 16–26.

Jowitt, Kenneth, 1992: *The New World Disorder: the Leninist Extinction*, Berkeley: University of California Press.

Kadritzke, Nils, 1992: 'Die überraschende Wiederkehr des Nationalismus in die Geschichte', *Prokla*, 22 (2), 166–88.

Kirchheimer, Otto, 1961: *Political Justice: the Use of Legal Procedures for Political Ends*, Princeton: Princeton University Press.

Kirschbaum, Stanislav J., 1992: 'Das Slowakische Problem', Munich, unpub. MS.

Klein, Dieter, 1993: 'Ost-West-Einflüsse im Gefolge östlicher Transformation', *BISS-Public*, 10, 63–70.

Klessmann, Christoph, 1984: *Die doppelte Staatsgründung: deutsche Geschichte 1945–1955*, 3rd edn, Göttingen: Vandenhoeck and Ruprecht.

Klingsberg, Ethan, 1992: 'Judicial Review and Hungary's Transition from Communism to Democracy: the Constitutional Court, the Continuity of Law, and the Redefinition of Property Rights', *Brigham Young University Law Review*, 42 (1), 41–144.

Knerer, Harald, 1992: 'Rückgabe oder Entschädigung in den osteuropäischen Staaten: Ungarn', *Recht in Ost und West*, 36 (11), 324–7.

Koch, Koen, 1991: 'Back to Sarajewo or beyond Trianon? Some Thoughts on the Problem of Nationalism in Eastern Europe', *Netherlands Journal of Social Sciences*, 27 (1), 29–42.

Kocka, Jürgen, 1979: 'Neubeginn oder Restauration? Deutschland 1945–1949', *L '76, Demokratie und Sozialismus*, 11, 112–36.

Kocka, Jürgen, 1990: 'Revolution und Nation 1989: zur historischen Einordnung der gegenwärtigen Ereignisse', *Tel Aviver Jahrbuch für deutsche Geschichte*, 19, 479–99.

Kolarova, Rumyana, 1992: 'The Tacit Agreement', Sofia, unpub. MS.

Kornai, János, 1990: 'The Affinity between Ownership Forms and Coordination Mechanisms: the Common Experience of Reform in Socialist Countries', *Journal of Economic Perspectives*, 4 (3), 131–47.

Kornai, János, 1992: 'The Principles of Privatization in Eastern Europe', *Economist*, 140 (2), 153–76.

Kosta, Jiří, 1991: 'Ökonomische Aspekte des Systemwandels in der Tschechoslowakei', in Deppe, Dubiel and Rödel 1991, 302–25.

Krüger, Hans-Peter, 1992: 'Ohne Versöhnung handeln, nur nicht leben', *Sinn und Form*, 44 (1), 40–50.

Kukutz, Irena, and Katja Havemann, 1990: *Geschützte Quelle: Gespräche mit Monika H. alias Karin Lenz*, Berlin: Basisdruck.

Laber, Jeri, 1992: 'Witch Hunt in Prague', *New York Review of Books*, 23 April.

Lendvai, Paul, 1992: 'Das Gespenst der Balkanisierung', *Frankfurter Allgemeine Zeitung*, 29 February.

Leonhardt, Peter, 1992: 'Rückgabe oder Entschädigung in den osteuropäischen Staaten: Rumänien', *Recht in Ost und West*, 36 (11), 335–7.

Linden, Ronald, 1991: 'The Appeal of Nationalism', *Report on Eastern Europe*, 2 (24), 29–35.

Linz, Juan, and Alfred Stepan, 1992: 'Political Identities and Electoral Sequences: Spain, the Soviet Union, and Yugoslavia', *Daedalus*, 121 (2), 123–39.

Lipset, Seymour M., 1981: *Political Man: the Social Bases of Politics*, expanded edn, Baltimore: Johns Hopkins University Press.

Lübbe, Hermann, 1983: 'Der Nationalsozialismus im deutschen Nachkriegsbewusstsein', *Historische Zeitschrift*, 236, 579–99.

Maier, Charles, and Stanley Hoffmann (eds), 1984: *The Marshall Plan: a Retrospective*, Boulder: Westview.

Markus, György, 1992: 'Parties, Camps, and Cleavages in Post-Communist Hungary', Budapest, unpub. MS.

Meuschel, Sigrid, 1992: *Legitimation und Parteiherrschaft in der DDR*, Frankfurt: Suhrkamp.

Meyerhoff, Hans, 1949: 'The Reconstruction of Government and Administration', in Gabriel A. Almond (ed.), *The Struggle for Democracy in Germany*, Chapel Hill: University of North Carolina Press, 185–220.

Michelman, Frank I., 1966/67: 'Property, Utility, and Fairness: Comments on the Ethical Foundations of "Just Compensation" Law', *Harvard Law Review*, 80 (6), 1165–258.

Miszlivetz, Ferenc, 1991: 'Central Europe: the Way to Europe', Budapest, unpub. MS.

Morris, Christopher W., 1984: 'Existential Limits to the Rectification of Past Wrongs', *American Philosophical Quarterly*, 21 (2), 175–82.

Müller, Klaus, 1992: 'Modernizing Eastern Europe: Theoretical Problems and Political Dilemmas', *Archives Européennes de Sociologie*, 33 (1), 109–50.

Munzer, Stephen R., 1990: *A Theory of Property*, Cambridge: Cambridge University Press.

Nairn, Tom, 1990: 'Beyond Big Brother', *New Statesman and Society*, 3 (105), 30–2.

Neuber, Alexander, 1992: 'Toward a Political Economy of Transition in Eastern Europe, with Particular Reference to Poland', Cambridge, Mass., unpub. MS.

Niclauss, Karlheinz, 1974: *Demokratiegründung in Westdeutschland: die Entstehung der Bundesrepublik 1945–1949*, Munich: Piper.

Obrman, Jan, and Pavel Mates, 1993: 'Czech Republic Debates Return of Church Property', *RFE/RL Research Report*, 2 (19), 46–50.

O'Donnell, Guillermo, Philippe C. Schmitter, and Lawrence Whitehead (eds), 1986: *Transitions from Authoritarian Rule*, vol. 5, Baltimore: Johns Hopkins University Press.

Offe, Claus, 1992: 'Die politischen Kosten der Vereinheitlichung des Gesundheitssystems', in W. Schmähl (ed.), *Sozialpolitik im Prozess der deutschen Vereinigung*, Frankfurt/New York: Campus, 59–90.

Offe, Claus, 1993: 'The Politics of Social Policy in East European Transitions: Antecedents, Agents, and Agenda of Reform', *Social Research*, 60 (4), 649–84.

Offe, Claus, 1994a: *Der Tunnel am Ende des Lichts: Erkundungen der politischen Transformation im Neuen Osten*, Frankfurt/New York: Campus.

Offe, Claus, 1994b: 'Moderne "Barbarei": der Naturzustand im Kleinformat?', *Journal für Sozialforschung*, 34 (3), 229–47.

Offe, Claus, 1995: 'Designing Institutions in East European Transitions', in Robert E. Goodwin and H. Geoffrey Brennan (eds), *The Theory of Institutional Design*, Cambridge: Cambridge University Press.

Okolicsanyi, Karoly, 1993: 'Hungarian Compensation Programs off to a Slow Start', *RFE/RL Research Report*, 2 (11), 49–52.

Oltay, Edith, 1993: 'Controversy over Restitution of Church Property in Hungary', *RFE/RL Research Report*, 2 (6), 54–7.

Paczolay, Peter, 1992: 'Judicial Review of the Compensation Law in Hungary', *Michigan Journal of International Law*, 13 (4), 806–31.

Pajor-Bytomski, Magdalena, 1992: 'Das ungarische Entschädigungsgesetz unter besonderer Berücksichtigung der Ansprüche der Auslandsungarn', *Jahrbuch für Ostrecht*, 33 (1), 55–71.

Pederson, Ove K., 1992: 'Selling the State or Building a Society: Private Property Reforms in West and East', Seminar Papers, no. 7, Cracow: Cracow Academy of Economics.

Pehe, Jirí, 1991: 'Czechoslovakia: Parliament Passes Controversial Law on Vetting Officials', *Report on Eastern Europe*, 25 October.

Pehe, Jirí, 1992: 'Czechoslovak Federal Assembly Adopts Electoral Law', *RFE/RL Research Report*, 1 (7), 27–30.

Pfetsch, Frank, 1986: 'Die Verfassungspolitik der westlichen Besatzungsmächte in den Ländern nach 1945', *Aus Politik und Zeitgeschichte*, sect. 22, 31 May.

Pickel, Andreas, 1992: 'Jump-starting a Market Economy: a Critique of the Radical Strategy for Economic Reform in the Light of the East German Experience', *Studies in Comparative Communism*, 25 (2), 177–91.

Pradetto, August, 1991: 'Der Zusammenbruch der DDR: ökonomische und politische Konsequenzen aus der Sicht mittel-osteuropäischer Länder', in Rolf Reissig and Gert-Joachim Glaessner (eds), *Das Ende eines Experiments*, Berlin: Dietz, 75–98.

Prazauskas, Algis, 1991: 'Ethnic Conflicts in the Context of Democratizing Political Systems', *Theory and Society*, 20 (5), 581–602.

Preuss, Ulrich K., 1993a: 'Die Rolle des Rechtsstaates in der Transformation postkommunistischer Gesellschaften', *Rechtstheorie*, 24 (1–2), 181–204.

Preuss, Ulrich K., 1993b: 'Restitution and Privatization of Property in the Former GDR: the German Case and Some Historical Precedents', Bremen, unpub. MS.

Przeworski, Adam, 1991: *Democracy and the Market: Political and Economic Reforms in Eastern Europe and Latin America*, Cambridge: Cambridge University Press.

Putnam, Robert D., 1993: *Making Democracy Work: Civic Traditions in Modern Italy*, Princeton: Princeton University Press.

Rodrik, Dani, 1989: 'Promises, Promises: Credible Policy Reform via Signalling', *Economic Journal*, 99 (3), 756–72.

Rodrik, Dani, and Richard Zeckhauser, 1987/88: 'The Dilemma of Government Responsiveness', *Journal of Policy Analysis and Management*, 7 (4), 601–20.

Rovan, Joseph, 1992: 'Das Erbe der Tyrannei', *Frankfurter Allgemeine Zeitung*, 8 August.

Sachs, Jeffrey D., 1992: 'Privatization in Russia: Some Lessons from Eastern Europe', *American Economic Review: Papers and Proceedings*, 82, 43–8.

Sanderson, Fred H., 1949: 'Germany's Economic Situation and Prospects', in Gabriel A. Almond (ed.), *The Struggle for Democracy in Germany*, Chapel Hill: University of North Carolina Press, 111–84.

Schieder, Theodor, 1991: *Nationalismus and Nationalstaat: Studien zum nationalen Problem im modernen Europa*, Göttingen: Vandenhoeck and Ruprecht.

Schneider, Gernot, 1988: *Wirtschaftswunder DDR: Anspruch und Realität*, Cologne: Bund.

Schönherr, Albrecht (ed.), 1992: *Ein Volk am Pranger*, Berlin: Aufbau.

Schöpflin, George, 1991a: 'National Identity in the Soviet Union and East Central Europe', *Ethnic and Racial Studies*, 14 (1), 3–14.

Schöpflin, George, 1991b: 'Nationalism and National Minorities in East and Central Europe', *Journal of International Affairs*, 45 (1), 51–65.

Schöpflin, George, 1991c: 'Post-Communism: Constructing New Democracies in Central Europe', *International Affairs*, 67 (2), 235–50.

Senghaas, Dieter, 1992: *Friedensprojekt Europa*, Frankfurt: Suhrkamp.

Sher, George, 1981: 'Ancient Wrongs and Modern Rights', *Philosophy and Public Affairs*, 10 (1), 3–17.

Siklova, Jirina, 1991: 'The Solidarity of the Culpable', *Social Research*, 58 (4), 765–73.

Sitzler, Kathrin, 1992: 'Ungarn im Spannungsfeld von Demokratie und Geschichte', in Margareta Mommsen (ed.), *Nationalismus in Osteuropa*, Munich: Beck, 96–117.

Sörgel, W., 1969: *Konsensus und Interessen: eine Studie zur Entstehung des Grundgesetzes für die Bundesrepublik Deutschland*, Stuttgart: E. Klett.

Staniskis, Jadwiga, 1991: 'Dilemmata der Demokratie', in Deppe, Dubiel and Rödel 1991, 326–47.

Stark, David, 1990: 'Privatization in Hungary: from Plan to Market or from Plan to Clan', *East European Politics and Societies*, 4 (3), 351–92.

Stark, David, 1992a: 'Path Dependence and Privatization Strategies in East Central Europe', *East European Politics and Societies*, 6 (1), 17–54.

Stark, David, 1992b: 'The Great Transformation? Social Change in Eastern Europe', *Contemporary Sociology*, 21 (3), 299–304.

Stark, David, n.d.: 'Privatization Strategies in East Central Europe', unpub. MS.

Statistics Committee of Latvia, 1992: *The Ethnic Situation of Latvia Today*, Riga.

Stokes, Gale, 1991: 'Lessons of the East European Revolutions of 1989', *Problems of Communism*, 40, 17–22.

Stölting, Erhard, 1992: 'Angst, Aggression und nationale Denkform', *Prokla*, 22 (2), 225–41.

Szelenyi, Ivan, and Balazs Szelenyi, 1994: 'Why Socialism Failed: toward a Theory of System Breakdown – Causes of Disintegration of East European State Socialism', *Theory and Society*, 23, 211–31.

Thränhardt, Dietrich, 1986: *Geschichte der Bundesrepublik Deutschland*, Frankfurt: Suhrkamp.

Troebst, Stefan, 1992: 'Nationalismus als Demokratisierungshemmnis in Bulgarien', *Südosteuropa*, 41 (3–4), 188–227.

Ulrich, David, and Gill Schröter, 1991: *Das Ministerium für Staatssicherheit: Anatomie des Mielke-Imperiums*, Berlin: Rowohlt.

Wagner, Gert, 1991: 'Zur Entwicklung der Marktwirtschaft in den neuen Bundesländern: Erwartungen und erste Schritte der Erwerbstätigen', in U. Gerhardt and E. Mochmann (eds), *Gesellschaftlicher Umbruch 1945–1990*, Munich: Oldenbourg, 81–92.

Walzer, Michael, 1992: 'The New Tribalism: Notes on a Difficult Problem', *Dissent*, spring, 164–71.

Wiesenthal, Helmut, 1992: 'Sturz in die Moderne: der Sonderstatus der DDR in den Transformationsprozessen Osteuropas', in Michael Brie and Dieter Klein (eds), *Zwischen den Zeiten*, Hamburg: VSA, 162–88.

Williams, Colin H., 1991: *Linguistic Minorities, Society, and Territory*, Clevedon: Multilingual Matters.

Winter, Gerd, 1986: 'Über Pflöcke im wandernden Rechtsboden: die Eigentumskonzeption des Bundesverfassungsgerichts und Ferdinand Lassalles Theorie erworbener Rechte', *Kritische Justiz*, 19 (4), 459–70.

Wolkow, Wladimir K., 1991: 'Ethnokratie: ein verhängnisvolles Erbe in der postkommunistischen Welt', *Aus Politik und Zeitgeschichte*, 41 (52–3), 35–43.

Zaslavsky, Victor, 1992: 'Nationalism and Democratic Transition in Postcommunist Societies', *Daedalus*, 121 (2), 97–121.

Index

Studies in Contemporary German Social Thought
Thomas McCarthy, General Editor